O.J.SIMPSON'S MOST
MEMORABLE GAMES

Books by Jim Baker

O.J. SIMPSON
THE BUFFALO BILLS
BILLIE JEAN KING

O.J.SIMPSON'S MOST MEMORABLE GAMES

Jim Baker

G.P. PUTNAM'S SONS
NEW YORK

SBN: 399-12108-0

Library of Congress Cataloging in Publication Data

Baker, Jim, 1941-
O.J. Simpson's most memorable games.
1. Simpson, O. J., 1947-   2. Football
players—United States—Biography. I. Title.
GV939.S47B34   1978   796.33′2′0924   [B]   78-1304

PRINTED IN THE UNITED STATES OF AMERICA

For Erin Elizabeth,
who will learn about O.J.
by reading this book.

Contents

O.J. and his "main man," guard Reggie McKenzie. They're a matchless combination.
Buffalo Bills Photo

Introduction

One Sunday afternoon in the fall of 1960, Cleveland Browns' superstar Jimmy Brown strolled into an ice cream parlor across the street from Kezar Stadium in San Francisco.

The place was packed with kids, most having just seen Brown perform his running magic against the 49ers. Some simply stared. Others milled around, asking for Brown's autograph.

One uninhibited 13-year-old boy stood out, however. He had something to say to pro football's greatest running back. Never shy, the boy walked over and blurted: "Mr. Brown, you ain't so tough. Some day, I'm gonna break all your records. Wait and see!"

Brown merely looked away without replying. Just a loud kid, he figured. And yes, the kid was loud, a sometimes troublesome type who had used his considerable speed to elude cops instead of linebackers.

What Brown didn't realize was the kid was dead serious and would someday possess all the brilliance to pursue that brash promise and erase one Brown record after another. His name was Orenthal James Simpson. Back then, he was merely the fastest kid on the block. Today, recognized universally as "O.J." or "The Juice," he is the king of running backs.

Nearly two decades after that chance meeting in the ice cream shop, O.J. Simpson has surpassed most of Jimmy Brown's legendary standards. A multi-millionaire with a career which has blossomed into movies, television and the business world, Simpson extended his playing days beyond the mid-1970's and into the twilight zone for essentially one reason.

Brown remains the alltime pro rushing king with 12,312 yards. The Juice has climbed into second place with 10,183 and wants to be No. 1.

O.J., an excellent team player, long proclaimed reaching and winning the Super Bowl as his primary target. Just one day after running farther in one season than any other player, he declared: "My goal in pro football is to be on a world championship team. Then there could be nothing else I could ask for in football. I've won the Heisman Trophy and the rushing crown, but the Super Bowl is the ultimate goal."

However, there appears to be no team title in O.J.'s future. The Buffalo Bills, his only professional team for nine seasons, reached the National Football League play-offs just once—and were quickly eliminated by Pittsburgh in 1974. A March 24, 1978, trade sent O.J. to San Francisco, but the 49ers aren't a contender either. Re-building a frequent loser into title status in one or two years just isn't done. The 49ers need time—time O.J. doesn't possess.

Two years could be sufficient, though, for him to surpass Brown as the sport's premier alltime running back. Then he could retire and reflect upon his trail of destruction of Brown's standards with glowing satisfaction, knowing he accomplished such incredible feats without the benefit of playing for a champion.

Instead of team laurels and because of O.J., Buffalo in the early-1970's became the home of football's top individual supershow. Bills' fans even called Simpson "The Franchise."

In 1973, he opened the NFL season by churning 250 yards, farther than any pro runner had traveled in one game, and he closed it by becoming the sport's first 2,000-yard rusher within one year.

A pair of superstars: Billie Jean King and O.J. Simpson.
UPI Photo

Two seasons later, O.J. dented the Super Bowl champion Pittsburgh Steelers' armor for 227 yards, probably his finest effort ever, considering the quality of team he devastated. It was a Three Rivers Stadium opener the Steelers will never forget.

In the bicentennial season, his year of team collapse, O.J. salvaged the spectacular by rewriting his own single-game rushing record, since broken by Chicago's Walter Payton. O.J. humbled the Detroit Lions, then leading the league in defense, by exploding for 273 rushing yards on Thanksgiving Day at Pontiac Stadium.

The Juice amassed a staggering 647 yards in his final three games of 1976. That's the equivalent of a full year's work for most NFL running backs. And in the end, after an unsuccessful trade request, his absence from training camp and an incredibly slow season start, O.J. still embraced his fourth league rushing title in five years.

O.J.'s penchant for the sensational has ignited him to 10 league records (seven still existing) and a virtual reprinting of the Bills' rushing standards. No player in history has dashed for more yardage in one season. He once held the single-game attempts yardage and single-season attempts records as well. No player claims more 100-yard games, total or consecutive, in a game or season. No player has scored more touchdowns in one year.

Perhaps most impressive of all, no player has accumulated more 200-yard games than his half-dozen from 1973-76. And he might have mustered another two or three with one more handoff or by staying in a game instead of leaving early with the outcome determined.

O.J. Simpson is so much more than a record runner, however. He is so representative of the many ghetto products who have been elevated to prominence through athletic greatness. He is a rare breed who caromed from the pinnacle of Heisman Trophy success in 1968 to three wasted years in pro football and back to the top again.

O.J. is the "main man" behind all those little and not-so-little boys wearing T-shirts with the famed No. 32. He is the charismatic type who never says no to kids seeking autographs. O.J.

The Juice at home: O.J. poses with his family. That's wife Marquerite, daughter Arnelle, son Jason.
Photo by John Kontos,
Williamsville, N.Y.

keeps even his own coach and teammates waiting on the team bus while he signs away.

Indeed, O.J. holds a special relationship with kids—whether they've met him only through television or in person.

There was a clubhouse boy in Atlanta a few seasons back who ran to get O.J. a Coke while newsmen interviewed him following a game with the Falcons. The youngster returned and waited until the last question was answered before handing O.J. the Coke.

"Hey, this is warm," the Juice blurted after taking a sip.

"Sure it's warm," answered the boy's father, the clubhouse custodian. "My son's been holding it for you for half an hour."

"In that case," O.J. smiled, "I'll not only drink it, I'll drink a toast to you."

The boy smiled and his dad nodded. "O.J. Simpson showed me something," he said. "He's got class and you can't coach that."

You also can't coach popularity with the young. O.J. not only has it, he has ranked at the top of popularity polls among the teenage set.

There never has been any question, either, of his affinity toward his teammates. One inkling as to how he feels about them came after the 1973 season finale in New York—that cold December afternoon when he set the football world on its ear by completing a record 2,003-yard season.

Here was Simpson, having not only eclipsed Brown's record of 1,863 yards in a single season (1963), but having just become the game's first 2,000-yard man. And what did he do in the postgame interview crush before almost 400 newsmen? Instead of letting the spotlight descend upon him in his greatest moment of glory, he shared it with the Bills' entire offensive unit.

The Juice escorted all the Bills' offensive players into a special interview room which was set up for him. "This is Joe Ferguson, our quarterback," he said. "He's a rookie and did he do a job!"

And on he went, introducing Jim Braxton, the fullback, and each lineman down to the last reserve. All shared his moment, from guard Reggie McKenzie—"my main man"—to little-used tackle Bob Penchion.

O.J. didn't stop there, either.

Spending about $25,000, he bought each member of that offensive unit and each offensive coach a gold bracelet commemorating not only his 2,003-yard trip but the team's 3,088 rushing yards. Just as he had become pro football's first 2,000-yard runner, the Bills were the game's first 3,000-yard rushing team.

The bracelets bore this inscription: "3,088—2,003 . . . We did it . . . Juice." It was a gesture without parallel in professional sports, yet one which Simpson attempted to keep private. He spent $1,000 for each bracelet to show his appreciation to his teammates and coaches, yet he wanted only them to know it. "I didn't do it for the publicity," O.J. later said. "I didn't want anything said or written about it."

All of which reveals another facet of the man's class and that special relationship with his peers.

O.J. seldom encountered difficulty being popular, but thousand-dollar bracelets were way beyond his league for most of his life.

O.J. was born July 9, 1947, the fourth child of Jimmy and Eunice Simpson. His legs were so pencil-thin, he had to wear braces, a fact which became more amusing later in life when that same set of wheels became million-dollar legs.

When O.J. was five, his mother and father separated, but his dad remained a caring parent. At age six, O.J. moved to Potrero Hill, his fourth or fifth home and the place where he did most of his growing up. His mother worked nights as an orderly in a San Francisco hospital. She'd work the midnight shift after putting the kids to bed.

It was a ghetto life which O.J. experienced, but not the worst of ghettos. "We always had money to eat," O.J. is quick to point out. But he did live in a project and he did live a rough existence, so rough that had he not turned toward his natural gift in athletics, O.J. might have ended up in jail.

He stole hubcaps, attended gang rumbles where there were beatings and stabbings, had friends who were into the drug scene. He attended the same high school, Galileo, where Joe DiMaggio went. But at school, he rolled dice, played cards and talked about stealing cars. Yet, deep down, O.J. was not a bad kid. He wanted to be famous and admired. As he told Al

Cowlings, his boyhood friend and teammate in high school, college and the pros, "I'm gonna amount to something."

Now, O.J. looks back on his misspent youth as a necessary way for him to mature. "I would never change it at all," he says. "I had fun. I stole cars and I used to fight all the time. I enjoyed it. I think it taught me things about relating to people."

When O.J. went out for the football team at Galileo, he soon discovered that winning was not a way of life there. Comprised mostly of lightweight Chinese students, Galileo was the doormat of its competition. The school hadn't won in three years and O.J.'s first opponent, St. Ignatius, hadn't lost in two.

O.J. lobbed a pass for one touchdown, raced 75 yards for another, then won the game as a safety (yes, he played defense, too). O.J. raced over from the other side of the field, lunged to intercept, then weaved his way 60 yards through most of his opponents for the winning touchdown. And so a star was born at Galileo.

O.J. enjoyed a fine Galileo career, but there was no real indication that he would someday become the game's greatest player. In fact, his football career could have ended right in high school. There were no scholarship offers because his grades were horrible. The newspapers placed him on the all-star teams, all right, but with a phrase such as: "And O.J. Simpson rounds out the backfield."

Disappointed, O.J. was on the verge of joining the Army, resigned to a fate which probably would steer him to Vietnam, where so many of his friends were fighting. Instead, he knew two friends who were playing football at City College of San Francisco. There, he could improve his grades and maybe attract a scholarship to a major college. He entered on the final day for enrollment.

O.J. was a smash hit from his first game at City College. He scored seven touchdowns in his debut, three being called back for penalties. He averaged an incredible 9.9 yards a carry and scored 26 touchdowns that season.

In two seasons at City College, O.J. amassed 54 TDs and broke every national rushing and scoring mark in junior college football history. He needed only six games to erase the school

Former New York Giant star Kyle Rote presents O.J. the Seagrams
Seven Crowns of Sport Award.
Photo by Van Horn

standards set by the great Ollie Matson. His rushing total was a
spectacular 2,552 yards. City College compiled a gaudy 17-1-1
record with O.J, the crowning achievement being victory in a
season-ending classic named, incredibly, the Prune Bowl. O.J.
found no easy going in the Prune Bowl.

City College trailed Long Beach, the defending national champion, 20-0, in the first half. Then O.J. scored three touchdowns,
earning most valuable player honors and stirring a comeback 40-
20 triumph.

"We did everything with O.J. at City College," said his coach,
Dutch Elston. "We used him as a running back and flanker. We
set him on the wing with the Wing-T. He's a tremendous pass
catcher, something many fans don't realize."

In one mud-caked game he scored six touchdowns—measuring
88, 73, 58, 16, 14 and 27 yards, the last via a screen pass. In all,
he carried 17 times for 304 yards in a 48-6 romp past San Jose
City College.

"I said when O.J. left he could succeed at any one of seven
positions in the pros," observed Elston. "He was a running back,

wide receiver, safety and cornerback with us and he was exceptionally good at returning kicks. I'm sure he could play a couple
of other positions if he had to."

The Juice heard bids from Arizona State, Utah and many
others after one junior college season, let alone two, but there
really was only one school he wanted. After the Prune Bowl,
that's where he went. It was the University of Southern California all the way.

O.J.'s success under Coach John McKay at USC is legendary. In
21 games, he carried 674 times for 3,423 yards—over five yards
per thrust. He scored 36 touchdowns. He severed 13 Trojan
records and revised their standards for rushing yards and attempts. USC compiled an 18-2-1 log with O.J. at tailback.

The Trojans made the Rose Bowl both of O.J.'s years on
campus, capping a national championship season in 1967 with a
14-3 victory over Indiana but bowing to Ohio State, 27-16, the
following year. In the race for the Heisman Trophy, O.J. finished
second to UCLA quarterback Gary Beban as a junior, but was a
clearcut victor in 1968.

He swept all kinds of awards, from the campus variety to
College Athlete of the Decade. After churning an NCAA-record
1,880 yards and scoring 23 touchdowns in 1968, he was most
everyone's "Player of the Year."

Or as McKay put it shortly following that season, "Simpson
was not only the greatest player I ever had, he was the greatest
player anyone ever had."

Clearly, O.J. was the toast of football as he headed toward the
1969 NFL draft.

There was no question where O.J. wanted to play as a
professional. He was a Californian, raised in San Francisco, with
Los Angeles his adopted home. The Rams were his favorite team.
However, it was just as clear that, because of the draft, Simpson
would not only not go to the Rams, but not even the NFL.

The American League was to be in existence for one more year
but, under merger terms, there was a common draft in 1969.
And Buffalo had the worst record in either league, thereby
qualifying to draft first. By being the worst, the Bills had won the
"O.J. Simpson Derby."

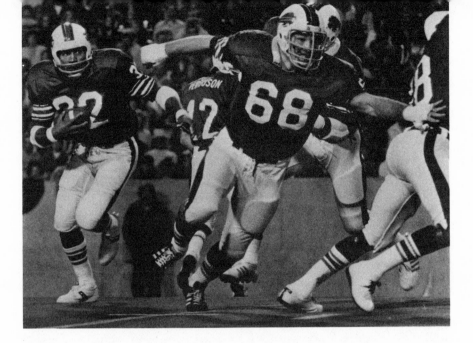

O.J. uses the blocking of All-Pro Joe DeLamielleure for many of his major gains. Joe D (68) is Bills' right guard.
Buffalo Bills Photo

O.J. did not accept his fate easily. "I was raised in an NFL town and naturally I would prefer to play in the NFL," he said. "My feeling has nothing to do with Buffalo as a city or team."

The Bills didn't hesitate in drafting O.J., but they did balk at even approaching his asking price. O.J., through his agent, sought a $500,000 loan. Bills' owner Ralph Wilson promptly labeled the request "outrageous," and O.J. became pro football's longest rookie holdout.

Simpson finally did sign, of course, but not before learning the hard way that Wilson wouldn't budge. O.J. agreed to play for only $50,000 a year—plus a $100,000 loan. And the loan windfall soon went "poof" in the stock market.

The major reason Simpson agreed to play for $50,000 was a collection of lucrative endorsements which hinged on his playing. Chevrolet gave him a three-year pact worth $180,000 and Royal Crown Cola came through with $37,500 per year. O.J. also signed a contract with ABC Sports.

Yet O.J. was anything but a smash success as a pro rookie . . . or sophomore . . . or junior. He led the Bills in rushing each of those three seasons, but was averaging only a dozen carries per game. Most of those were on obvious third down and short-yardage situations.

The cold, brutal fact was O.J. was being limited by a coach who did not appreciate his incredible talent, a coach who refused to revolve his offense around one man, a coach who made O.J. Simpson a virtual decoy. That coach was John Rauch and to say that he and Simpson did not get along is putting it mildly.

"I couldn't build my offense around one man, no matter how good he is," Rauch insisted. "That's not my style. It's too easy for the pros to set up defensive keys. O.J. can be a terrific pass receiver and we expect him to block, too."

Translated, that meant the stubborn Rauch wasn't going to give college football's greatest runner the ball very often.

"I never could understand why they wouldn't give it to me," Simpson recalled later. "I knew I had to learn how to block and follow pass patterns, but I thought I'd be running at the same time."

Simpson ran for 697 yards as a rookie and the Bills won four games. He gained 488 and suffered a knee injury which abbreviated his 1970 campaign, when the Bills won three games. In 1971, after Rauch was fired, O.J. accumulated 742 yards and, under coach Harvey Johnson, the Bills triumphed but once.

"I was playing the game but not enjoying it," the Juice says of his "three wasted years." He candidly admits, "By the middle of the season, I couldn't wait to get back to California."

In those three years, O.J. was a good running back with a very bad football team. He was accused by Bills' fans of stutter-stepping, hesitating too long before hitting the hole. He heard boos directed at him for the first time in his career. The lucrative business deals he enjoyed were expiring with no anxiety by sponsors to renew. Friends were asking O.J., "Whatever happened to you?" One wag even mailed him a one-way boat ticket to Africa.

O.J. clearly wanted out of Buffalo, but into the breach stepped Louis Henry Saban, the Bills' next coach. Here was a man with a history of building his offense around a solid rushing attack. Under Saban's direction, the careers of Cookie Gilchrist in

O.J. checks his totals on Rich Stadium scoreboard.
Photo by Bob Bukaty

Buffalo (mid-1960's) and Floyd Little in Denver soared. Simpson realized Saban could do the same for him.

O.J. reviewed Saban's playbook soon after arriving at the Bills' 1972 training camp and quickly did what he had vowed never to do—sign another contract with the Bills. "I've cried with these guys. Now I want to drink some champagne with them," O.J. quipped.

Simply put, the playbook showed the Bills' attack would revolve around Simpson. "There's your meal ticket," Saban told the regrouping, young club early in camp. "Block for him!"

Simpson referred to Saban often as "the man with a plan," and Saban explained his plan this way: "Offenses and defenses have to tie themselves around certain players. They must have a hub and then, one by one, the other players become spokes. It makes the unit better because others want to reach the heights, too.

"We have a very young, impressionable team," Saban went on.

"All the talking in the world is of no consequence. You need examples and you want to use a man to set high standards who's capable of reaching them. If you continue to hope that a player with potential might reach a certain level, he probably never will. But O.J. had been there once. The better he gets, the better the team gets."

That's precisely what happened with the Bills during 1972–74. Saban's wide receivers became blockers first and pass catchers second, with O.J. the beneficiary. If a receiver balked, he was traded, as happened to Denver-bound Haven Moses. Saban drafted Reggie McKenzie in the second round, and the guard from Michigan joined New York Jet reject Dave Foley (obtained on waivers) in giving a new look to the offensive line.

Saban further helped O.J. by using the I-formation, in which the Juice would have six yards behind the line of scrimmage to freelance and time to wait for holes to develop. His teammates became drive blockers, taking their defensive man whichever way he wanted to go and allowing O.J. the option of darting in the other direction.

It was no accident, then, that O.J. captured his first NFL rushing title in 1972, amassing 1,251 yards and rolling up six 100-yard games. That's twice the 100-yard efforts he mustered in the previous three seasons combined.

The Bills showed a glimmer of improvement in 1972, upsetting San Francisco and closing strongly by shocking the Super Bowl-bound Redskins in Washington. O.J. realized his first pro rushing crown in "The Year of the Running Back," and the Bills rose to a 4-9-1 record.

Simpson went on to his first Pro Bowl, a game many players look upon (and even avoid) with disdain. O.J. didn't. He was named Player of the Game, and Pittsburgh All-Pro defensive tackle Joe Greene reacted: "Man, if that guy had some blocking in Buffalo, they'd have to ban him from the league."

Saban worked on that blocking, drafting Michigan's Paul Seymour and Michigan State's Joe DeLamielleure one-two. Seymour, drafted as a tackle, instead became one of the game's best blocking tight ends and DeLamielleure (dubbed Joe D for obvious reasons) teamed with McKenzie as one of football's best guard tandems.

With Seymour at tight end, the Bills used an unbalanced line, flavored with three No. 1 draft choices and five Big Ten products. All were over 6 feet, 3 inches and under 25 years of age. To juice up the Juice's blocking even further, wide receiver J.D. Hill became one of the league's best crackback specialists.

The results were evident as soon as the 1973 season began. The Bills followed a winless preseason with O.J.'s 250-yard rushing effort, an all-time NFL record, to initiate the 1973 campaign against the Patriots in New England.

This was one of three times the Juice surpassed 200 yards in 1973. He did so both games against the Patriots and once in an historic season finale with the New York Jets, the snowcapped December day in Shea Stadium that O.J. became the first player in football history to rush 2,000 yards in a single season.

The Juice rambled 2,003 yards in 1973, the Bills became the sport's first 3,000-yard rushing team and blossomed toward a 9-5 record. They missed the playoffs—barely—but the future promised much. Buffalo had football's ultimate weapon, Simpson. And he was talking Super Bowl.

"When we go back to camp next summer, my goal will be the world championship," Simpson said. "At Buffalo, we're dedicated to attaining that."

In 1974, the Bills edged closer, again going 9-5 but reaching the NFL playoffs for the first time. However, the eventual champion, Pittsburgh Steelers, ousted them in the first round, 32-14. For O.J., the defeat climaxed a frustrating season. A severe ankle injury which forced him out early in the opener with Oakland never mended completely, and O.J. played hurt throughout the season. He finished with 1,125 yards and lost the NFL rushing title to Denver's Otis Armstrong.

In 1975, the Bills' highlight film was entitled "They Sure Were Exciting." They were—as O.J. and the offense rolled up a club record of 420 points. The Juice regained the rushing diadem with 1,817 yards, and there wasn't a more explosive offense in the game. Yet there was hardly a more porous defense. The Buffalo team slid to 8-6, missed the playoffs, and the downward slide had begun.

O.J. not only led the league in scoring, but outrushed nine NFL teams and established a record for single-season touchdowns

(23) in 1975. He realized a career high with 2,243 combined net yards, gained 227 rushing in keying an upset of the champion Steelers, became the second player in history to score at least a TD in every game, registered eight 100-yard games—and still the Bills couldn't reach title contention.

"One thing that season proved was that I couldn't make them a champion," O.J. later stated. "The Bills were the best offensive team in football and broke an all-time record for first downs, but we were eliminated from the playoffs with two games left in the season. Obviously, the team needs defensive players."

Simpson shocked the football world in 1976 by declaring he'd played his last game with Buffalo—that either he would be traded to a West Coast team, preferably Los Angeles, or he'd retire. O.J., super-rich with a wealth of endorsements and promising careers in television and the movies, wanted no more of a six-month separation from his family to play football. He wanted to play at or near home.

However, a trade never happened and Simpson returned to Buffalo just in time for the season opener, out of shape but richer with a record $2.2 million contract for three years.

Simpson was booed lustily by Buffalo fans as the Bills lost their opening-night game to Miami. Worse, fullback Jim Braxton was injured and lost for the season. Inner-squad dissatisfaction with management exploded over the courting of O.J. while others' requests were rejected.

Saban had long since felt his power eroding and, after an embarrassing loss to the New York Jets in the fifth game, decided to step down. Soon, quarterback Joe Ferguson suffered a broken back and was lost for the season.

It was near total disaster and the Bills won only two games, one over expansionist (and winless) Tampa Bay and none with Jim Ringo their head coach over the last nine games. Still, O.J. salvaged something big—breaking his own single-game rushing record with an astounding 273-yard performance Thanksgiving Day in Detroit.

O.J. wound up collecting 647 yards the final three weeks of the season, won his fourth NFL rushing title in five years with 1,503 yards and advanced to second place among all-time NFL rushers—behind Brown.

Two happy millionaires: O.J. and Bills' owner Ralph Wilson following the 1973 record 250-yard game in New England.
Photo by Robert L. Smith,
Elma, N.Y.

O.J. entered the 1977 campaign realizing his football career had entered the twilight zone. And then some. The point was driven home when knee surgery cost him the last half of the season. He never scored a 1977 touchdown, but he did manage to pass the 10,000-yard career rushing plateau—the second player to claim that achievement.

Yet, the sad season prompted O.J. to again meditate over his future. The average life of a running back in the NFL is five years and, originally, that's all O.J. planned on playing. But those three wasted years altered the plan and now, with Jim Brown's all-time yardage reign his only realistic goal, he needs two more seasons to surpass that.

He would have preferred the twilight years to be filled differently.

"Getting 2,000 yards satisfied my ego and left me with only one thing to attain in football—playing on a championship team," O.J. said in 1975. "Once a player wins an individual title, I don't know if it means so much to him after a while. I know what I want—that ring. That's all I need to complete my career."

Now, Simpson realizes the team trip to glory probably will never happen for him. In early 1978, he was traded to the San Francisco 49ers, another non-contender, and the trade means a new start, a new system, new teammates and all that adjustment—too late for that coveted team trip. Yet, he could still be No. 1.

"Brown's record has been in the back of my mind for some time," O.J. admitted after that devastating 273-yard game on Turkey Day in Detroit. And if the record comes, O.J. then will retire as many already consider him: The greatest running back in history.

He has already proved so much to so many. He has starred in several motion pictures—from *The Towering Inferno* with Paul Newman to *The Klansman* with Richard Burton and Lee Marvin. He has provided television commentary on numerous sports events, including the Montreal Olympics, and now owns a lucrative contract with NBC-TV.

His film fee exceeds $100,000 per appearance. His endorsement world couldn't be better. He has sold everything from autos

O.J. runs the obstacle course en route to $54,000 Superstars triumph in Rotonda, Florida. The Juice is an all-around champion.
AP Wirephoto

to sunglasses, and his Hertz airport rushes won a national advertising award. His per-game salary is pegged at $50,000 plus, and his after-dinner fee is $7,500.

In 1975, O.J. won ABC's "Superstars" (and $54,000) by taking the 100-yard dash in 9.69 seconds and capturing the bowling title. He was second in weight-lifting, tennis and rowing, and third in baseball hitting and the obstacle course.

When the dust finally settled, pole vaulter Steve Smith summarized the O.J. Show this way: "A guy who can run 9.7 and lift 260 pounds in the same day can't be from this planet!"

That's roughly the type of sentiment NFL defensive players have been expressing about Simpson since 1972. His is destined to go down as the most legendary career among running backs in NFL history.

Many of his games are or will become legends in themselves, beginning with those fabulous two seasons at the University of Southern California and onto the team which caught him in the draft—the Buffalo Bills.

Certainly, those half-dozen trips above the magical 200-yard plateau will be relived through films and stories for years to come. And yet, there have been so many other incredible, record-setting, pulsating moments in the career of the fabled No. 32.

The following chapters will recapture the most memorable of O.J.'s football exploits in games that marked the path of development for perhaps the most exciting gridiron player of all time. These games range in nature from "firsts" to disappointments to the spectacular.

CHAPTER ONE

The Fastest Trojan

O.J. Simpson entered the University of Southern California in 1967, tabbed not only as a sure-fire All-American but widely acclaimed as the most sensational junior college football player of all time.

As he stepped from two seasons at the City College of San Francisco, where he severed every national rushing and scoring mark in junior college grid history, Simpson was treated as a virtual messiah before his first major college game.

A writer who had covered Simpson for the San Francisco *Examiner* labeled him "the spittin' image of Gale Sayers." Dutch Elston, his junior college coach, claimed: "He has the balance of Jon Arnett." And Ray Willsey, the University of California coach, said O.J. reminded him of a young Ollie Matson.

And so, long before even that initial handoff, a love affair blossomed between the Juice and USC. The roots grew deeply for O.J. "I always wanted to go to USC," he said. "As a kid, I remember watching them on television and my dad talking about them. It was always embedded in my mind. Then I really got interested in 1962, the year they won the national championship. That's when they had Ben Wilson, Willie Brown, and all.

"When I was being recruited, everybody kept telling me USC already had so many good backs that I'd be better off going elsewhere," O.J. smiled. "That made me want to go there all the more. I wanted to compete with the best."

Legends travel quickly in. football, and word that the Trojans were about to feature a back who had scored 54 touchdowns in two years spread like wildfire. So did some of the details—such as one game against San Jose State in which he carried 17 times for 304 yards and six touchdowns. That was a freshman performance.

His sophomore blitz of San Jose was almost as overpowering, but this time he scored only five touchdowns, including one jaunt measuring 97 yards. Yes, he would be welcome indeed at USC.

To be sure, the majority of games in Simpson's two seasons as a Trojan could be singled out as highlights. In only his second game, he scored an early tying touchdown against Texas and legged 30 of 56 yards in a drive leading to a winning field goal. In game three, he arched a touchdown pass off a fake sweep which overcame Michigan State, 21-17. O.J. was humble. "Just to play Michigan State is a privilege," he said. This was a junior who had amassed 190 yards in 36 carries.

In game four, O.J. carried 29 times for 160 yards, caught two aerials for 52 and fired a 10-yard TD strike in a 30-0 blitz of Stanford. In game five, he carried six consecutive times inside the Notre Dame 18 to score a knotting six-pointer and, later, had 11 consecutive thrusts before scoring from 36 yards and igniting a 24-7 triumph over the Irish.

This was the pattern of O.J.'s great tailback career at USC. These were the usual exploits, spectacular for almost anyone else but commonplace for the Juice. Beyond this type of greatness, there were eight games in which O.J. reached yet a higher plateau. These were O.J.'s greatest games as a Trojan.

The first came midway through O.J.'s junior campaign, and the apex of the afternoon's excitement was his longest run of the season, an 86-yarder against the University of Washington.

O.J.: The way he was at USC, en route to the 1968 Heisman Trophy.
USC Photo

The Juice discusses his plans with his college coach, John McKay. McKay guided Simpson's fortunes in 1967-68.
AP Wirephoto

With the Huskie defense pinched tightly to defend an expected Simpson burst up the middle, O.J. accepted a handoff from quarterback Steve Sogge and swept toward the weak side. Adrian Young crumbled a linebacker and O.J. spun into the hole, cut back toward the middle and sped toward paydirt.

When the day was done, Simpson had rocketed a robust 235 yards in 30 carries. He added a 10-yard TD to the 86-yard game-breaker and lofted his third scoring pass of the season (a 16-yarder to Earl McCullough), and USC breezed, 23-6.

"I got 235 yards," O.J. beamed in the dressing room to Tim Rossovich, the huge defensive end. "That's only 16 short of the school record. I wish I could have broken the record, but the coach took me out. We got some big games coming up and he didn't want me to get hurt."

The sterling performance buoyed Simpson toward a sensational 13-touchdown season (rushing), one in which he led the collegiate nation with 1,543 yards off 291 trips (a 5.3 yard average). He became UPI's "Back of the Year" and "Player of the Year." He replaced former USC Heisman Trophy winner Mike Garrett as the Trojans' top single-season rusher. He finished second to UCLA quarterback Gary Beban in the Heisman race. And this was only the beginning.

O.J.'s sensational Trojan story peaked again in the annual war with UCLA, which usually boiled down to a Pacific Eight title clash. This time, it was different. The national championship was at stake.

USC had lost its last game, a 3-0 squeaker at Oregon State in which a foot injury bothered Simpson, who tasted defeat for the first time as a Trojan. The setback gave UCLA an opportunity for the NCAA crown, and O.J. was ready for the challenge. Some billed it as the "Game of the Decade."

With the score 7-7 in the first half, McCullouch worked an end-around for a 52-yard sprint to the Bruin 26. UCLA braced to bottle up Simpson with an eight-man front, but a pass to McCullouch foiled that defense and the Trojans were at the 13. Now it was O.J.'s turn.

As the deep back in the I-formation, O.J. took a pitchout and faked a sweep—as if to try to outleg the Bruins to the corner of the end zone. Instead, he utilized Danny Scott's wipeout of a defensive end and cut back inside, breaking several tackles. Before the defenders could recover, the Juice was at the five and carrying safety Sandy Green into the end zone on his shirt tail. USC led, 14-7.

However, this was to be one of those classic see-saw struggles. The Bruins not only battled back, but two Beban bombs lifted them into a 20-14 lead (a PAT being missed) with five minutes to play. USC was desperate and Simpson was the answer.

Quarterback Toby Page noticed the UCLA defense switch to double coverage on a receiver, potentially opening the middle. He switched to an automatic call at the line of scrimmage and he yelled O.J.'s number. O.J. was to carry up the gut.

He hugged the handoff, faked one way and followed Scott into a large gap under full steam with head bowed. Scott obliterated a linebacker and the Juice bolted right—toward open field. McCullouch, who had battled O.J. for honors as the fastest Trojan (and lost), raced upfield to provide an escort.

O.J. saw only one man to beat—Green—and darted left to place McCullouch between the safety and himself. Green was no match for the two 0:09.4 trackmen, his lunge netting only air, and Simpson completed a spectacular 64-yard TD trip which, with a conversion, won the game, 21-20. It also captured the title.

Afterward, O.J. revealed he adopted a tactic which enabled him to spring loose for the 64-yard game-winner. "It was nothing that I told the linemen or backs," he said. "I was getting hit pretty good, so I decided to fake into the wrong hole in the line when I carried, then cut back to where I was supposed to go."

UCLA tried a special tactic in the showdown game, too. But this one didn't work. Bruin coaches noted Simpson liked to lie on the ground a few extra seconds after rushing plays—to rest and catch his breath. The coaches instructed their defenders to quickly help O.J. to his feet. This was no act of sportsmanship, but a maneuver designed to prevent O.J. from resting.

Unfortunately for the Bruins, O.J. liked the pickup service. "It gets harder to get up as the game goes on, so I didn't mind," he said. He even laughed at the Bruins while they were coming to get him.

When the game ended, the Los Angeles Coliseum was aglow. O.J. had dazzled the huge crowd with an absolutely brilliant piece of broken-field running for a 13-yard score, breaking five tackles. "It seemed tougher on film," he quipped.. He had watched his team fall behind in the waning minutes, then captured victory and the nation's top collegiate rung with a magnificent 64-yard breakaway. Trojan fans had carried him off the field in typical collegiate football hero's style. O.J. relished every moment, but there was one more step before the USC slogan—"All the Way With O.J."—could be fulfilled. There was the Rose Bowl.

O.J. accepted handoffs 25 times against Indiana in the 1968 "Granddaddy" of all bowls at Pasadena. He barreled 128 yards, unstartling by Simpson standards. But he scored both touchdowns and USC won, 14-3. The thrill was matchless.

The Hoosiers were bracing for O.J. all afternoon, so coach John McKay crossed them up by ordering frequent passes on first down. In the first half, the Juice's outside running helped USC to the Hoosier two, where he used blocks by Scott and Bob Miller for a plunging score.

Later, O.J. sped 15 yards down the sideline with blurred vision and had it jolted clear by a crackling tackle. He and Scott took turns carrying, and USC reached the eight. There, O.J. took a handoff and bolted into a hole surrounded by a mass of humanity. He tunneled to the two, then spun off a defensive back and into the end zone.

O.J. was named the Rose Bowl's Most Valuable Player and he responded with comments which were to become his trademark in later years—superlative praise for his blockers. He told newsmen, many who were interviewing him for the first time, exactly who opened the holes for his key runs and pair of touchdowns. This was clearly no prima donna, no selfish limelight hugger. He knew that without those linemen who so often went unnoticed, he was nothing. All who listened were impressed.

The Heisman Trophy eluded O.J., but he expected that. Beban was a senior and, though his final year had not been spectacular, he compiled an outstanding three-year record at UCLA. "People tell me they're sorry, but I'm not," runner-up O.J. said. "I accomplished more than I ever thought possible this year. The happiest moments were reading the final polls, when we were first, and knowing I made All-America."

Besides, O.J. still had a senior season to grasp the Heisman, and how he wanted it!

Noting O.J. carried the ball seven of every 10 plays in 1967, and pointing out his special abilities, McKay thought he deserved recognition as college football's best player. So did numerous others.

"I have never been associated with, or seen, a player who could dominate a football game as much as O.J.," McKay lauded. "O.J. can chart the course of almost any game he plays in, if you get the ball to him often enough.

"Give O.J. one step and there's no way you can catch him," McKay praised on. "He's too fast. He's the best broken-field runner we've ever had at USC, and we had Mike Garrett and Frank Gifford."

Johnny Pont, the Indiana coach, echoed McKay's sentiments. "Simpson is one of the few runners I've seen in 12 years of coaching who can make a 90-degree turn and generate full speed within a step or two," he said. "He gets to the hole faster than any back I've ever seen. Your defensive linemen have to slow him or stop him. He's too big, too powerful, too quick for a linebacker or defensive back to bring down one-on-one."

There were different words awaiting O.J. when the Trojans opened the 1968 season at Minnesota. This greeting was posted in the Gopher dressing room: "Here Comes O.J. So What? He's Only Human."

The Gophers were about to find out just how "human" Simpson is.

Oh, he fumbled early in the game on his 15 and Minnesota took advantage for a 7-0 cushion, but that only served to arouse O.J. He wound up carrying 39 times for 236 yards and all four USC touchdowns in a 29-20 Trojan triumph. He also snared six passes worth 57 yards and answered three kickoffs for 72 more. That's a total yardage of 365—not a bad way to open the season.

His touchdowns? Well, the first was a 36-yard sweep around right end. The second was a one-yard dive. With Minnesota ahead, 20-16, O.J. carried six straight times in a personal drive from the Gopher 45 and scored from the seven by bolting for the sideline, pivoting and striding into the end zone. Soon he added a fourth, anticlimactic, insurance TD.

Yet, despite the quartet of scores, his most memorable run that afternoon didn't net a point. It came with four minutes to play and Minnesota holding that 20-16 edge. It was Juice's fourth straight carry. It was second-and-seven from the Gopher 27.

O.J. was bruised aplenty after being belted and piled upon most of the game by the large Minnesotans. He had suffered a deep thigh bruise, yet no one knew but him. Still, upon accepting the handoff, he swept right with the usual blazing speed. Only when he reached the right sideline, there was no more room to run. Or at least, that's the way it seemed.

Five Gophers had O.J. trapped. Suddenly, he put on a burst on the wet grass and darted 20 yards to the seven. The Metropolitan Stadium crowd in Bloomington, Minn., couldn't believe the move. It was that fantastic.

O.J. scored the go-ahead, winning touchdown two plays later— after his option pass to an open receiver fell short. When the game was over, O.J. had that thigh bruise, another on a shoulder, his ribs were badly battered and there were welts all over his body. And yet he had grown stronger as the game progressed. It was a performance which swung over witnesses who doubted whether O.J. was the greatest.

Murray Warmath, the Gopher coach, paid O.J. a handsome tribute. "They all say O.J. is the greatest, but he's been misrepresented. He's greater than that," Warmath declared.

Despite the thigh injury which slowed O.J., the Trojans breezed past the Miami Hurricanes the following weekend, 28-3. Losing coach Charlie Tate claimed: "O.J. makes running backs in our area look like a bunch of ribbon clerks."

O.J.'s second sensational day of the 1968 campaign came against Stanford, quarterbacked by Jim Plunkett. This performance was something special because of the way O.J. came onto the field. The thigh bruise had been aggravated against Miami, but almost no one realized how badly. Assistant coaches Marv Goux and Craig Fertig had to help Simpson through a tunnel at one end of the stadium. Pain lined his face. It hurt to walk, yet soon he was trotting.

Some three hours later, O.J. had rushed an incredible 47 times for 220 yards and three touchdowns, and USC barely won, 27-24. O.J. played 22 games in his two-season USC career and, considering the pain, this was his finest show.

Each time O.J. ran this day, he had to brace mentally to ignore the pain. He limped back to every huddle. In the third quarter, after a Plunkett pass bagged a 17-10 Stanford lead, O.J. took a pitchout and bolted 46 yards through a swarm of players to score his second TD, and USC tied, 17-17.

Soon the Indians were back in front, 24-17, but once again Simpson was the answer. A bomb from Steve Sogge to Jim Lawrence, with Stanford expecting O.J., set up USC on the four. On first down, O.J. smashed into the line, caromed high and sprang past several reaching defenders to score touchdown no. 3. Again USC had tied, 24-24.

Time was nearly gone when USC drove downfield to the Stanford 22. O.J. smashed into the line and, once again, bounced off. This time, he retreated, stumbling. He gained his balance and swung wide. Suddenly he spotted Scott waving his arms at the seven. O.J. fired on the run and Scott caught the toss, setting up Ron Ayala's winning field goal.

Afterward, friend and foe marveled at Simpson's super show under the duress of tremendous pain.

"I guess he showed us on a couple of those runs why he's 'the Man,' " marveled Stanford's Bob Moore. Teammate Don Parish agreed. "You might think a man as great as he is would be conceited and arrogant," Parish said. "But not him. He even complimented me when I hit him. Maybe he was trying to psych me out, I don't know. But he did it."

What he also did was establish a USC record for most carries (47) in one game and vault USC into the no. 1 national ranking in both wire service polls.

The sixth highlight game in O.J.'s Southern California career came the following week against Washington. He carried 33 times for 172 yards and both Trojan TDs in a 14-7 triumph. Yet what made this game special was O.J.'s comeback from nearly being adorned with "goat horns."

In the first quarter, the Juice worked a fourth down smash of one yard for a touchdown and 7-0 USC lead. The Huskies tied in chapter three on Buddy Kennamer's eight-yard scamper. Washington threatened to win midway through the fourth quarter after O.J. fumbled on his own 20, but the Trojan defense held at the one.

Given a reprieve, O.J. came alive in an awesome 99-yard march for the winning score. Simpson accumulated 57 yards off seven carries during that decisive march and cut outside left tackle for the winner, a nine-yard burst behind Jack O'Malley and Bob Miller. It was this kind of garrison finish, inspired by O.J., which was becoming almost a weekly habit for the Trojans, causing one scribe to dub them "the Cardiac Kids."

O.J. knew the game with Oregon State would require a special effort from him. For one thing, the winner would go to the Rose Bowl. For another, Oregon State had delivered his only defeat as a Trojan, that 3-0 squeaker of '67.

The Juice was even more certain when the fourth quarter started with USC trailing, 7-0, after he had fumbled on the Beaver 36. He just had to take matters into his own hands and hold on. The opportunity came on third-and-three at the Beaver 39. O.J. smashed the right side of the line, broke three tackles and scurried 11 yards for a first down. Three plays later, the score was tied. Not long after, a field goal handed USC a 10-7 edge. But the game was far from finished.

It needed a clinching touch or the Trojans were in danger of being overcome by a closing burst. Once again, Simpson provided the formula with less than two minutes remaining. O.J., who just cracked free for a first down, swung around right end. Bob Chandler, his future teammate in Buffalo, and Scott provided the key blocks as the Juice spurted 40 yards down the sideline for his 18th touchdown of the year.

The score was needed, too, because Oregon State did register a late touchdown. Because of O.J.'s run, it was meaningless, and USC was Pasadena-bound with a 17-13 victory.

O.J. had mustered another 47-carry effort, matching his own school record, and blazed a trail of 238 yards in pacing USC's eighth success and 11th in a row since that 1967 loss to the Beavers.

Yet the special nature of this performance among O.J.'s Trojan highlights was the rebound from that apparently disastrous fumble at the Oregon State 36—by far USC's best penetration at that point.

Instead of sulking, despairing or asking the coach for forgiveness, O.J. only became more determined. The thought that he might have blown the Rose Bowl trip did not faze him. After all, the fourth quarter had not yet begun.

And in that final period, O.J. lugged the ball no less than 20 times and rolled up 138 yards, including that brilliant 40-yard TD. After that fumble, he had gained 147 yards. That's a season's production for some players.

Victim No. 9 of the 1968 season was UCLA, and this game belongs among the Juice's most outstanding collegiate efforts for a unique reason. When this day was done, O.J. Simpson had rushed more times for more yardage in one season than any player before him in the 99-year history of college football.

This was also the occasion of USC's final triumph with O.J. at tailback, and it was another heart-pounder in the true tradition of the Cardiac Kids. In one striking way, it was similar to the victory over Washington.

The Trojans led by five points late in the game when UCLA advanced to the one-yard line, only to watch the Trojan defense halt the advance right there. O.J. took over, dashed three times for 47 yards and tallied an insurance TD which provided a 28-16 victory.

The Juice rushed 40 times for a walloping 205 yards against the Bruins, leading USC to its ninth victory without defeat. Just a half-week later, the Heisman Trophy winner would be announced, and O.J. was more than hopeful. Most experts thought he had a lock on the honor, but there were a few who observed that Purdue's Leroy Keyes played defense as well as offense.

McKay had the perfect answer for such people.

"If Jay played defense, he'd be the best tackler on the squad," the white-haired coach opined forcefully. "We watched Jay play defense in junior college. He was one of the best safetymen I've ever seen. But I'll guarantee you one thing. You will never see O.J. Simpson play defense for USC. We happen to believe he is a home run hitter. And you don't tell home run 'hitters to bunt."

It was a quotation many would remember during O.J.'s subsequent struggling years in Buffalo.

O.J. soon was revealed as the Heisman winner, and the Juice was aglow with college football's no. 1 individual prize. Yet his happiness soon was tempered because the Trojans ended his senior season on two downbeat notes, being tied by Notre Dame (21-21) and losing the Rose Bowl to Ohio State, 27-16.

Yet even those disappointments couldn't tarnish the indelible mark O.J. had left at USC. He finished with 1,709 rushing yards, an NCAA record which North Carolina's Don McCauley erased two years later. He equalled or bettered some 13 USC game, season and career standards.

Included were marks for career rushing (3,423 yards), single-season rushing (1,709 plus 171 in the '69 Rose Bowl), career total offense (3,471), one-season total offense (1,895), single-season TDs (23) and points (138), carries in a game (47), season (383) and career (674); most career rushes and passing plays (685), single-game TDs (4), career rushing TDs (36) and career points (216).

And so with 3,423 yards off 674 carries, O.J. averaged more than five yards per rush in smashing all the college standards for attempts and production. And USC had amassed an 18-2-1 record in two years because of him.

O.J. became most everyone's "Player of the Year" in landslide fashion and, naturally, headlined all the All-America selections. All were dwarfed by the ultimate award—College Athlete of the Decade.

The tributes poured in, none more glowing than one from his own coach. "I have never been around a man I admired more," McKay beamed. "He's a warm person, the most popular man on campus, and he goes out of his way to make friends. He isn't

O.J. poses with his old college jersey and the Heisman Trophy. They're treasures at O.J.'s Los Angeles home.
AP Wirephoto

noisy, although God knows he has every right to be loud, boastful and a little above everybody else. I think so much of O.J. that if he called me from across the country and said he wanted to talk to me, I'd take the next plane.''

CHAPTER TWO

A Debut with Buffalo

Winning the Heisman Trophy, being considered the No. 1 college athlete of a decade and becoming the most coveted prize of a football draft can have its drawbacks.

For one thing, it means the team with the worst won-lost record in the game holds draft rights to your professional career. It means leaving a climate where victories are commonplace and a championship feeling abounds and going to a town where losing has become a way of life.

Further, it means tough and extensive contract negotiations, perhaps spiced by hard feelings if a settlement doesn't come easily. It means sudden wealth but also a change in coaches, with a need to prove yourself all over again. And, just maybe, that new coach won't appreciate your finest abilities.

All of the above happened to O.J. once his Southern California days were finished. All that and more. There was a cultural change as well. Instead of playing in his native California and for the Los Angeles Rams, as he had wished, he was bound for wintry Buffalo. In place of Hollywood, he would find a blue-collar town in the industrial Northeast his football home. Instead of the established National Football League, he would play as a rookie in the American League. The merger, which cost him thousands of dollars in salary, wouldn't take effect in the schedule until 1970. Instead of the famed Coliseum, his home games would be played in a ghetto house of horrors named War Memorial Stadium.

To put it mildly, the transition was an incredible shock to this gifted young man at the impressionable age of 22.

There was another notable ingredient to the Juice's eastward ho movement—a 193-day holdout period. Chuck Barnes, O.J.'s agent, had strolled into Bills' owner Ralph Wilson's Detroit office and asked the following for Simpson's services: $650,000 spread over five years and a $500,000 loan.

Wilson blanched, then invoked one of his favorite adjectives: "That's an outrageous demand," he stormed. Wilson offered $250,000 over five seasons, take it or leave it, and the stalemate was on.

Days turned into weeks and O.J., growing restless, considered a million-dollar offer from a Texan to sign a personal services pact. He didn't consider it for long, however. The man could have O.J. washing dishes for the money, if he wished.

There also was a $250,000 offer from Indianapolis of the Continental League, but that was a minor circuit. O.J. even talked of sitting out of football for a season—he grew that disgusted. Finally, there was a break, and it came at O.J.'s end.

Simpson realized his lucrative endorsement contracts—a three-year, $180,000 agreement with Chevrolet, another for $37,500 annually from Royal Crown Cola and an announcing pact with ABC-TV—depended on his active football career. And so he signed.

Wilson declared he would shell out to O.J. "more than any rookie has been paid since the NFL-AFL merger [1966]." Most experts took that to mean he would surpass Steve Spurrier's reported three-year windfall of $200,000 from the San Francisco 49ers.

Some pegged O.J.'s four-year contract at $250,000 plus a $100,000 loan, but the Juice later said Wilson didn't budge from his $50,000 per-year pitch plus the loan. He knew the NFL's

Here's how O.J. looked as a 1969 Bills' rookie. All the Buffalo recruits had their heads shaven.
Buffalo Bills Photo

longest rookie holdout had to sign or risk losing those fantastic side deals. This was Simpson's invaluable indoctrination into the shrewdness of Wilson, a millionaire insurance and trucking executive.

"All those other deals were tied to my football career, which is why I always tell Ralph that he got me cheap," Simpson said. "I finally agreed to play for $50,000."

"I'm awfully glad it's over," O.J. stated upon the end of the record rookie holdout run. "I never wanted to lay out a year, and I've always wanted to play in either the AFL or the NFL, the best level possible. I know I'm getting to training late, but I'm anxious to get started."

The Bills had not only undergone the most basic phase of training camp by the time Simpson signed but played two exhibition games. It was Aug. 9, 1969, when O.J. finally inked a contract in the office of a Los Angeles attorney.

Finally, O.J. would make his first appearance as a professional, as a Buffalo Bill. And, ironically, that appearance would come in Detroit, Ralph Wilson's home town, in an exhibition with the Lions.

First, there were problems during the early days of O.J.'s crash course into pro football. Problems such as the Bills had no helmet large enough for his head . . . such as O.J. had to switch from his famed No. 32 to 36 because Gary McDermott, another running back, already had the former uniform . . . and such as O.J.'s inability to grasp coach John Rauch's system, a pass-oriented setup which turned off the Juice from the outset.

As anyone might expect, all kinds of jokes were cracked about O.J.'s head being too large for a Bills' helmet, but the rookie merely grinned and a rush order went out to USC for his old helmet. O.J. considered the uniform number problem "no big thing" and accepted No. 36. As for Rauch's system, it would bother and hamper O.J. for two years.

Rauch made it plain that he wasn't about to compromise his setup just to accommodate the NFL's premier draft pick. Running may have been the name of the game at USC, but O.J. would be expected to block, be a receiver and a decoy for the Bills. Rauch would employ the same system with which he

The rookie arrives: O.J. scans field with Bills' Coach John Rauch. O.J. wore No. 36 until Gary McDermott's departure left No. 32 available. *Photo by Robert L. Smith, Elma, N.Y.*

coached Oakland into the 1968 Super Bowl—under Al Davis' wing.

But Rauch tried to soften the blow to O.J. And O.J.'s responses were mild. "We like to throw often," the coach explained. "We like to throw to our backs. To tell the truth, I'm really impressed by O.J.'s pass catching. We should be able to exploit his ability to catch the ball."

O.J. was in a turmoil inside, but publicly he uttered statements such as: "In junior college, I was mainly a pass receiver and I have always liked to go out for passes."

And so after just three practices, it was time for Simpson's long-delayed debut, on Aug. 15, 1969. He did not expect to see much action in Tiger Stadium, but he was surprised. He played only two downs or 12 seconds in the first half, but Rauch used him most of the fourth quarter.

Wilson, as excited as a kid, felt lucky. He had good reason. His Oxford Stables had just captured its first stakes victory in the East after 18 years. A horse which had cost Wilson $2,000 to enter had just captured the $23,578 Sanford Stakes at Saratoga. O.J.'s salary was coming home at the track.

Soon there was another omen. The first time O.J. made an appearance in the game, the Bills scored. He came on with 5:41 gone in the first quarter and stayed for one play.

It was first down and 15 at the Lions' 20. Rauch sent in O.J. to replace Max Anderson, a diminutive running back. Quarterback Tom Flores dispatched O.J. to the left flat and Haven Moses was the inside man in a slot formation. Moses received single coverage from safety Mike Weger because Detroit could not afford to help Weger—not with O.J. opposite Ed Mooney, a 240-pound linebacker, on the other side of the field.

"I faked a post pattern and broke to the outside," Moses related. Flores passed to him in the right corner of the end zone for a touchdown. Moses lost Weger completely. And for O.J., it was one play, one touchdown. "O.J. was open, too," Flores commented.

Detroit, en route to a 24-12 triumph, had game control by the fourth quarter, but the 34,206 Lions' partisans weren't thrilled.

In fact, they were bored. They had come to see Simpson and the chant of "We want O.J." rolled up from those craving excitement.

Rauch answered the request and inserted Simpson in the same backfield with rookie quarterback James Harris, who received a sound second-half audition. O.J. carried four times in that final quarter, gaining 19 yards. Included was a 14-yard burst off-tackle, a dash which the Juice nearly broke open.

Simpson's biggest moment came late in the game, setting up Buffalo's last TD. "We worked on the play along the sideline," O.J. explained. "Cornerback Lem Barney was picking me up from the linebacker when I ran a long pattern down the sideline. So they had me kind of loaf as if I was just running out into the flat. Then, just before Barney picked me up, I was to break loose."

The Juice breezed past Barney, who was then probably the best cornerback in the game. Harris rocketed a perfect pass for a 38-yard gain before Weger belted O.J. out of bounds as he made the grab.

"O.J. said I really laid it out there, but he made a great catch and made me look good," Harris lauded. Soon Harris rifled a 22-yard scoring strike to Earthquake Enyart, another member of this all-rookie backfield, and O.J. contributed by leveling a Lion trying to sack Harris.

When the game was over, Harris had completed seven of 13 aerials for 87 yards, playing all the second half. The rocket-armed quarterback had three passes dropped. Some of his aerial attempts looked like they were launched by a mortar, but Enyart managed to grasp four for 44 yards. "There's no way he can throw too hard to suit me," said Rauch, a statement to be long remembered around Buffalo.

While Harris' audition dominated Buffalo's statistics, Detroit's showed Mel Farr with a four-yard TD, Bill Munson with a 10-yard TD pass to tight end Charley Sanders, Earl Mann with a 20-yard field goal, and Altie Taylor with a late 48-yard TD off a draw.

And yet the attention grabber was O.J. He had to be convoyed off the field afterward and Bugsy Engelberg, the Bills' rotund kicking coach, was dumped unceremoniously.

In the bustling dressing room, a hand thrust through a maze of sports writers at Simpson's stall. "O.J., welcome to the squad," smiled Ralph Wilson.

"Yes, sir," O.J. replied. "Thank you very much."

"You're going to help pull us out of the cellar," Wilson quipped, thinking of Buffalo's 1-12-1 campaign of 1968.

"Well . . . ," O.J. answered. He certainly wasn't very confident of that. Witnesses laughed—even Wilson. He wasn't so sure, either. Soon after he left O.J., a writer asked the Bills' boss his impression of his team's overall effort. "We played like a bunch of bums," Wilson scoffed. He was not thrilled at seeing his team undressed before his neighbors, even in preseason.

Simpson, used to being physically spent after his USC games with as many as 47 carries, wasn't a bit tired afterward. Though this was to bother him after other games, it didn't this night. He hadn't expected to see much activity.

"I was surprised I played so much," he said. "I was nervous at first because they put me in sooner than I expected. I was standing in the wings and didn't know whether to sit down or stand up. But once I got in and got bumped a little, I was all right.

"I'm pleased with my effort, but you can't be too pleased when you don't win," the Juice went on. "Some of the plays I knew thoroughly. But while I knew them, I wasn't immediately reacting to the necessary patterns. I need more work to do that."

Rauch explained that the Bills' ragged appearance was due to the large number of players used. "This was our third game [after a loss at Houston and victory over Vince Lombardi's Washington Redskins] and we played many more people than we did in the first two," Rauch said. "This, naturally, broke our continuity. We made far too many mistakes. However, we must build reserve strength and you only do that by using all your material. We have three weeks before the regular season, and we'll have a respectable team by then."

His listeners doubted that.

Rauch was still in the courting stage with Simpson, however. After all, this was only game one in the rookie's career.

"I played him longer than I planned to because he seemed to be enjoying the workout," the coach observed, recalling that O.J. still had to feel the effects of a cross-country flight, moving his family and only three days in camp. "He was confident, so I let him stay in."

Rauch seemed enthusiastic when asked if he spotted flashes of greatness in Simpson's abbreviated performance.

"Sure," Rauch replied. "He runs tough in the middle, he runs good to the outside, he explodes upfield, he can follow his blockers and he'll always be a threat as a receiver. But this is no new find. He's done it all a hundred times before."

There was one more debut confronting O.J. and it came the following weekend—his introduction to Buffalo's home fans at War Memorial Stadium, the antiquated facility Buffalo writers referred to as the "Monument to Decay." O.J. was to find the stadium disgusting, an incredible comedown from the Coliseum, but the fans were rabid—and extremely loud!

The crowd of 45,750—largest ever for a preseason game at the old stadium—roared at the mere sight of Simpson. The Baltimore Colts, champions of the NFL but shocked Super Bowl losers to Joe Namath and the New York Jets, were the opponent. O.J. was the object of the fans' admiration, but he was clearly in awe of the Colts.

He had grown up marveling at the exploits of Johnny Unitas, Lenny Moore, Gino Marchetti, Big Daddy Lipscomb and company. All the memories came back when, during the warmup, O.J. glanced downfield at the Colts. Now, in his first game at Buffalo, O.J. would actually oppose the great Unitas.

Unitas didn't disappoint the Juice—he fired a 70-yard touchdown bomb and converted five of eight third downs as the Colts, showing their great experience advantage, notched a 20-7 triumph. Baltimore made the big plays while the young Bills struggled.

It was a learning adventure for O.J., still wearing No. 36. He carried five times for just 25 yards, but flashed his brilliance twice by making a sharp cut and squirming free for decent gains. Yet he was nabbed holding, he missed assignments and was smashed with a forearm to the head by blitzing linebacker Sid Williams.

Further, as in Detroit, O.J. got a taste of his role as a decoy on aerial patterns. It didn't bother him yet—not after two exhibitions and missing most of training camp as a rookie. But he didn't understand, either. He never would.

CHAPTER THREE

The First 100-Yard Game

After six weeks, O.J. was beginning to wonder if the Bills were ever going to win a game with him in the lineup. The preseason ended with a ragged loss to Chicago, 23-16, in a head-to-head clash with Gale Sayers and an embarrassing 50-20 shellacking by the Rams in O.J.'s celebrated return to the Los Angeles Coliseum. That defeat was to mark the beginning of a long line of frustrations for O.J. in West Coast visits.

Then the season bell rang and lopsided defeat continued. The Bills lost their opener to the Super Bowl champion New York Jets, 33-19, and then Houston posted a 17-3 triumph.

Next, Lou Saban was bringing the Denver Broncos to town to finish Buffalo's three-game homestand. And "finish" seemed the appropriate word for the lethargic Bills. For veterans, the victory drought lasted far longer than six weeks. To be precise, it was 364 days or 12 games since Buffalo last realized success in a regular season game.

It seemed the pattern would continue as Pete Liske's 11-yard TD pass to Mike Haffner gave Denver a 14-3 cushion after one quarter. However, thanks to O.J. and veteran quarterback Jack

Kemp (now a western New York congressman), the Bills suddenly lived up to their billing and became offense-minded. They exploded for 38 points in the middle periods.

Kemp, playing his final season, took to the air and launched an 80-yard drive which was capped by a three-yard pitch to the wide-open Simpson for a touchdown. O.J. (wearing no. 32 with McDermott waived) had lost a linebacker. Bruce Alford's 30-yard field goal brought the Bills within 14-13 and then Kemp hit Haven Moses on a streak pattern for a 55-yard TD which netted a 20-14 halftime advantage.

O.J. was to score two touchdowns this day, yet said the Kemp-to-Moses touchdown heave "gave me more satisfaction than both." He had good reason.

The Broncos had a safety blitz on and O.J., who had been encountering trouble with his blocking assignments, wasn't fooled by the linebacker trying to draw him out. O.J. tucked back in and really popped the charging safety. Because of that blitzing safety, only one Bronco was covering the fleet Moses and he fell down. Moses snared Kemp's toss and was home-free. And O.J. was proud of his role.

Denver regained the lead in the third quarter when Liske's underthrown pass fooled corner Booker Edgerson and Al Denson turned to make the grab, then wheeled for a 62-yard score. But O.J. ignited the Bills with a 28-yard burst up the middle. Kemp contributed three completions, and, with the Broncos expecting O.J., he handed off to fullback Wayne Patrick for a four-yard TD. The Bills led, 27-21, and never looked back.

Butch Byrd's interception and 12-yard return bagged another score and, after strong safety John Pitts made a lunging interception at the Bills' one, the Bills drove for their final score. O.J. barreled 12 yards in two tries and the Broncos contributed holding, face-mask and interference penalties. Kemp then rifled a seven-yard TD pass to tight end Billy Masters. The Bills outscored Denver, 38-7, in the middle periods and won, 41-28, despite Liske's three touchdown passes.

The reasons for the form reversal were Simpson and Kemp. O.J., given a rare opportunity to carry 24 times, responded with 110 yards, his first pro game over the magic 100-yard plateau and the first Buffalo player to exceed 100 in three years.

O.J. hurdles teammate Earthquake Enyart en route to first pro 100-yard game. The Bills trampled Denver, 41-28, for their first 1969 victory.
Photo by Robert L. Smith,
Elma, N.Y.

Kemp, who had directed the Bills to American League championships in 1964 and 1965, reached back for his old expertise, completing half of 38 passes for 249 yards, three TDs and with no interceptions. Five passes went to Simpson for 45 yards and Buffalo's first touchdown.

Many observers couldn't believe O.J.'s reaction to his initial pro 100-yard game. Again, he focused on his blocking—especially that first-half crunch of the blitzing safety, allowing Kemp to throw the TD pitch to Moses.

"Naturally, I was glad to go over 100 yards for the first time," the Bills' prize running back declared. "But I'm really most happy with my blocking. I had my best day blocking against Denver."

O.J. was ecstatic over the initial victory as a professional. "It turned a year of frustration into a day of hope," he later said. "That hope was short-lived, as things worked out, but its brief intensity left its impression. I never imagined that winning one game could mean quite so much. How sweet it was!"

Suddenly, after those early disappointments, some were already mentioning O.J. in connection with the AFL rushing title. The only rookies who had won the league crown were Dallas' Abner Haynes (1960) and Cincinnati's Paul Robinson (1968), but certainly the widely heralded O.J. could become a third. The questions started about his goals.

"I never set any goals, though everyone uses 1,000 yards as a plateau," O.J. answered. "After this game, I see no reason why I shouldn't have more 100-yard days—in which case there'd be no problem reaching 1,000. The big thing is to keep progressing and avoid injuries."

O.J.'s optimism was refreshing. "Your whole outlook changes after winning, especially when you score so many points," he said. "It was the best thing that could have happened to us. We suffered no injuries and now we feel we not only can do it again, but that we have the potential to score from anyplace on the field."

Even Rauch, troubled after other games, was bubbling. "You had a good game," he told the Buffalo players. "You went after people. We had some mistakes, but there was nothing we can't work on and correct."

Clearly, O.J. and Rauch figured the Bills would go on toward better things, but what followed were five defeats in the next six games and a 4-won, 10-lost season. As far as high scoring went, the Bills never reached 30 points again that year, let alone 40.

O.J. thought he surely would eclipse 100 yards several more times that season, but his second century game didn't come until the mid-mark of the 1970 campaign. The rushing title went poof, as well. O.J. finished sixth with 697 yards. AFL Rookie-of-the-Year honors went to a running back, but not O.J. The winner was Boston's Carl Garrett, and Patriot fans were yelling with glee: "O.J. Who?"

"It wasn't a good season, either for me or the team," the Juice admitted. He wasn't complaining—not yet—but was perplexed when he glanced over his rushing attempts. Against Oakland, he carried six times. Against Miami, he ran but 10 and realized a paltry 12 yards. He never approached the 24 carries he had against Denver, and here was a fellow who had lugged the ball 47 times in two USC games a year earlier. He had been drafted to run with the ball. And yet he wasn't getting it. Why?

He couldn't figure it out and no one could tell him, except he knew Rauch didn't believe in building a team's attack around one man. Even so, O.J. reasoned, why only seven carries in a season-ending game at San Diego? Sure, a team can't run when it's playing catch-up and the Bills were blown out, 45-6, but what about earlier? What about changing the game plan?

At season's end, the rushing figures read 181 carries, 697 yards and two touchdowns. For a Heisman Trophy winner, the College Athlete of the Decade and pro football's most heralded rookie, this was the epitome of deflation. O.J. would never forget it.

How could he forget a season in which 110 yards rushing represented his finest game—by far? That first season of one 100-yard game would become microscopic by his standards of the Seventies. After 1977, he would own some 41 such 100-yard efforts.

Clearly, O.J. and Rauch were at odds. The coach told him that, unlike college ball, a successful team needs an effective aerial game to win. O.J. argued that to be successful, a team must have a solid rushing attack and wasn't that why he was drafted No. 1?

"Namath is the best passer around, but the Jets have been

winning with a running game," O.J. remarked. "We've been trying to win with passes and we don't even have a Namath. Also, when the Chicago Bears get behind, you can be sure they're going to give the ball to Gale Sayers."

O.J. had made his point, but it fell on deaf ears.

CHAPTER FOUR

Injury and an Early Trip Home

It was 1970, the second year of John Rauch's reign in Buffalo, and the Bills began the season as they had 1969—by dropping the first two games at home. This time the defeats went to Denver, 25-10, and Los Angeles, 19-0. The Broncos held O.J. to 52 yards, the Rams 24.

Yet, as they had the previous season, the Bills rebounded in game three—with O.J. the catalyst. O.J., used on the suicide unit in his early pro years, electrified a Buffalo sellout crowd of 46,206 by racing 95 yards to paydirt with a kickoff just after the New York Jets had taken a 7-0 lead.

Simpson bobbled the ball at the Bills' five, then let go with a burst of speed that left rookie George Nock chasing him into the end zone. Al Andrews and Dick Cunningham provided the key blocks. It was the only kickoff-return touchdown of O.J.'s pro career.

Significantly, it came just before a Joe Namath milestone—his 100th touchdown pass, a 72-yard connection with tight end Rich Caster.

O.J., hooted in 1970 because of an outbreak of "fumbleitis," was magnificent as the Bills outscored New York, 34-31. O.J. carried 21 times for 99 yards, caught three passes for 63 yards and amassed 141 (including the long TD) off two kickoff replies. That totaled 303 yards—then the 10th highest aggregate in NFL history.

This was also the day Dennis Shaw, eventually the NFL Rookie-of-the-Year, realized his initial pro start—and was an immediate, smash success. Shaw outplayed the fabled Namath, mixing his plays well and completing 12 of 21 aerials for a robust 317 yards. Shaw lofted two scoring strikes to Marlin "The Magician" Briscoe measuring 19 and 25 yards.

A tremendous Buffalo comeback netted the surprise victory, with Shaw, Briscoe and Simpson playing the lead roles. New York, usually snake-bitten in War Memorial Stadium, held a 24-13 halftime advantage.

Shaw's 19-yard heave to Briscoe and a PAT cut the margin to four, but Emerson Boozer rambled six yards to score and the Jets seemed golden. They led by 31-20 entering the final quarter.

However, the Jets never scored again, and O.J. rallied the Bills within striking distance with a one-yard TD smash after 5:20. Exactly two minutes later, Shaw faded and flung a 25-yard TD pass to Briscoe, winning the game, 34-31.

The Bills bowed to Pittsburgh (23-10) and Miami (33-14) and seemed back in their familiar shell at 1-4 when suddenly they broke out. They edged the Jets in New York, 10-6, and followed with an incredibly strong effort in walloping the Patriots at Boston, 45-10. The Bills owned a 31-0 halftime margin and fans watching via television from western New York couldn't believe their eyes. This hardly seemed like the Bills they knew.

O.J. turned the game in a lopsided direction with a brilliant 56-yard scoring burst which bagged a 17-0 second-quarter lead. He finished with the best rushing day of his first three pro years, gaining 123 yards in 17 carries—a 7.2 average.

Suddenly O.J. ranked third among American Conference rushers with 448 yards. Suddenly the Bills were 3-4 and looking sharp. Suddenly they had a passing threat in Shaw.

Into Buffalo came Paul Brown's Cincinnati Bengals, reeling with a 1-6 record and six-game losing skein. They had scored but

Bengals sandwich O.J., leading to 1970 knee injury. His 1970 season ended after eight games.
Photo by Robert L. Smith,
Elma, N.Y.

10 points in the two previous games. The situation appeared ripe for Buffalo to reach the .500 level and a crowd of 43,587 showed hoping for just that. Instead, disaster resulted.

There were plenty of omens, too. Shaw fumbled the first center snap. On the very next play, Wayne Patrick dropped an easy swing pass. In all, the Bills fumbled five times and were penalized seven without ever touching Bengal quarterback Virgil Carter. But these were far from the major problem.

The first half began innocently enough, with Shaw looping a 29-yard TD pass to Briscoe. After Cincinnati gained a 13-7 lead, O.J. raced 51 yards with a kickoff and followed Austin Denney's great 24-yard catch with a one-yard TD slant. The Bills led, 14-13, late in the first half.

Then, just 17 seconds after O.J.'s score, rookie Lemar Parrish accepted a kickoff at his five, rammed full speed into and through a wall of tacklers at the Bengal 40 and zoomed to a 95-yard TD return. Shortly, Horst Muhlmann came in to kick his third of five field goals that day and the Bengals led, 23-14, with just 11 seconds left in the half. There was time for a kickoff, a return and that's about all.

That was just enough to scramble the Bills' season at its midpoint.

Muhlmann kicked off to Simpson, who caught the ball near the sideline and ran ahead five yards. He was grabbed around the ankle at the Bills' 20, tried to squirm free but could not. Then Ron Lamb and two other Bengals sent him sprawling in pain.

O.J.'s right knee was injured—so badly that he could not get up. Al Cowlings, his boyhood friend and USC teammate, and guard Joe O'Donnell carried him off the field. He was taken immediately to a hospital.

"We had a right return play on," Simpson explained. "I ran way left to catch the ball, couldn't get back to the right and started up the sideline. Muhlmann grabbed me. I was mad—a classic case of not concentrating on what I was doing. If I'd have just gone down, I'd have been all right. But my mind was on other things and the knee was twisted when others hit me.

"I think if a runner gets hurt, it's his own fault," O.J. went on. "I've only been hurt this once and it was my own carelessness. I caught the kickoff near the sideline and my blockers didn't adjust over to help me. I got so mad at them I stopped concentrating on what I was doing. Muhlmann got ahold of me and I just stood up there and let some of the people hit me."

Just that suddenly, halfway through the season's seventh game, O.J. was finished for 1971. At first, the injury was diagnosed as a "moderately sprained outer knee." Later that was amended to a "light tear of the capsule in back of the knee."

The impact on the Buffalo team was overwhelming. The Bengals, capitalizing on a steady stream of breaks, scored 20 unanswered points and went on to a 43-14 rout. The Bills never won another game that season and finished 3-10-1. The Bengals, incredibly, never lost again. They completed the season with a seven-game winning streak, and not only reached the playoffs but won the AFC Central Division title with an 8-6 record.

O.J., meanwhile, stayed around Buffalo for a month after the

Boyhood friend Al Cowlings (right) helps O.J. toward dressing room
after knee injury on kickoff return shelved him.
Photo by Robert L. Smith,
Elma, N.Y.

injury, suspecting he would undergo surgery which never came. In fact, while at the hospital that Sunday evening after the game, O.J. was prepared physically and psychologically for an operation. He was examined for 45 minutes while under anesthesia. He didn't learn until he awoke the next morning that no surgery would be required.

The loss of Simpson was just the headliner of unfortunate incidents which befell the Bills this game. Moses was helped off the field with a badly pulled leg muscle. Shaw, belted by Ron Carpenter with his arm cocked, found his apparent forward motion ruled a fumble, which Royce Berry retrieved for an eight-yard TD. Then Rauch, ordering a field goal despite a 22-point deficit late in the game, looked on in horror as the attempt was blocked by Ken Riley and scooped by Parrish, who was off to the races for a closing 83-yard TD.

It was one nightmare after another for the Bills and a dramatic season turn for Cincinnati. "We went six games without a real break, and now we get them all in one afternoon," observed linebacker Larry Ely with a broad grin in the Bengal boudoir.

Paul Brown echoed the sentiments. "The things that happened to the Bills today—like losing O.J. and then Haven Moses—happened to us in early season when Greg Cook and Mike Reid were injured," the Bengal boss declared. "I was sorry to see the two Bills' stars get helped off the field. Maybe the Bills weren't up for this game because we had lost six straight and they won two in a row. Anyway, the momentum turned after Parrish's run."

Lost in the Simpson saga and the surprise, lopsided score was the fact that Cincinnati with 43 points scored only one offensive touchdown all afternoon. Rauch tried the stiff-upper-lip approach. "We didn't play that bad football, but a lot of unfortunate things happened to us," he reasoned. All about him, the Bills' dressing room resembled a tomb and it stayed that way the rest of the year.

Two weeks later, O.J. was still limping around Buffalo suspecting surgery would be ordered any minute. The swelling had not gone and he was restless. "This sitting around, wondering what will happen, is killing me," he complained.

Finally, one month after the mishap, O.J. was told he could go home. He departed just as the Bills' tension with Rauch was reaching a new peak. In the last six seconds of a 14-10 loss to Boston, after Jim Harris had marched the Bills into scoring position, Rauch yanked Harris and reinserted starting quarterback Shaw for one last play, which failed. On the sidelines, helmets were hurled and shouts rolled out at Rauch's decision, which some players termed "callous."

O.J. was happy to be leaving such controversy and ill feeling behind as he flew home to California.

"Personally, I was feeling good about this season until that Cincinnati game," the Juice declared. "Dennis was throwing well, I was running well and feeling more comfortable than I had since turning pro. I even think I was starting to do some of the things people expected of me.

"We're a young team and a lot of our question marks have been resolved," O.J. claimed, perhaps kidding even himself. "I think we were much better this year, yet we had an easier schedule. Some things you just can't figure. Right now, I intend to go home and rest. I'd like to forget football for three or four months, say until next May or June, but it will be tough to forget this season."

Dr. Joseph Godfrey, the Bills' physician, stated O.J.'s knee injury would heal by itself in four to six weeks, which it did. But the tensions with Rauch never eased and neither did the team's injury problems. Five Buffalo players followed O.J. to the sidelines with season-ending mishaps. And O.J., despite missing a half-season, wound up the Bills' leading rusher.

Simpson, finishing with 488 yards in 120 carries, had also hauled in 10 passes for 139 yards and returned seven kickoffs for 333 yards—a resounding average of 47. But returning kickoffs also led to his season lasting 7½ games instead of 14.

O.J. departed Buffalo without saying much about Rauch, but others talked openly about a "mutual disrespect" between the coach and his players. They called him cold, indifferent to their feelings and attitudes.

It wasn't until later years that O.J. really bared his feelings about Rauch. "He and I never hit it off," O.J. declared. "We never hit it off starting from the day I reported to Buffalo, when he tried to make me a receiver instead of a runner. I was a rookie and so I had to go along, but Rauch and I really began having run-ins in my second season.

"I knew then the offense wasn't working and I figured we should try something different. Rauch tried to impress the players with his system and was determined to stick with it, regardless of our record or what it cost the players."

O.J. said his relationship with Rauch grew as hot as it could, but he never asked to be traded—even in times when he wanted out very badly.

Yet, as much as O.J. disliked Rauch and what he was doing to his football career, the Juice grew hotter over something else.

"I hated the damned excuses most of all," O.J. admitted. "Some people said I'd do better with another team, like the Rams. I said I'd do better if they'd just give me the ball more— and it all left a bad impression of me.

"Sometimes I wonder how I got through it without giving up on myself. But I learned a lesson. I promised myself that if things ever got turned around, I'd never forget the bad times that some guys have to go through. Even today, there might be some rookie someplace listening to a coach like John Rauch, who wanted to teach me to hit the holes in the line faster and give up my stutter-stepping style.

"I don't think styles should be tampered with," O.J. said. "Take Anthony Davis [another ex-great USC tailback now reunited with coach McKay in Tampa Bay]. He's what I call an 'insane runner,' and he's one of only five or six in the country. A lot of guys can fake you, give you a leg and take it away. But A.D. and a few like him [O.J., for example] do things you don't expect. That's something you can't teach. It's instinctive. And it shouldn't be changed."

As O.J. flew home to California, following an aborted, second disappointing season in Buffalo, he didn't realize it yet, but Rauch would be his coach no longer. Yet, a third year of frustration awaited his return to the Bills.

CHAPTER FIVE

The Ultimate Embarrassment

When O.J. and other Bills veterans strolled into the team's Niagara University training camp in the summer of 1971, they were greeted by a new but familiar head coach, Harvey Johnson.

Johnson was a friendly, loquacious player personnel director who twice was a "disaster" coach in at least two ways: (1) the appointed coach departed suddenly and at a time when no replacement from the nation's coaching ranks could be found, and (2) disastrous won-lost record resulted each time.

In 1968, Wilson fired Joel Collier after the season's second game. Johnson took over and the Bills finished with a 1-12-1 record, just horrible enough to be the worst in pro football, qualifying the Bills to draft O.J. Simpson with the NFL's premier pick.

Now Johnson took over again after Rauch went on a Buffalo television show and criticized two of the Bills' most popular players of the 1960's. Rauch labeled Paul Maguire "the clown of the team" and criticized the play of Ron McDole. Both Maguire, a star punter, and McDole, a tremendous defensive end who went on to much greater heights with Washington, had been dropped from the team by Rauch. Wilson heard about the show, came to Buffalo to view a tape and promptly told Rauch he would publicly defend the players.

Rauch responded: "Do that and you can find yourself another coach." Wilson did. He beckoned Harvey Johnson.

To put it mildly, O.J. was not sorry to see Rauch gone, but he was surprised—the blowup not happening until the day he arrived back in Buffalo and veterans not learning of Rauch's exit until they entered camp.

O.J. turned hopeful his career would take a positive turn. Things seemed to be improving. Rauch, the coach Buffalo players called "Satan," was gone. After much ado, Erie County legislators passed a $20.5 million bond resolution for a new 80,000-seat stadium in suburban Orchard Park, meaning 1972 would be the Bills' last season in rundown War Memorial Stadium. And, most important to O.J., Johnson seemed determined to build an offense around him.

"We'll give the ball to O.J., get out of his way and watch him run," Johnson declared. "We'll have three new plays: O.J. to the right, O.J. left and O.J. up the middle."

That's all the Juice needed to hear. He was ebullient. He liked Johnson's approach and said so. "Rauch used to have long practices, long meetings, long everything," he said. "We'd even have to stay in a hotel the night before home games. Harvey has short practices and short meetings. He has honed the system down to fundamentals. I look forward to practice now. I feel like I'm back in high school again."

The Bills split six exhibition games, and O.J.'s optimism grew. He even admitted to being cocky. "On any given day we can beat the best and we've proved it," he claimed. He connected the apparent turnabout to Johnson. "We used to be a dull team, but now we can score from anywhere on the field," he said. "I'm being used more in situations where I can get some open-field running. I'm used more like I used to be in college with flares, draws and sweeps. This year, everybody is psyched up to play. The line's blocking is a hundred times better."

O.J. forgot one thing. He was basing all this optimism on preseason appearances—and those can be mighty deceiving.

Colts' linebacker Ray May helps O.J. to his feet. This 1971 game was
O.J.'s most embarrassing: minus 10 yards.
Photo by Bob Bukaty

The season began and the Bills were, to borrow a phrase from horse-racing terminology, left at the post. The offense moved in the mud-caked opener with Dallas, but O.J. gained only 25 yards rushing and the defense collapsed as the Cowboys won, 49-37. Then the offense began to sputter and the defense never did come around. Miami rolled, 29-14, and Minnesota breezed, 19-0.

Yet things never became as dark as on Oct. 10, the fourth game of the season. A capacity turnout of 46,206 showed in Buffalo to watch the winless Bills battle the Super Bowl champion Baltimore Colts.

From kickoff to the final play, the Bills were never so embarrassed. Norm Bulaich and Don McCauley ran almost at will, each scoring twice. Don Nottingham, the back resembling a bowling ball, dashed 36 yards to paydirt. Earl Morrall and John Unitas completed half their passes. The Colts amassed 214 yards rushing, 193 through the air and owned a yardage advantage of 407-125. The final score was 43-0.

The large crowd wasn't disappointed or peeved at the Bills' performance. It was downright furious. O.J. seemed to be loafing on two incomplete passes. Or at least the crowd thought he was dogging it. He was booed as he was never booed before. The hoots cascaded from the old rockpile, ringing in his ears.

It was the kind of day when Dennis Shaw, unable to muster a semblance of offense, took himself out of the game. It was the kind of day the Bills gained four yards rushing. And, in what later years would be viewed as the height of the ridiculous, O.J. Simpson ran seven times for *minus* 10 yards.

Now the Colt defense was exceptional as every Super Bowl champion's has been. But no defense is that strong and the Bills, to a man, knew it.

The Bills were not only horribly beaten and booed loudly by their fans but actually laughed at. That's the ultimate negativism a fan can express—laughter. And the Bills' followers, disgusted at their team, were splitting their sides en masse.

Along a row of bowed heads in the tomblike Bills' dressing quarters sat O.J. "I admit there were times I felt bad, but today I was humiliated," he admitted.

O.J. even took a shot at the Buffalo fans. "Booing doesn't bother me," he claimed, not too convincingly. "I play football for my team, my family and the crowd—in that order. I've learned in three years here not to pay attention to the fans."

The Juice noted that West Coast fans get behind their teams when they sputter, citing the Rams and 49ers as beneficiaries of such support. He said that Eastern teams get no such backing.

O.J. just couldn't get over it—and neither could those who had witnessed his years of greatness on the West Coast. Here was a Heisman Trophy winner, College Athlete of the Decade and a player some had judged as potentially the greatest running back of all time being not only blanked, but limited to minus 10 yards in a game. It was just too much.

Shaw seemed to have one answer in a one-sentence response to a reporter asking why he removed himself from the game. "We can't do anything right that's merely fundamental," the quarterback stated.

Simpson wondered something else: whatever happened to Johnson's system of O.J. right, left and up the middle? Against the Colts, he carried seven times and the Bills, as a team, only 11. Once again, when the Bills fell behind—even in the first half—they abandoned the rushing game and, in effect, they abandoned Simpson. They played catchup only through the air, and Shaw was plainly inept.

So now, after the Colt game with the team 0-4, O.J. no longer talked positively about Johnson. He didn't knock him either, because he genuinely liked the man. He just didn't view him as a coach and neither did his teammates. "You had to like Harv," O.J. would say. "You also had to laugh—just to keep your sanity—because we were really losers."

All semblance of confidence and self-respect gone, the Bills now entered each game wondering what new way they'd discover to lose. Without exception in the first 10 games, they found a way. They went 0-10, and some were predicting a perfect season, 0-14.

Finally, in week no. 11 they found a victim—their only conquest in a 1-13 season. New England, which O.J. would come to know as his "cousin" opponent, was outscored, 27-20. "We knew that our slump had to end," O.J. reasoned. The Bills had gone 15 games over two seasons without a triumph.

Yet, even in this one success, O.J. was not the star. He scored a seven-yard touchdown in the fourth quarter. It was the winning score, but O.J. gained only 61 yards in 14 carries. J.D. Hill, the first-round draft choice who suffered a broken back in an exhibition, returned to catch two touchdown passes in his NFL debut.

The Juice realized just one 100-yard game in 1971—an 18-carry, 106-yard performance at San Diego. But even that was mired in negatives. Neither he nor the Bills scored a touchdown in a 20-3 defeat. And, after gaining 91 yards in the first half, he rarely saw the ball again.

When the season ended, the Bills had become not only a laughing stock, but its supposed strong suit—offense—had evaporated to the tune of four shutouts. O.J. had 742 yards and five TDs to show for 183 carries. He ranked seventh among AFC rushers. In three seasons, he had achieved only three 100-yard games.

O.J. was not only disgusted, he plainly wanted out of Buffalo.

"I came out of USC as a running back, but I haven't gotten the same opportunity as other major pro running backs," he said. "Some are carrying the ball 50 to 100 times more a season than I am. I've only averaged 13 carries a game. At USC, I averaged 32."

O.J. glanced at the names of the six runners who finished ahead of him. The man at the top was Denver's Floyd Little, guided by a coach named Lou Saban, who built his offense around Little. Floyd had 284 carries, 101 more than O.J., and 1,113 yards. The others were Larry Csonka (Miami), Marv Hubbard (Oakland), Leroy Kelly (Cleveland), Carl Garrett (New England) and John Riggins (New York Jets).

"I know I'm a better runner than Csonka, Hubbard, Garrett—all of them," O.J. stated. "If I were running for Miami, I'd gain 100 yards a game. You really get down when you look around the league and see runners who aren't as good as you doing better."

Quite clearly, O.J. just didn't have the blocking. It was far less than inadequate. But now there was more than that. After three years of frustration, he started second-guessing himself. He wondered why he ever committed himself to four years in Buffalo—and felt "committed" was precisely the verb.

No one was knocking on his door for endorsement contracts anymore. The old arrangements with Chevrolet and Royal Crown expired and there was no quest for renewal. Here was O.J., who came into the pros in 1969 as the most publicized college football player of all time, faded into the background three years later. Where once his name, face and voice appeared almost everywhere, now people asked him whatever became of his career.

"I was to the point where all I wanted was out," O.J. later acknowledged. He pictured himself a fallen star. Further, he had never warmed up to Buffalo as a city. "It's a lot different from LA," he said. "There's nothing wrong with it, but it has a different way of life—one I'm not accustomed to."

Trade rumors began, including one that had quarterback Roman Gabriel coming to Buffalo and O.J. to the Rams. None materialized, but O.J. told friends he would never sign another contract with the Bills.

The memory of that minus 10-yard game, a one-win season, too few carries for paltry yardage combined with O.J.'s "bush" image of his own team—a team disorganized, practicing in public parks, holding team meetings in the hall of an ice-skating rink and playing in a stadium with dressing rooms so horrible that visiting teams often dressed at their hotel before a game.

No memory, however, would be as repulsive as that minus-10-yard afternoon amidst all those cascading boos against the world-champion Colts. It was the bottom of the pit for No. 32.

CHAPTER SIX

Turnabout Against the Old Hometown

During the lean years, when he felt especially down, O.J. would visit or call his USC coach, John McKay, for advice. They were and are exceptionally close, and O.J. has retained a deep respect for the opinion of the field boss who steered him toward the Heisman Trophy.

Invariably, McKay would soothe O.J.'s hurt feelings and encourage him.

"It was clear to me that he was playing for a coach who didn't understand the running game, and wasn't aware he had the greatest threat in football," McKay said. "I told O.J. not to let the situation get him down, that things would change for the better."

Soon after the 1971 season ended, McKay learned the Bills' new coach would be the same person who guided the 1964 and 1965 Bills to the American League championship, and the coach who shaped the careers of Cookie Gilchrist and Floyd Little. Soon O.J. and McKay held another chat.

"When I found out that Lou Saban was going to coach Buffalo, I told O.J. that was a guy who understands what makes up a sound running game, and that with Saban there was no way he could fail to make it big."

O.J. decided to reconsider his desire to exit Buffalo at the earliest possible moment.

"I sat alone in my living room at home [a $100,000-plus layout in the exclusive Sky Crest section of Bel-Air, Calif.] and did some deep thinking," O.J. remembers. "I decided I'd just been kidding myself about running away from the situation. For one thing, I wasn't ready for all the bitterness and hassling I would have to go through to play out my option. More than that, I just didn't want to make the move. The Bills were changing and I was changing even more. Simply, I'd grown up."

O.J. soon met Saban on a plane en route to Hawaii and the Hula Bowl, where O.J. would do the color commentary for ABC-TV. Quickly he remembered that Saban was Floyd Little's coach in Denver and Little just won the AFC rushing crown. He remembered that Little had 101 more carries than he and figured those attempts would be worth at least 350 yards . . . and 350 additional yards would mean a 1,000-yard season. Perhaps even the rushing title.

Simpson told Saban his college playing weight was 205, but Rauch wanted him at 217 so he could block and absorb pro-style hitting. He told Saban that weight deadened his legs and feet, that he would like to return to 205. Saban agreed and he added something O.J. would relish the whole off-season: "Be in shape because you're going to carry the ball a lot more. When you see our playbook, you'll see ours will be an offense geared to running the football."

Saban quickly went to work in the draft. His second pick would become more important than the first to Simpson. With the NFL's first choice, the prize for finishing with the league's worst record, Saban selected Walt Patulski, the All-America defensive end from Notre Dame. With choice No. 2, he tapped Reggie McKenzie, the prize guard from Michigan who would become O.J.'s "main man."

A wheeler-dealer, Saban swapped, scoured the waiver wire and started to rebuild. One of his waiver acquisitions was tackle Dave Foley, who was considered expendable by the New York Jets for ineffective pass blocking for Namath. But it was rush blocking which most interested Saban and that was Foley's strong suit,

O.J. eludes 49er linebacker Dave Wilcox during a long jaunt in this 1972 upset over his old hometown team.
AP Wirephoto

steeped in a tradition of powerhouse running attacks at Ohio State. Foley joined McKenzie in the restructured offensive wall tutored by Jim Ringo, former All-Pro center at Green Bay.

The goal was clear: build a crackerjack rushing attack by placing first-rate blockers in front of the Juice. Then one strategy change was necessary. "It is my philosophy," Saban said upon taking over the Bills' reins, "that when you have a great runner, you give him the ball."

To give a star running back the ball on a long-term basis, a coach must be sure the featured attraction will remain on the scene. And so, with Saban closing quick negotiations, Simpson did what he vowed never to do. He shocked his West Coast friends by signing another Buffalo contract, this one spanning three years.

O.J. explained he didn't want to go through a whole season constantly being asked if he would play out his option. He decided that, with Saban coaching, he wanted to be in Buffalo with him. "It looks as though I'll be playing for just one team in my career and that's the Bills," O.J. declared. He noted, however, his original estimate of a five-year pro career would be expanded because of those "three wasted years."

Clearly, O.J. no longer considered the Bills "rinky-dink," as he called them on one occasion, or an "operation not run as well as my high school program," as he said on another. Clearly, he was no longer disillusioned with the team. And as far as that horrible stadium went, there would be only one more season before moving into spacious Rich Stadium.

With Saban, the players were treated like men, a departure from the Rauch era. There was no more staying at hotels sans wives the evening before home games, bed checks at 11 P.M., hair and dress codes and elementary pregame written tests.

The preseason was an immediate indication better things were in store. O.J. ran for 173 yards against Chicago and finished the six exhibitions with 420 and six TDs off 84 attempts. The Bills upset the Minnesota Vikings and went on to a 3-2-1 record, their first winning preseason since 1966. "The system is ball control and I love it," O.J. enthused.

Saban had his wide receivers wearing caged face masks and

blocking. Moses balked and was dispatched to Denver. Bob Chandler, the Juice's USC teammate, started with J.D. Hill and both blocked like demons. "O.J. will gain more than 1,000 yards this year," Saban predicted. "I guarantee it!"

O.J. was aiming for 1,500—and his first rushing crown.

Still, there was disappointment as the Jets routed Buffalo, 41-24, in the opener. The Bills were obviously poor defensively and had to resort to tricks and surprises. Saban, with first call on other teams' waiver rejects, constantly shuffled personnel. And there were crippling injuries, such as losing middle linebacker Edgar Chandler and center Bruce Jarvis for the season on opening day.

This was the backdrop as the Bills entered the second game of the season against the San Francisco 49ers, the team O.J. used to call his favorite as a boy on San Francisco's Potrero Hill. O.J. glanced downfield before the game and saw several veterans he and Al Cowlings cheered as young boys. "It was unreal," O.J. smiled. "There were John Brodie, Len Rohde and Charlie Krueger. I was out there with guys Al and I used to jump the fence to see when we were kids."

Saban, disgusted with the effort against New York, made purchasing a program an absolute necessity for the 45,845 witnesses in War Memorial Stadium. Old-timers couldn't remember such an in-season roster shakeup. He installed eight new starters, including recent waiver products Jerry Patton and Don Croft as defensive tackles. He switched the positions of three players. He added four new bodies. And Mike McBath, who started at defensive tackle the previous Sunday, was out of a job.

O.J. offered a great line upon running into the first huddle. "All right, guys," he grinned, "does everyone here know everyone else?" Suddenly, everyone was loose.

The 49ers were highly regarded in the NFC West and had opened the season by crushing San Diego, 34-3. Here was a veteran-packed team, a contender, up against an exceptionally young band of players, many of whom had just been introduced to their teammates. The official spread was 13 points, but some figured the 49ers might be able to name the score—say a 30- or even 40-point difference!

The 49ers soon discovered that these new Bills weren't the rollover type. In the second quarter, Croft walloped Brodie to the ground, forcing the veteran quarterback out of action with a sprained wrist. Steve Spurrier had to finish the game and he was punished repeatedly by the new tackle combination, Croft and Patton.

O.J., taking pitchouts and sweeping frequently, was accumulating yardage as never before in his pro career. McKenzie, the rookie from Michigan, was his chief escort, his main man. With nine minutes remaining, San Francisco led, 20-13. It seemed, despite promising signs, the Bills were destined to lose again.

Unlike similar circumstances in the Rauch and Johnson years, however, there was no panic by the Bills. Even when Shaw was sacked by Cedric Hardman and the Bills had a second-and-23, they didn't press the button. To the contrary, they mustered a play which turned their fate.

Shaw faded to throw again, sucking Hardman and friends on top of him. But this time, the play was a screen to Simpson and O.J. trampled All-Pro cornerback Jimmy Johnson and another 49er on a 25-yard burst all the way to the 49er 28.

Shaw, looking sharp this day, passed to J.D. Hill for a 13-yard gain and the Bills were knocking at the 15. The 49ers began to crack as Krueger jumped offside. Then O.J. juked a couple of defenders and sliced to a first down at the four.

From there, second-year fullback Jim Braxton, a powerful sort from West Virginia, bulled over in two plays. John Leypoldt kicked the PAT and the heavy-underdog Bills had tied, 20-20, with 4:08 to play. The stunned, happy crowd was going wild.

Now it really was panic time. And the 49ers, particularly Spurrier, did exactly that. Attempting desperately to salvage a victory which was almost taken for granted, Spurrier passed from his own 10. The throw went directly to strong safety John Pitts at the 49er 28. He raced to the 18 and now, incredibly, the Bills were in position to notch an astonishing upset.

O.J. gathered in a pitchout and swept eight yards to the 10. That was O.J. left. On second down, he lost a yard. That was O.J. right. On third-and-3, he barreled five yards to the six. That was O.J. up the middle. Saban was showing his offense—O.J. left, right and middle—and the Bills were nearing a sensational form reversal.

With two minutes left, Braxton bulled to the one on first down. Then 49er linebacker Skip Vanderbundt jumped offside. Finally, with 1:16 to play, Braxton smashed across for the decisive touchdown. Leypoldt converted, Spurrier threw four desperate incompletions and the Bills prevailed, 27-20.

Braxton had scored the tying and winning touchdowns, but O.J. was the major catalyst. The Juice finished with his finest pro rushing day yet—138 yards. Under Saban's new system, he had carried the ball 29 times. Shades of the USC days, O.J. figured. He had never rushed so often as a pro and he was elated.

"I'll tell you what," quipped Vanderbundt in the 49er dressing room. "I was on the Oregon State team which upset O.J.'s Southern Cal team, 3-0, a few years ago. I said then that he was the greatest back I've ever seen. After today, I'll repeat it. We had him trapped time after time. There was no way he could have escaped. But he did."

O.J. was grinning from ear to ear in the Bills' boudoir. He realized the folks back home in San Francisco witnessed his turnabout day and he realized Saban was coming through on his promise. His career was being reborn.

"This has to be my greatest thrill in pro football," O.J. beamed. "And boy, did we ever need this one! I'm almost sorry we had to beat the 49ers because I rooted for them as a kid. I didn't miss a game from 1957 to 1965. That's the reason today's victory was so personally satisfying to me."

O.J. also pointed out the 49ers were the first winning team (above .500) the Bills defeated in over four years. While he gained almost five yards per carry, the Bills' patched-together defense held San Francisco's highly respected ground game to 33 yards. "It's my most satisfying triumph as a head coach," Saban declared. "We had so many tough personnel problems to overcome."

Without question, at least for one brilliant afternoon, the Bills certainly did overcome. And the message went out through the entire NFL: the real O.J. has arrived at last!

CHAPTER SEVEN

A Record and a Championship

Through most of the 1972 season, the name of the Buffalo Bills' game was misfortune. There was a seemingly endless run of injuries, particularly to offensive linemen and middle linebackers. Promising starts turned into defeats, largely due to inexperience. A scoreless streak against Baltimore reached 17 quarters and O.J.'s one-yard touchdown with a half-minute left in a 35-7 defeat averted a fourth straight shutout by the Colts.

The Bills were 2-2 and respectable after four games, but then lack of staying power hurt them against two powerhouse foes on the road. Faced with a suicide schedule of mostly contenders, the Bills went to Oakland and mounted a 13-0 halftime advantage. Amazingly, they still led the potent Raiders, 16-7, after John Leypoldt's third field goal two minutes into the fourth quarter. Then the Raiders scored three touchdowns, two by Clarence Davis, within 10 minutes and won, 28-16. A 28-carry, 144-yard rushing show by O.J. was wasted.

The following Sunday, the Bills led Miami, 13-7, at halftime in the Orange Bowl. But early in the second half, Shaw reached out to hand off and the charging Manny Fernandez stole the ball, setting up an easy touchdown. Miami went on to a 24-23 triumph.

Meanwhile the Bills were in the process of going through four centers and seven guards—due to injuries and illness. The resulting turmoil throughout the offensive line derailed Saban's master plan, but O.J. was ready for such bad breaks. "I've come to expect bad things to happen to us," he said. He didn't let them bother him.

It was in this setting that the Bills hosted the fast rising Pittsburgh Steelers Oct. 29 before 45,882. The Bills, entering with a 2-4 record, didn't even begin impressively this day. The Steelers, led by Franco Harris, took charge quickly and enjoyed a 17-0 cushion at intermission.

Harris, who would finish with 131 rushing yards and three touchdowns, scored on a two-yard slant, quarterback Terry Bradshaw on a one-yard dive and Roy Gerela on a 29-yard field goal to provide the halftime gap.

The stadium, except for visiting Pittsburgh partisans, was quiet. It grew downright solemn when Bobby Walden punted to the Buffalo one in the third quarter.

Mike Taliaferro, quarterbacking the Bills, tried a sneak but didn't gain an inch. Then L.C. Greenwood edged offside to provide five yards of daylight. But Braxton gained nothing on second down. So it was third-and-five at the Bills' six and punter Spike Jones was warming his right leg.

Suddenly O.J. took a pitchout, swept right, cut sharply and— whoosh—he was gone down the right sideline! The Steelers, expecting a pass or another slam into the middle, were caught by surprise. O.J. raced 94 yards for the longest touchdown in the Bills' annals and fifth longest from scrimmage in NFL history.

The crowd cheered O.J. for several minutes and repeated the plaudits throughout the second half as he exploded for 189 yards in 22 carries. For the third time that season, O.J. realized his best pro game rushing.

However, the Bills never could draw closer than 10 points and incurred their third straight setback, 38-21. O.J.'s run was the game's feature highlight, however, and Bills' fans savored that for several days. Of particular interest to them was that O.J.

Linebackers Henry Davis (53) and Andy Russell (34) corral O.J. Bills'
Reggie McKenzie (67) can't help here, but O.J. later broke 94-yarder
against Pittsburgh.
Photo by Bob Bukaty

never thought the play, called a "Misdirection 26," would work.

"I told Jim Ringo [offensive line coach] before the game it
would never work," O.J. smiled after the sting of defeat wore
away. "I thought Jim Braxton would hit his block too slow for it
to break open. But it caught them by surprise. It was like our first
counter play. We hadn't shown it at all in the first half and they
didn't think we'd run it. Then we almost broke another one on
the next series."

The play developed this way: O.J. lined up in the I-formation,
grabbed a handoff and started toward left guard (McKenzie).
Then he cut, following McKenzie, who was pulling right. O.J.
had the option of slanting over right tackle or sweeping outside,
around right end.

O.J. reviewed the play as follows: "Braxton had the first big
block and Reggie and J.D. had key ones. J.D.'s was just enough
for me to get by the corner. If we had tried the play sooner,

things might have been different—because after it, I think we averaged five yards a carry. We found out something a little late."

The Bills entered the game wondering how to combat "Mean" Joe Greene, the Steelers' vaunted All-Pro defensive tackle—especially with that injury riddled right guard slot opposite him. Saban's answer was an unbalanced line—left tackle Donnie Green and tight end Jan White on the weak side of center Remi Prudhomme and Reggie McKenzie becoming the strongside guard alongside tackle Dave Foley and Paul Costa. The three-tackle setup worked and it didn't work. It held the Steelers to only one sack (by Greene), but it failed to produce a score until O.J.'s 94-yard jaunt after the Steelers assumed command.

"They never reacted to the unbalanced line properly all day," claimed Costa, the outside tackle. "They undershifted and played me like a tight end. When a team uses an unbalanced line, the opponent is supposed to consider the strong guard like a center. But they considered the center as a center."

Still, except for O.J.'s run, the Steelers fared excellently even if they didn't diagnose the unbalanced line precisely.

Saban, in his dressing room post mortem, was disappointed with his two quarterbacks, Shaw and Taliaferro, who split four interceptions. He yanked Shaw in the second quarter, but had to return him after Taliaferro was shaken up. Shaw came back to fire touchdown passes of 11 and four yards to Bob Chandler.

"I was disappointed in the quarterbacking," Saban emphasized. "We didn't get off to a very good start, although our offense was much better in the second half. This also was our worst game since the opener from a defensive standpoint. I thought the unbalanced offensive line worked out pretty well once we got it going. I'd been thinking about using it for a couple of years. We thought it would create problems, but we just stayed behind and couldn't catch up."

Ringo indicated the Bills, considering all the offensive line injuries, would use the unbalanced system again. "Every once in awhile, we'll mount two tackles side by side on the strong side to confuse our opponents' linebackers," Ringo said. "Because we run so many dives over left guard, this misdirection play will look like another dive."

There was one after-effect of the Steeler game that O.J. enjoyed. He was tired—which meant he was contributing the way he did at USC—as the team leader. Noting the mud-splattered field as one reason, O.J. commented: "It was tough running in that heavy grass with all that mud and on one particular series, I was dragging. But it didn't last long," he laughed.

The following morning, O.J. liked another after-effect of the Pittsburgh affair. He was the NFL's leading rusher at the season's midpoint with 723 yards. Already, with half a season to play, he had nearly matched his best year rushing. The Bills' fortunes hardly matched his, however.

Their losing skein reached five, and Saban erupted after an embarrassing 41-3 setback to the Jets in New York. "We don't have an offensive line—we haven't had one since the beginning of the season," he fumed. The streak was snapped as 10 points in the final minute, including Leypoldt's winning 45-yard field goal with five seconds left, provided a 27-24 triumph at New England. O.J. ran 22 times for 103 yards and one TD.

Then came a 27-10 setback in Cleveland, O.J. eclipsing the magical 1,000-yard plateau on the final play, capping a 93-yard rushing effort. A 35-7 defeat in Baltimore ensued, Saban vowing afterward to "clean house" following the season.

The Bills tied Detroit, 21-21, in their final War Memorial Stadium game and entered the season finale at Washington with a 3-9-1 record. O.J. amassed 116 rushing yards in 27 thrusts against the Lions and had 1,150 in 266 runs to comfortably lead the American Conference race. But the Redskins' Larry Brown, a hard-driving runner who absorbed tremendous punishment, was the league leader with 1,216 in 285 carries.

The Bills were loose, with nothing to gain but pride and O.J.'s first NFL rushing title. The Redskins rested in a far different position. They had clinched the NFC Eastern championship and owned a glossy 11-2 record, but just lost the previous game to Dallas. Coach George Allen, who never takes any game lightly, certainly did not want to enter the playoffs with back-to-back defeats.

From an individual viewpoint, the game seemed a natural. This was the "Year of the Runner" and here was O.J. and Larry Brown in a showdown game for the league rushing title. That's how it appeared right up to kickoff. Brown had missed the Dallas game with knee and heel injuries, but practiced all week and was supposed to oppose the Bills. After all, he certainly wanted the rushing crown, he realized a 68-yard lead over O.J. wasn't safe and he just might break Jim Brown's record of 305 carries in one season (1961). Larry needed 21 attempts to crack the mark.

But Allen had other ideas. With the playoff opener against Green Bay a week away, Allen did not want to risk his star runner in a season-ending game which meant nothing in the standings. "I don't care a bit about individual titles," Allen declared, stating his and the team's goal was strictly to win the Super Bowl.

For three quarters, it seemed highly likely that Brown would capture the rushing crown even though he sat out a second straight game and O.J. was playing. The Juice was being shut off by the "Over-the-Hill Gang," showing just 38 yards off 17 attempts. The Bills, who mounted a 10-0 first-quarter lead on cornerback Alvin Wyatt's interception and 49-yard TD return and Leypoldt's 23-yard field goal, trailed 17-10. Herb Mul-Key had barreled in for an eight-yard score in the second quarter, Bob Brunet clicked from two yards in chapter three and Curt Knight followed with a 35-yard field goal.

Hardly anyone gained 100 yards against the Redskins and Ron McDole and friends wanted to deprive O.J. of that and the 67 yards needed to eclipse Larry Brown. Laverne Torgeson, the Washington defensive coach, had all but made it a team crusade during that week's practice sessions.

Yet in the fourth quarter the Juice began to flow. In a sustained march from their own 20, the Bills tied the game 3:43 into the final period and O.J., his stutter-stepping days long gone, was the driving force. He carried five times, amassing 44 yards and capturing the league rushing crown.

Simpson kept the drive rolling past midfield with a 12-yard burst, then drew the Bills even with a sensational 21-yard touchdown sweep behind a crushing block by right tackle Donnie Green. That was the play which vaulted O.J. past Brown and netted his first league ground-gaining diadem.

Still, there was the matter of winning the ball game. The Bills

O.J. dives headlong toward his first NFL rushing title in 1972 as Redskins Diron Talbert (72), Verlon Biggs (89) and Harold McClinton reach for him. *AP Wirephoto*

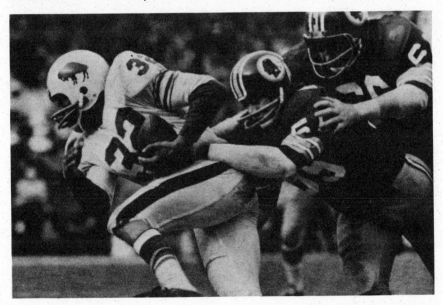

O.J. sheds Redskin linebackers Chris Hanburger (55) and Myron Pottios (66) in 1972 season-ending 24-17 upset of Super Bowl-bound Washington. *AP Wirephoto*

seemed headed for a second straight deadlock when Redskin quarterback Billy Kilmer tried a lateral pass which Mul-Key only deflected. Linebacker Dale Farley stole the ball in mid-air and rambled 42 yards to the Redskin three. Myron Pottios threw O.J. for a one-yard loss on first down, but Braxton bulled in from the four on the next play with just 46 seconds remaining. Leypoldt's conversion capped a most satisfying 27-20 season-ending upset of the Redskins, stunning a sellout throng of 53,039 at Washington's Robert F. Kennedy Stadium.

Irony played a major role in this upset. Farley, a teammate of Braxton at West Virginia, was activated from the Buffalo taxi squad the morning of the game and his interception set up Braxton for the winning touchdown. Further, Mul-Key had been activated only a week earlier as the roster replacement for Larry Brown, and Mul-Key wound up proving one of George Allen's cliches correct. "Rookies make mistakes," Allen often says, and Mul-Key was only his third rookie in two years at Washington.

"I didn't touch Mul-Key," the happy Farley said in Buffalo's dressing room. "He just fumbled the ball in the air. I saw him looking at me and trying to turn the corner. Then the ball just popped into the air."

"It was a good pass from Kilmer," said Mul-Key, a free-agent acquisition playing in his second pro game after no college experience. "I was pulling it in and just didn't have a good hold on it."

Further irony was the circumstance which placed Farley on the field for the big play. Saban closed the season by experimenting with his linebackers—using one unit in the first and third quarters and another (with Farley) in the second and fourth. Next season, Farley would be an almost forgotten hero. He would be gone from the squad.

It was the type of afternoon in which just about all of Saban's decisions were right. Spotting the Redskins using five defensive backs (a "Nickel Defense") in the closing minutes, he instructed Shaw not to throw. Some thought the Bills were playing for a tie, but Saban explained his strategy.

"If you're passing against five defensive backs, you're taking a chance," Saban pointed out. "I told my quarterback, 'Let's not lose it by giving up the ball in good field position for them.' We might get a break, get the ball back and score."

Which is precisely what the Bills accomplished against a Redskin contingent that built a reputation on taking advantage of such errors.

"We led the league in mistakes," quipped Dennis Shaw. "And today, we didn't make many—only two interceptions."

Washington went on to the Super Bowl, bowing 14-7 to Miami in the Los Angeles Coliseum, and the Bills, though only 4-9-1 for Saban's first season, were elated to finish on an upbeat note.

In fact, one member of the Washington press corps, visiting the Buffalo dressing room, commented that it had the atmosphere of a team which had just taken a championship. O.J. made a short speech with the keynote message: "Get your buckets in shape for next year!"

O.J. finished with his sixth 100-yard game of the season (26 carries, 101 yards), doubling his total of the three previous seasons combined. His title totals were 1,251 yards in 292 carries. Both represented Bills' records. And that game-tying TD, on which he entered the rushing throne room, was his sixth of the year. All these figures seemed earth-shaking to O.J. after those "three wasted years," but in so short a time they would be almost ordinary to the popular No. 32.

After the reporters' postgame crush subsided, O.J. walked over to the Washington dressing room and told Larry Brown: "I really didn't want to win the rushing title that way, with you on the bench." They shook hands and went their own ways.

Saban smiled broadly after the victory and alluded to the team's history of carefree performances and rout defeats in season finales. "We've been known as the Run-for-the-Bus-Gang, and now I think we're past that," he laughed.

Before leaving the stadium and in the days to follow, O.J. heard repeated questions about his emergence after three years in virtual obscurity. What was he doing differently? "I'm not running any differently," he maintained despite what seemed a scrapping of the hesitation and a move to the cutting, sweeping style which led him into the holes quicker. "I had better blockers this year and a coach with a system geared to running. Man, I'm tired of hearing that O.J. is just coming back. It makes me remember how frustrating those years were. It makes me remember not getting along with a coach who wouldn't let me do what I was drafted to do.

"My first three years, man, I'd look at those cats in Dallas and say to myself, 'Hey, if I was there, I'd be doing three times as good.' I looked at some of those backs and knew they'd be on the bench if I was there. I'm just glad coach Saban is here now and I don't have to think that way anymore."

Saban responded in the true mutual admiration style that he and O.J. cultivated. "When you consider all the problems we've had with our offensive line, it's remarkable we could get him over 1,000 yards," the coach declared. "And I don't think he's even scratched the surface yet. He can do so many outstanding things."

Louis Henry Saban was never more correct.

CHAPTER EIGHT

The Pro Bowl Beckons

So many National Football League stars own a negative attitude toward the Pro Bowl, the annual all-star affair which pits the American Conference's premier players against the cream of the National Conference crop.

Many of the high-salaried superstars scoffed at the $2,000 winning player's share and the $1,000 loser's take. Some considered the trip to Texas Stadium and daily practices in mid-January, long after the season, a nuisance. They thought so even though their own Players Association was a chief beneficiary of the game. A growing number offered feeble excuses for failure to attend after being selected.

O.J. Simpson displayed no such attitude. After those "three lost years," being chosen to the American Conference squad for the first time was a distinct honor. He said so and played just that way.

This Jan. 21, 1973, clash in Irving, Tex., also would be a game the Juice and his followers would never forget.

It was the second quarter and the National Conference team held a 14-0 advantage on two touchdowns by Green Bay's John

Brockington, who plunged a yard for the first and speared a three-yard pitch from Billy Kilmer for the second.

Suddenly the Juice took matters into his hands. O.J. spearheaded a steady, impressive march downfield and capped it by taking a pitchout and stepping over several NFC defenders for a seven-yard TD.

The touchdown not only rallied the AFC back into contention, but ignited an incredible explosion of 33 unanswered points. Pittsburgh's Roy Gerela kicked field goals of 18 and 22 yards and Oakland's Marv Hubbard put the AFC ahead to stay with an 11-yard burst. In the fourth quarter, a pair of Kansas City Chiefs turned the game into a rout. Otis Taylor snared a five-yard TD pass from Daryle Lamonica, and linebacker Bobby Bell rambled 12 yards with a pass theft. The AFC was rolling, 33-14.

Brockington's third touchdown, a one-yard dive, and San Francisco tight end Ted Kwalick's 12-yard TD pass from Norm Snead only made the final score close, 33-28. The AFC had clearly dominated, and the player doing the dominating between those many scores was O.J. Simpson. Showing he surely belonged playing among the stars, O.J. carried 16 times for 112 yards, a 28-yard breakaway being his longest. He was the Pro Bowl's first 100-yard gainer. He also hauled in three passes for 58 yards, including a 39-yard reception.

O.J. was the game's runaway, unanimous Most Valuable Player!

"Mean" Joe Greene, Pittsburgh's stellar defensive tackle, sat by his dressing room stall afterward and told reporters: "You've heard people say whatever became of O.J. Simpson after he won the Heisman Trophy. But he showed them today, didn't he? Man, if that guy had some blocking up there in Buffalo, they'd have to ban him from the league."

Merlin Olsen, the Los Angeles Rams' longtime star defensive tackle, echoed those sentiments in the NFC quarters. "He's a helluva runner," Olsen said of O.J. "If he were with the Rams, he'd gain about 2,000 yards."

Olsen didn't know it, of course, but he had just mentioned the magic number O.J. would surpass in 1973—as a Bill!

The Juice still heard such comments about what he could do

as a star with other, more prominent NFL teams, but he wasn't listening any longer. He was happy now playing under Saban's direction, and he was convinced the Bills were turning the corner—having won only 12 games in his four years on the roster.

"I used to think how much more I'd like to be with my friends in LA or San Francisco," O.J. smiled. "But your best friends should be the guys you play with. That's what football is about, and that's the way it is now on the Bills."

The accolades were beginning to pour in, too. In addition to being the NFL's leading rusher and Pro Bowl MVP, O.J. was chosen American Conference Player of the Year. And he made all the All-Star teams.

Football for O.J. Simpson was fun again. His confidence was back. He was taking charge as the Bills' team leader. In interviews, he declared flatly he could carry the Bills toward the heights of success.

"Just give me the ball, and the more the better," he declared. "Ever since I got to Buffalo, that's all I've been saying. I'll get it in there some way. My first couple of years, I didn't get the ball but two or three times a quarter—and then it was usually on third down and short yardage. I know we didn't have that good a line then, but I don't care. All my blockers don't have to be the best in the business. If they're just consistent, if they make their blocks most of the time, or even miss them most of the time, I'll adjust. Just give me the ball."

O.J. was sure a virtual one-man offense could be successful in the NFL and wanted to prove it.

"I don't want to sound like I'm carrying a big head, but there usually are one or two guys around who can carry a team," he said. "They set the tone for a whole football game. Jim Brown used to be like that. Joe Namath is like that. I used to do it in college and I believe I can up here, too. I think with Lou Saban coaching us now, I'm going to prove it."

The Juice stated his 1,251 yards of 1972 were not really proof, even though he led Buffalo to its best record (4-9-1) in six seasons. "That's not doing it like I can," O.J. insisted. "We've got an offensive line now. I looked at our line in training camp last season—guys like Irv Goode, who came from St. Louis, and young guys like Reggie McKenzie and Donnie Green. I took a look at Saban's playbook and told everybody if I didn't gain 1,500 yards, I'd have a bad year.

"Well, I got 1,251 but the whole line got hurt. Everybody, man. But look out this year. Saban is a run-oriented coach. He's the coach I've needed."

Even in January, Simpson was talking about next season. He was enthused and excited. His attitude was such a marked departure from previous off-seasons. He not only didn't want out of Buffalo now, he was anxious to return.

"For the first time in a long time," he said, "I really want to play football. I never started working out as early as I did this year. We've got a new stadium, we like Saban and we've got a group of guys who would love to win together. Saban is doing the things it will take to make us a winner. I think his running game is very well conceived, for one thing. And when I walk into the locker room now, I see guys I know, guys I understand and get along with.

"I predicted I could gain 1,500 yards last season and missed, but if we can keep our line healthy, I really believe I can make close to 1,700 this season. Lou told me he plans to give me the ball about 25 times a game. That's all I want."

Little did he realize, a history-making season was just around the corner. O.J. Simpson was about to become the toast of football.

CHAPTER NINE

A Record Explosion in New England

The date was Sept. 16, 1973. The Bills were about to open the season against the New England Patriots in Foxboro, Mass., and Lou Saban and his team seemed in a quandry.

The Bills' finest draft ever—10 of the 21 players picked making the final roster—had O.J. so enthused, he predicted a 10-4 season and playoff entrance. Some fans hearing that wanted to give the Juice a saliva test.

Yet he certainly had reason for such optimism. The first two draft choices, Michigan's Paul Seymour and Michigan State's Joe DeLamielleure, entered the offensive wall as starters. Seymour, drafted as a tackle, moved in at tight end and Joe D joined with McKenzie in what would become pro football's finest guard tandem.

The draft produced quarterback Joe Ferguson from Arkansas, a rifle-armed kid who wrested the starting job from Shaw for this opener. There also was a talented linebacker from Penn State named John Skorupan.

Saban, nicknamed "Trader Lou," had initiated a season of 23 trades by completing a six-player deal with these Patriots which produced middle linebacker Jim Cheyunski, ultimate starting center Mike Montler and Halvor Hagen, a reserve lineman. Saban acquired Earl Edwards from San Francisco and Mike Kadish from Miami in moves for strong, talented defensive linemen. Certainly, the roster picture looked upbeat and, surely, the schedule was easier.

And yet, the Bills appeared horrible in preseason. They lost all six games and O.J., who missed the early portion of training camp when hospitalized with a stomach virus, suffered a cracked rib in the second exhibition. He missed two games, returned for the final two of the preseason and impressed in neither. With O.J. unsteady, the Bills produced more than two touchdowns in only one exhibition and were bombed that night, 37-21, by Washington in the Rich Stadium inaugural before 80,020—a sellout.

Saban, shuffling players in and out of camp in a scene which resembled a railroad depot, never panicked. "We wanted to play everyone and we did," he said about the 0-6 preseason. "We took it on the chin six times, but we found some players. The preseason is a proving ground and kids like Skorupan, Kadish and Ferguson proved they can play."

Most observers thought Saban's talk was just that, idle chatter. The team looked disorganized and punchless, the fans were howling and the press was negative. Then Cheyunski, the starting middle linebacker, suffered a serious knee injury and was lost for the opener against his old team. Saban had to go with a 13th round draft choice, Merv Krakau.

Things looked bleak, indeed. And then the season started in Foxboro.

Jim Plunkett, the Patriot quarterback, was out to impress former Oklahoma coach Chuck Fairbanks, making his debut as New England's head pilot. He went to work on Buffalo's rookie linebackers immediately, hitting Bob Adams for 14 yards and Sam "Bam" Cunningham for 10. Then Plunkett found Josh Ashton open over the middle for 51 yards, Ashton barreling all the way to the Bills' seven. It seemed another typical Bills' opener when Cunningham scored from the seven on first down, carrying safety Leon Garror into the end zone with him. The Pats

O.J. darts off on power sweep right during record 250-yard game in New England.

Photo by Robert L. Smith,
Elma, N.Y.

didn't look worried when the conversion failed and the score was 6-0.

Just 18 seconds later, the Patriots and all in Schaefer Stadium were plenty worried. After the kickoff sailed out of the end zone, the Bills started from their 20 and Ferguson's first-down handoff went to the Juice. O.J. probed right, bounced off defensive tackle David Rowe and linebacker Steve Kiner, and took off down the right sideline. He didn't stop until 80 yards had passed under his feet and he was in the end zone. O.J. was mobbed by his ecstatic teammates, screaming "Juice, Juice, Juice!" Leypoldt's PAT put the Bills in front, 7-6, and they never looked back.

The attack didn't even sputter when Ferguson was knocked cold by defensive end Julius Adams in the second quarter. The attack didn't stall because the attack was Simpson. All Dennis Shaw needed to do was hand him the ball.

The Bills' lead was only 10-6 at intermission, Leypoldt hitting a 48-yard field goal one second before it. O.J. had 125 yards in 13 carries at the break and the 56,119 Schaefer fans knew something special was happening—with their team the victim.

O.J. continued to run magnificently in the third period and the Bills marched 71 yards in nine plays to take a 17-6 lead on fullback Larry Watkins' four-yard burst up the middle. Seconds earlier, O.J. nearly broke away, but Sandy Durko caught him by the shirt after a 22-yard jaunt. The Pats climbed back into contention as Canadian League export Mack Herron swept 10 yards to score, and the three-quarter margin was only 17-13.

On the fourth quarter's initial play, O.J. swept right (it was always right this day) behind blocks from McKenzie and Hill to score his second touchdown on a 22-yard burst. O.J. had 184 yards in 20 carries, and the Bills held a 24-13 lead at that point—with 14:53 remaining.

The next time the Bills gained possession, O.J. swept right again for 33 yards, breaking his own single-game pro rushing record and becoming the Bills' all-time top career rusher. Shaw fumbled away the snap on the next play, however.

With 9:01 to play, the Patriots gambled on fourth down and seven at the Bills' 49. Left end Walt Patulski crashed through to smear Plunkett for a 14-yard loss and Buffalo took over. Five plays later, Watkins bulled past Bolton 15 yards to score his second touchdown and put the game on ice. The scoring was over and the Bills would win, 31-13, but the story was far from complete. There were still 5:55 remaining on the scoreboard and O.J. had a date with destiny.

Members of the Bills' offense stood along the sideline shouting to their defensive teammates: "Get the ball back, get it back!" Cornerback Tony Greene complied, intercepting a Plunkett pass at midfield. O.J. trotted into the huddle, already having accumulated 217 rushing yards. He needed 31 to break the NFL single-game standard of 247 established Dec. 5, 1971, by the Rams' Willie Ellison against New Orleans.

Shaw just kept calling O.J.'s number and the Juice carried four of the next five plays, collecting 27 yards and approaching Ellison's mark with 244. Hot after the record, O.J. kept going on a steady diet of those power sweeps to the right.

Once again, McKenzie pulled out in front to block, obliterating Kiner, and O.J. picked up seven yards with his 28th carry. He had an astounding 251 yards and 1:10 still remained. O.J. was oh, so weary but equally happy. He carried once more and lost a yard to finish his record-setting afternoon with 29 attempts and a fantastic 250 rushing yards

O.J.'s initial postgame remarks were so typical of this great athlete. He shared the limelight. He heaped praise upon his teammates. After three seasons without blocking support, he was learning it had arrived in abundance. And he was so grateful.

"We just went at them, and Larry Watkins took the pressure off me," the Juice declared. "Those counters Larry was running for big 10-yard pops made the Patriots play an even defense, and I don't think any team can stop us with an even defense. Up front, our offensive line just manhandled 'em. I want to credit the entire line for a tremendous job in making this league rushing record possible.

"I don't think anyone will ever bad-mouth our offensive line again. Larry Watkins also went over 100 yards. That's a tribute to the line when two backs go over 100. Our guys up front really did the job, just blowing people out of there. So give them credit—we have some great offensive linemen.

"Give Larry a major assist, too," O.J. continued. "He took so much pressure off me—not only keeping their defense honest with the counters but by the tremendous job blocking ahead of me. And Dennis Shaw did a heckuva job, doing a lot of audiblizing at the line."

The aftermath of assembling a list of records Simpson and the Bills toppled that fateful day at Foxboro was just incredible.

Together, O.J. and Watkins staged one of the most awesome two-man rushing shows in football history. They combined for 355 yards and all four Buffalo touchdowns (two each) in 47 carries. Watkins, a five-year veteran obtained from Philadelphia a month earlier, amassed 105 yards in 18 thrusts.

"The Simpson and Watkins Show" enabled the Bills to establish three club single-game records: (1) most yards rushing, 360; (2) total rushing plays, 51; and (3) most first downs rushing, 18.

Further, this was the Bills' first opening-day triumph on the road in the team's history, which dates to 1960. It was their first opening-day success anywhere since 1967. The Buffalo offense totaled 459 yards (to the Pats' 297), averaged 7.1 yards per play and punted only twice. The rushing difference alone was an unbelievable 360-107. It was pure destruction! That winless preseason was all but forgotten, and O.J. hinted strongly the Bills all along were awaiting the season bell to show their true arsenal.

"I'm ecstatic about the league record and becoming the Bills' career rushing leader, and I'm especially glad this came when it did," he said. "This is a great thrill, both personally and as far as the team is concerned. We both have a history of getting off to a slow start, you know. We took a lot because of our preseason record. But I kept saying (privately) we'd run off-tackle sweeps once the season began and that's the way it turned out."

The 250 yards gave O.J. 3,428 in 805 carries one game into his fifth pro season. That total erased the Bills' career record of 3,368 set by Wray Carlton in 819 rushes from 1961 to 1967. The 250 yards were seven more than the previous Buffalo single-game mark set by Cookie Gilchrist against the Jets in 1963. O.J.'s previous best was the 189 against Pittsburgh in 1972. His 80-yard TD trot was the longest ever in Schaefer Stadium and matched the second longest in Bills' history, tying another

O.J. runs away from Ray "Sugar Bear" Hamilton in 1973 opener. He's off for a touchdown in his record 250-yard game.
AP Wirephoto

Carlton mark and ranking behind O.J.'s 94-yard burst against the Steelers the previous season.

And on, the records and near-records went. Of course, most coveted was the league standard and few experts, if any, felt the 250-plateau would be surpassed.

"It looked like a track meet out there," quipped Fairbanks, horrified at his NFL coaching debut. "It was like Grant going through Richmond."

It seemed an ideal afternoon for punchy quotes. Others, in both dressing rooms, joined right into the spirit of the moment.

"O.J. had more yardage than Secretariat!" declared Pats' middle linebacker Edgar Chandler, a Buffalo restaurateur and former Bill. "It was embarrassing!"

Even Shaw, now a second-string quarterback who came on to hand off practically all day, was in a jocular mood. "I feel like a catcher who just handled a perfect game," he declared.

O.J. turned toward McKenzie and revealed to reporters two previous night happenings. First, the telephone rang frequently in O.J.'s hotel room. "My roomie, Reggie, kept answering it and the message was always the same," O.J. said. "The message was 'Tell O.J. that Julius Adams is going to kick his butt tomorrow.' " They laughed about that, and later Reggie told O.J.: "Tomorrow, we're going to get you 200 yards."

It turned out that Reggie was conservative. Now Simpson wondered about another McKenzie prediction, made before training camp. Reggie told O.J. the offensive line would get him 2,000 yards that season. Could he be correct on this count as well? Could it be possible? No one, not even Jim Brown, had approached 2,000.

Now McKenzie was talking to the crunch of reporters. Glancing at a statistics sheet which showed O.J. with 8.6 yards per trip, the star guard grinned: "He'll run for 300 yards someday. The Patriots were O.J.-conscious. They tried to key on him, which is why Watkins could run inside so well. But hell, any team has to be O.J.-conscious. He's the best."

Saban held a humorous view of the record proceedings. Possessing a two-touchdown lead late in the game, the coach was mainly interested in getting O.J. out of action and onto the bench, where he was safe. After all, 13 games remained and he didn't want to risk losing his superstar needlessly, after a game was clinched.

Suddenly a Bills' publicist dispatched word that O.J. needed 15 yards to break Ellison's single-game rushing record. All right, Saban figured, an NFL record is something special.

After Greene's interception at midfield, O.J. went in with the offense and slashed three yards on first down. The power sweep right netted seven more, giving him 227. Shaw provided a breather by keeping and then Simpson swept right again for nine.

Ah, Saban thought, that's more than 15. He has the record. Now I'll pull him. But, no.

"The figures were wrong—he still needs 15 yards," someone told Saban. The coach was upset, but how upset could he get with this overwhelming victory and a league record at the doorstep? O.J. ran his favorite play again and shuffled eight yards to the Pat 30. Now he had 244. After the two-minute warning and a Watkins two-yard burst, O.J. carried again. And, once more, it was the power sweep right—this time for seven yards and the record.

Saban even left the Juice in for that one last play in which he lost a yard. After all the commotion, the coach never did yank his star. "I didn't know about the record until late in the game when somebody on the bench said he needed just 15 more yards," he said. "I was reluctant to risk injury, but I put him back in and he got the 15 yards. Then somebody said he needed 15 more. I was really exasperated then because I was so afraid of needless injury.

"But he got the record and I'm glad he did. He deserves it. He had a great game and deserves all the accolades. Records aren't all that important, though—not worth risking injury. I was more concerned about his safety. You don't find many like O.J. around.

"And let me tell you something," added Saban, warming to the occasion. "He's a man. He's also a great team man. He knows no other way to play. And he had help today. Watkins gave him a lot of help. The offensive line deserves a lot of credit for doing a great job blocking. And Shaw called as fine a game as he's ever called."

There were differences of opinion as to how large a role the offensive wall played in that steady stream of power sweeps to the right. "He did it all alone," charged Julius Adams, one of many Pats grasping at air most of the day. "His blocking wasn't that great—he was!"

O.J. would hear none of that. He credited McKenżie with key blocks which sprang him for the 80- and 22-yard touchdowns. And he mentioned nearly every player on offense after Reggie.

"Our guys thoroughly handled the Patriots up front," O.J. declared. "Reggie was pulling out great all day. There were things you don't see, like Bruce Jarvis [center] blocking ahead on Edgar Chandler. Larry Watkins got all those yards up the middle on that counterplay we just put into our attack. Give Donnie Green and Paul Seymour a lot of credit. Much of the yardage came to that right side.

"Reggie has that tremendous athletic ability which allows him to bounce in and out as a blocker," the Juice went on. "He was just blowing them out. Both he and Watkins were hitting Kiner. For me, it was just a matter of picking my way once I got there."

O.J. observed that 102 of his yards came via the pair of touchdowns runs, and he proceeded to describe for posterity how both plays developed.

"My first, the 80-yarder, could have gone inside or out," he said. "It helped having a guard like Reggie, who can move either way. Watkins threw a good block and I swept in. Rowe hit me and then Kiner hit me. But the second guy knocked me out of the first man's grasp and gave me impetus. Fortunately, I kept my balance and then it was just a matter of outrunning everyone. I went down the sideline from there. My only thought was not to get caught. I got caught after a long run against Philadelphia during the preseason and I felt that if it happened again, my teammates would never let me live it down.

"The second TD [22 yards] came off tremendous offensive line blocking, particularly from Seymour and Green. I was supposed to go inside the tackle, but Watkins hit Kiner in such a way that I went outside and Reggie screened me out from Kiner. He couldn't touch me. McKenzie and I got beyond the line—just him and me—all alone. There were about three guys waiting at the goal line, and we just bowled into them."

Fairbanks disagreed with Adams' assessment of the Bills' line, declaring Buffalo's marines had landed. "They blew us apart," the new head coach admitted. "Even when we stopped O.J. inside, he had the speed and quickness to bounce outside. We didn't force the issue, either. We weren't aggressive enough."

O.J. loved hearing that! He couldn't recall opposing coaches and players criticizing themselves so graphically after a Bills' game. How sweet it was! The rollover Bills were gone. These were the new, punishing Bills.

"O.J.'s breaking 80 yards didn't really bother me because you expect it of him," Fairbanks moaned on. "What really discouraged me were those six, seven, eight yards at a clip they were gaining on us, inside and out. We couldn't slow them down."

O.J. was thrilled. Imagine, after four years plus, an enemy coach finally complaining the Bills couldn't be slowed . . . that his defense was inept. How sweet, indeed!

Simpson answered and reanswered endless questions as wave upon wave of reporters descended upon him. An hour after the game, he was still surrounded—still in full uniform, clutching the game ball.

"What a day," O.J. summarized, realizing the reporters were the first to have him really trapped all afternoon. "And I had it figured all wrong. Against the defense I figured the Patriots would use, I thought I'd be doing a lot of decoying today."

The Boston and Buffalo writers roared in laughter. Then O.J. got serious.

"I gained a lot of yardage against San Francisco and Pittsburgh last year, and I was especially happy with the San Francisco game because that was my home town," he said. "But I'm happiest with this record. We needed this so badly. We played to win in preseason, but the coach played a lot of people. Even after we went 0-6, I kept saying we'd run the ball down some people's throats.

"This is our first opening-day win since I've been here, and that really feels good," O.J. went on. "I think we can take it from here and have an outstanding season."

O.J. bolted away to the showers at last. His teammates were already on the bus awaiting the long ride to the airport. Saban had long since postponed his postgame message to the team because of all the happy commotion. "What I've got to say to you, I'll say on the plane back to Buffalo," he laughed.

On the ride to the airport, a reporter leaned across the aisle and asked Watkins, almost a forgotten man, how his 105 yards ranked among his best career outputs. "It was my best game ever," he responded. Kidded that the effort was obscured by O.J.'s phenomenal game, Watkins grinned: "That's all right. We won!"

The comment was symbolic of a new spirit among the Buffalo Bills.

Meanwhile back in western New York, Bills' fans hashed over what they watched in amazement on their TV screens. They now realized all their team needed to win was strict adherence to the game plan.

And the game plan—for any and all opponents was: Snap the ball to the quarterback, who turns around and hands it off to O.J. Simpson. Then all hell breaks loose!

CHAPTER TEN

A Thousand Yards at Midseason

It was almost the halfway point of the 1973 season and the Bills were about to realize a long overdue "first": their initial appearance on ABC's nationally televised Monday night Game-of-the-Week.

Though some may refuse to admit it, Monday games are special to the players. All the other teams around the NFL are idle that evening and most of the players are watching. Members of the two combating teams know their peers are tuned in. This is the showcase game to them.

It's like being at center stage at the only play in town and practically all your fellow actors are in the audience. Special care is taken to perform at one's very best. After four years, the Bills were about to receive their baptismal appearance.

When the Kansas City game was scheduled to be beamed by Howard Cosell and friends, the Bills really had only O.J. and the luster of the new 80,000-seat Rich Stadium for attractions to a national viewing audience. They were coming off a 4-9-1 season and hardly anyone had predicted a winning record for them.

Yet now they grasped so much more. Simpson was more than a

league rushing champion yearning for another title. He was exploding. Two weeks earlier, in a 31-13 victory over Baltimore which capped a three-victory homestand, the Juice enjoyed a 22-carry, 166-yard afternoon—an NFL-record seventh consecutive 100-yard game spanning two seasons.

The Bills were now a winning enterprise, playing before sellouts in their vast new stadium. Miami had just halted O.J.'s string of 100's at seven and breezed past the Bills with a 27-6 Orange Bowl victory, but still the Buffalo record was 4-2. The Bills were destined for their best season since 1966.

There was enthusiasm most everywhere the Bills became a conversation topic. Ralph Wilson was especially excited. "Lou Saban is building this team the same way he built our championship teams of the mid-Sixties," the club owner observed.

O.J. was making a shambles of the league rushing race. After that 250-yard bombshell in Foxboro, he mustered 103 yards in 22 rushes at San Diego. The lowly Chargers romped, 34-7, O.J. scoring the Buffalo touchdown.

Then, in his first Rich Stadium season appearance, O.J. mustered a 24-carry, 123-yard effort against the Jets. Buffalo won, 9-7, on three Leypoldt field goals and held the Namath-less Jets scoreless with a makeshift defensive backfield until a bomb with two seconds to play. The following Sunday, O.J. had 27 carries and 171 yards as the Bills edged Philadelphia, 27-26, despite being outgained, 451-276 yards.

The domination of Baltimore followed, including a 78-yard O.J. touchdown sweep, but at Miami the Bills were held without a first-half first down for the second straight year. O.J. finished the day with 14 carries, 55 yards and a right-ankle sprain.

Simpson thought he broke the ankle at first, unable to place weight on the foot. But he rested it five days and was ready for the Chiefs. "I can't disappoint Howard," O.J. quipped with a wink, thinking of his friend Cosell.

Still, even with O.J. sound, Saban was worried. The Dolphins had simply shut off his high-voltage offense and O.J. had virtually nowhere to go. And Buffalo's quarterbacks were sacked a resounding nine times. Coach Don Shula explained what his team accomplished.

"What we wanted to do was get O.J. running toward the sidelines," the Miami coach said. "That way, he has only one way to go—outside. We didn't want him squirting through the line and getting position to use those moves of his. To do that, you have to play defense from the inside out, stringing out the play. Your support men have to come up fast. We did it—all our people played well on defense."

Saban knew longtime rival coach Hank Stram and his Chiefs were listening. And watching via film.

The Juice, however, remained confident. He knew the Dolphins were able to accomplish feats no other team could perform. "Let's face it," he said. "They beat us in every way. They are the world champs, you know."

O.J. was certain the Dolphin derailment was only a temporary thing. And he was talking about the Bills as a team, not his own efforts—even with 868 yards in six games and many writers around the nation already writing about the possibility of his breaking Jim Brown's single-season record of 1,863 established in 1963.

"Before the season, Jim Ringo told me if I stay healthy I'll get 1,700 yards this year," O.J. commented. "That sounds great, but I remember as a kid I wanted to play in the Rose Bowl someday. I didn't even think of a national championship. That was something way, way out. Even in my junior year at USC, I didn't think about it.

"But that's what I like to think about now," O.J. went on. "Let's get the team going. When we go to the Super Bowl, my career will be complete. The world championship is my goal right now. Not too many players ever have gone that far."

As Saban stated—he's a team player.

The skies opened and rain descended in virtual buckets until minutes before kickoff. However, with a local television blackout in effect, the stadium was filled. It was the Bills' third 80,020-sellout in four home appearances.

At kickoff, an enthusiasm filled the air that Bills' players had never before experienced. Yes, there was something about these Monday night games, they thought. Even before a ball was kicked or thrown, this shivering throng was screaming. It was a game later referred to as "Pneumonia Night," for obvious reasons. The fans stayed warm by yelling, stomping, drinking and waving a sea of signs.

It took new arrivals at least 15 minutes to read all the handwritten messages. Many of them heralded Simpson and chided Cosell. "O.J. and Howard are Alike—They Both Run On and On," proclaimed one. "Buffalo has the Juice, Don and Frank Have the Lemon," said another.

Indeed, the ABC trio of Cosell-Meredith-Gifford stoked the crowd's fervor. Cosell was bombarded with confetti when he walked out onto the TV deck outside the press box. When Howard went into his pregame show, one fan held up a banner which read: "Tons of useless Information." It was a carnival atmosphere.

Soon a fan on· the press box side held up a large picture of a naked baby lying on a bearskin rug with Cosell's head superimposed on the picture. Cosell merely glared with a firm grip on his cigar. Alongside, Meredith broke out laughing. A few moments later, Meredith evoked a roar by waving his cowboy hat at about 40,000 fans on the stadium's south side.

When the Bills took the field, the crowd was at fever pitch. "The atmosphere out there was just unbelievable," guard Joe DeLamielleure said later. "It was like electricity—you could almost reach out and touch it. The whole place was alive. I never saw anything like it before."

The large gallery spent most of the first quarter on its feet— and what a quarter it was!

Leypoldt kicked off to Warren McVea at the one, and when Steve Jones belted McVea to the turf, the roar was near-deafening. The din continued as Len Dawson, KC's veteran quarterback, saw his first-down pass batted incomplete by linebacker Dave Washington. On second down, the Chiefs indicated they were being rattled—and not by a four-linebacker defense Buffalo was using for a second week. The crowd frenzy was showing its effect as Dawson, encountering difficulty with the signals, fumbled the snap. Middle linebacker Jim Cheyunski pounced on it at the Chief 15, and the crowd was ecstatic.

Immediately, Saban indicated what his offense would contain—

The Juice looks for running room as Willie Lanier holds on. O.J.
eclipsed 1,000 yards at midseason against Kansas City.
AP Wirephoto

Simpson and more Simpson. O.J. carried all four plays, starting
with a fake reverse for nine yards and capped by his one-yard
burst off right tackle for the first touchdown after only 2:33.
Leypoldt converted and the Bills led, 7-0.

On the crowd roared, and three plays after the kickoff,
Cheyunski was there for another Chief turnover. Dawson faded
to throw on third-and-9 and Cheyunski cut in front of Otis Taylor
to intercept. Playing with a heavily taped knee to protect torn
cartilage, the gutsy middle backer dashed 31 yards to the KC
four. Now the crowd sounded delirious.

If it wasn't then, it became so on the next play as O.J. swept
right four yards to score. Everything seemed to be going right for
Buffalo. After only 3 minutes, 37 seconds, Cheyunski had a
fumble recovery and interception and Simpson had two touchdowns. What a combination! It was time for conversion. Holder
Bob Chandler couldn't set up the wet ball and so he took off—and
scored! Yes, everything was going right. The Bills led, 14-0.

The Chiefs never recovered from that whirlwind start. In fact, they never protruded from their own end of the field until Ferguson fumbled a snap late in the half and linebacker Jim Lynch recovered at the Bills' 43. Pete Beathard replaced Dawson and worked a screen to Wendell Hayes for 27 yards, and Hayes scored a one-yard TD with 1:20 left in the half.

That cut the margin to 14-7 at intermission, but Leypoldt put away the game with a trio of third-quarter field goals—from 31, 17 and eight yards—for a 23-7 advantage. The final score was 23-14, but the significance of the game rested in much more than the point differential. Never before had the Bills rushed so often, a resounding 65 times. And never before had one player run so frequently in an NFL game. O.J. carried 39 of those 65 times, cracking the league record of 38 set by the New York Giants' Harry Newman against Green Bay in 1934 and matched by the Patriots' Jim Nance against Oakland in 1966.

O.J. established two league records that day—most rushes in a game and fewest games required to reach 1,000 yards in a season. O.J. accumulated 157 yards (and the two TDs) in those 39 romps and became the first player in NFL history to reach 1,000 at midseason. O.J. now had 1,025 yards, an average of 146 per game, and still he insisted he wasn't running for records.

"I'm aware of Brown's record and, yes, I feel I have a good shot at it, but it's not on my mind really as much as people think," O.J. declared in the happy dressing room scene. "I'm not running for records. I'm just running. If you do that . . . if you keep running, the records might come."

One standard O.J. established that day—the 39 rushes—lasted only a year. Baltimore's Lydell Mitchell broke it the following October by running 40 times against the Jets. But the 1,025-yard half-season figures to stand for many years.

The Bills, in raising their record to a glossy 5-2, echoed their main point of O.J.'s 250-yard game in New England. They were telling all of pro football they could dominate an entire game via a rushing attack . . . through ball control . . . through O.J.

The game's comparative statistics proved this point. While the final score was respectable, the yardage figures told a lopsided tale. The Bills amassed 246 yards by land, Kansas City a meager 37. The total yardage difference was 309-104 and the first-down margin 21-8, 15-3 by rushing.

In destroying the Chiefs, the Bills also proved they employed versatility, even with the sameness indicated by O.J.'s record 39 carries and Watkins' 19 thrusts for 81 yards. Saban scrapped his conservative approach this night and the Chiefs were ultraconfused.

Saban sent wide receiver Bob Chandler in motion left and right, he altered the spacing between the wide receiver and tight end, he ran Watkins 15 times in the second half, he employed the reverse and fakes off it, with O.J. keeping the ball. And defensively, he used that four-linebacker setup with the outside backers aligned within the ends and with a safety yanked for the extra linebacker. Johnny Ray, the linebacker coach, was using the same defense which worked for him at Notre Dame.

No longer could the Bills be accused of unimaginative play.

O.J., meanwhile, zoomed 54 yards ahead of Jim Brown's 1963 record pace. His contemporaries weren't even close. While the Juice was No. 1 with those 1,025 yards, only one other NFL running back had topped the 600-plateau. That was Dallas' Calvin Hill, a distant second with 662 yards. Cincinnati's Essex Johnson was third with only 580.

Such figures underscored one fact of life to O.J. He was only as effective as his line allowed him to become. He knew what it was to operate virtually without one. He decided one thing: regardless of his season's yardage, he would not play in the next Pro Bowl unless the Bills' line was recognized properly—unless at least one Buffalo lineman went with him, preferably McKenzie.

"Last year, they called the Pro Bowl the Dropout Bowl," the all-star game's 1973 MVP declared. "Once a player gets a reputation, he makes that Pro Bowl year after year, whether he deserves it or not. Particularly linemen, who don't get noticed so much. A guy can live on his reputation and get away with it.

"Well, I'll tell you," O.J. continued, "I won't play in it this coming year if someone from our offensive line isn't chosen with me. Last year, they said there were only two consistent guys in the offensive line when I got all those yards (1,251), but someone up there must have been playing well. I think it's only right that one of the Bills' linemen gets to play."

O.J. then made a personal pitch for his roommate.

"Reggie's my main man," he declared of the line's imposing No. 67. "It's rare when you get a guard with ability like that. There aren't many with the physical capacity to go in and out with the play and keep it up. He does it continually."

The Bills' publicity department chimed in with a nickname for the offensive line. "I've got it," declared L. Budd Thalman, the public relations director. "We'll call it the Electric Company! Why? Because they turn loose the Juice."

Some winced at the suggestion, but the tag was affixed. And so Dave Foley, Reggie McKenzie, Mike Montler (replacing injured Bruce Jarvis at center), Joe DeLamielleure, Donnie Green and Paul Seymour became the well-known Electric Company. And O.J., after most every game, made sure through his statements to the press that this line received plenty of recognition.

"We have the cockiest offensive line in football," O.J. boasted after the Chiefs were walloped. "They think they can do anything for me. They're always cheering me on. Reggie is always telling me, 'Run it my way. I'll open it up for you.' Reggie also keeps saying I'm going to get 2,000 yards.

"Heck, I got 1,200 last year and the line wasn't healthy. If Reggie and the guys say I'll get 2,000, I've got to believe them, because they're the guys who'll get it for me."

O.J. was gearing himself for a great second half-season. He already had six 100-yard performances in seven games, a total of 1,025 rushing yards and eight touchdowns. The records were starting to tumble and yet there was much more to come.

A sign behind the Kansas City bench after that first-quarter explosion presented the Bills' happy situation as it was and no one understood it better than ABC's telecasting trio. The sign read: "Howard, Let's Be Frank—Everything Is Going Dandy!"

CHAPTER ELEVEN

Turnabout in Atlanta

O.J. will long remember the game on Dec. 2, 1973, in Atlanta, not so much for what he accomplished, but for how an exceptional over-all team performance revived the Bills toward a won-9, lost-5 season—making them seasonal winners for the first time in the NFL and for the first time with Simpson their mainstay.

It wasn't that O.J. didn't enjoy a tremendous game against the Falcons. To the contrary, he carried 24 times for 137 yards and tied the NFL record for most 100-yard games within one season—nine by Jim Brown in 1958 and 1963.

However, there was so much more to this upset victory which cast a lasting effect on this young, effervescent team. The Bills were not expected to stand much of a chance against an Atlanta express which was rolling toward the playoffs. O.J. had just been insulted by Falcon coach Norm Van Brocklin and, with enemy defenses stacked against O.J., the Bills had stalled after the midseason victory over Kansas City.

The Bills became New Orleans' first shutout conquest ever, 13-0, and then Cincinnati edged them, 16-13, on Horst Muhlmann's 33-yard field goal. O.J., facing seven- and even eight-man fronts, was held under 100 yards each time. Saban, with a rookie quarterback, wouldn't risk doing what the enemy dared—throw! The Bengal defeat would eventually cost a playoff berth.

Then the Miami Dolphins came to town. O.J. dashed 120 yards and Jim Braxton, recovered from a back injury which had idled him a half-season, barreled 119 yards in only 17 carries—sensational for a fullback, especially one just off an injury list. Amazingly, though, the Bills were blanked, 17-0, and their outstanding half-season had deteriorated into a 5-5 record.

One week before the Atlanta game, the Bills seemed headed for a fourth straight setback in Baltimore, despite O.J.'s "picturesque" 58-yard touchdown run and 124-yard day. But an errant punting snap led to a pair of touchdowns in the final two minutes and Buffalo escaped with a 24-17 victory on cornerback Dwight Harrison's interception and 31-yard TD return.

Still, the Bills appeared a troubled team, coming so close to defeat by the lowly Colts. Atlanta, by contrast, was closing the season with a three-game homestand against the likes of Buffalo, St. Louis and New Orleans. The Falcons were 8-3, winners of seven straight and considered golden for the playoffs.

Van Brocklin, never the quiet type, aroused the Bills with this pearl: "Simpson could never play for me because he won't put his nose in there. He doesn't like contact."

O.J. countered: "If he means he doesn't like it because I'd rather run away from a tackler than over him, then I guess I'll never play for Van Brocklin."

The Juice and his teammates offered a more tangible reply to the Dutchman at Atlanta Stadium that Sunday.

After being stopped on their first series, the Bills received a break when Spike Jones' 52-yard punt was fumbled by Ray Brown and recovered by Buffalo's Fred Forsberg at the Falcon 27. Seven plays later, Braxton churned a yard to score and Buffalo led, 7-0.

Nick Mike-Mayer, the NFL's leading scorer, interrupted with 26- and 16-yard field goals, Atlanta's only scores of the afternoon. Leypoldt's 20-yarder bagged a 10-6 halftime lead. In the second half, a tremendous effort by Buffalo's suddenly stingy defense zipped the Falcons and Braxton punched over another one-yard TD to cap a 54-yard march and give Buffalo a 17-6 triumph. Braxton scored in five straight rushes from inside the 17 after Hill recovered O.J.'s fumble following an 18-yard rip.

O.J., Braxton, Ferguson and a sensational defensive effort had replied to Van Brocklin—by starting his team on a slide which barred Atlanta from a "wild card" berth in the playoffs. The Bills, however, were gaining tremendous momentum. And O.J. quickly explained the reason.

"We lost to New Orleans because we played the run all day long," he declared. "We won the last two with Joe throwing the ball." O.J. noted Ferguson, who completed seven of 12 aerials and ran seven times for 22 yards, connected on 20 of 31 passes the last two games. He said that was enough to give the Bills the balance they lacked during their three-game slide against those stacked defenses.

"Joe's coming into his own now," O.J. declared about the Arkansas rifle. "We had to keep the reins on him early in the year, but he's starting to throw well now. We can run and beat anyone if we play them straight up—running AND passing. They're the keys," he said, pointing to Ferguson and Braxton. "They're the ones who take the pressure off."

Braxton, scoring the first two touchdowns of his injury-abbreviated season, carried 23 times (one less than O.J.) for 80 of the bruising-type yards. O.J. compared Braxton to Miami's Larry Csonka. "They're a lot alike," he said. "Look what Csonka does for Mercury Morris. Look at his average gain per play. I don't know what mine was today [5.7] but with Jim going inside, it helps me a lot outside. I can do more things."

Next Simpson gave the Atlanta scribes a lesson in types of running backs—something to counter Van Brocklin's blast, if the game pattern wasn't graphic enough.

"There are two kinds of great running backs—side-steppers and challengers," O.J. said. "I'm a side-stepper. I never challenge a great defensive player, never let him hit me square and if I can avoid him altogether, I do. I always look for the baddest dude and get it in my mind he's never going to hit me. My favorite tacklers are the little cornerbacks and safetymen. I run at those guys and sidestep the linemen.

"How often do you see O.J. on his head?" Simpson asked his interviewers. "My game is to juke the tough guys. I put the okey-doke on them, bounce around and look for daylight. If I can't find a hole, I won't just slam in there. I refuse to hit a wall. I'll run out of bounds first. Coaches criticize me for it, but those cats want me to put my head in [Dick] Butkus' lap. Not me. All great running backs are insane, but I'm not that crazy."

The writers roared. O.J. had made his point—on the field and in the classroom which was the space in front of his locker.

O.J. now had accumulated 1,584 yards by rushing, the second best total in NFL history. The 137 yards against Atlanta vaulted him past Brown's 1,544-yard season in 1965. Now the ultimate target remained—Brown's record of 1,863 yards in 1963. There was still an ever-so-slight hope for the playoffs, too, the Bills now owning a 7-5 record and clinching at least a .500 record. Second place in the AFC East was already assured.

Few seriously believed the Bills could make the playoffs, even with a 9-5 record. It was mathematically possible, but they needed too many other breaks—help from other teams to upset other contenders for the American Conference "wild card" berth.

O.J.'s quest of the rushing record was no longer a long shot. He was 280 yards away. "He needs that one big game and I feel he can get it," declared McKenzie with emphasis. "Atlanta has the best defensive line we've faced all season—rugged and exceptionally strong with cats like Claude Humphrey and John Zook—but we beat it for 239 yards on the ground.

"Around the country, people know who the Buffalo Bills are now," McKenzie declared. "This was the best game the offensive line has played collectively. The defensive front had a tremendous day, too, and that's where we beat them—on both fronts. On offense, we came off the ball quickly together and beat them continually at the line of scrimmage. It wasn't just one or two of us, but everybody.

"We used the double wing to keep their ends down and the move worked," McKenzie continued. "They have two great defensive ends in Humphrey and Zook. Braxton came out of the backfield to double-team one of them and Seymour helped this way, too. Late in the game, Humphrey said he didn't know what to do next. You know you're getting great blocking when the quarterback gets four to six yards on a sneak."

The Bills' star guard talked of Simpson's two long runs, 18 and 32 yards. "I was out front on both," McKenzie said. "The 18-yarder was supposed to be a power sweep, but they strung us out. Juice cut back against the grain and Tommy Nobis [Atlanta middle linebacker] overran the play. But he took a good pursuit angle and came back to make the tackle. He was the last guy who could have stopped the run from going all the way. If Juice would have stayed to the outside, he would have got it—an 82-yard touchdown [and a 200-yard day]. We settled for a 20-yard field goal just before halftime. On the first play from scrimmage in the second half, we used our 27-play that we ran quite a bit. Juice got 32 yards, running along the left sideline after I kicked out a linebacker and Joe D took out the strong safety."

You could almost see O.J., McKenzie and the other Bills rubbing their palms in anticipation as the Patriots, victims of O.J.'s 250-yard opening game, were to close Buffalo's home season the following Sunday. This could be that big game, McKenzie figured.

Already, the club records were falling like tenpins. The 17 first-downs at Atlanta had included 12 by land, increasing the season total to 123 and breaking the club record set by the 1962 Bills. The 239 rushing yards gave them a 12-game aggregate of 2,491—another season standard, erasing a 1962 log. And the Bills still had two games to play.

Further, there was something called defense, particularly the aerial variety. With an aggressive front four chasing quarterback Bob Lee most of the afternoon, the NFC's top-rated aerial outfit was held to nine completions in 22 attempts. Lee, nicknamed "the General," surrendered to sacks four times and the hottest NFL thrower suddenly was very cool. Atlanta was out of the NFC Western title race and soon to be out of the playoff picture, and a large airport gathering was readying a hero's welcome for the two-touchdown underdog Bills in Buffalo.

Already the Bills' thoughts were focusing on the Rich finale with those generous Patriots. "Nothing could be finer than to lay a block on Kiner," quipped McKenzie, with visions of that awesome power sweep right.

The Juice was smiling broadly.

CHAPTER TWELVE

The Juice Flows in Snow

The goal was 280 rushing yards in two games for O.J., and when the Bills awoke the morning of Dec. 9, 1973, they figured on gaining the lion's share against their "cousins," the New England Patriots. What they didn't figure on, however, was doing it in snow.

"We were a little worried with the weather and all," admitted rookie guard Joe DeLamielleure. "As it turned out, though, the weather gave us an advantage."

O.J. reported to Rich Stadium, looked out onto the Astroturf carpet, felt the snowfall increase in intensity and knew the white stuff couldn't be kept off the field this day. "My first reaction was disappointment because we had such great weather all year long," O.J. said. "When I came out on the field before the game, I was worried. I couldn't cut and I tried five different pairs of shoes—some from Hong Kong, Canada, France and a pair of regular American-made turf cleats. I finally went back to my original ones from West Germany. They're rubber-cleated."

Soon O.J.'s concern over the weather abated. "Once we started playing, we found the traction wasn't all that bad," he revealed.

And yet, although the Bills had little difficulty pulling away, O.J.'s large-yardage quest looked shaky for a half. He had only 43 yards in eight attempts before the break. With New England driving for an early 14-yard Jeff White field goal and Wallace Francis responding with a 90-yard TD kickoff return, the Buffalo offense didn't step onto the field until 6:57 elapsed. O.J. carried only twice in the first quarter, including a 24-yard sweep. It was the power sweep right—what else?

O.J.'s second-quarter highlight was a six-yard TD rip through the right side behind McKenzie, giving Buffalo a 14-3 cushion. After Leypoldt and White traded field goals, the halftime difference was 17-6.

In the third quarter, O.J. went to work. He darted five yards twice and then Braxton bulled for 10. O.J. opened up, sweeping 25 to the Pat 30. After a holding penalty, Ferguson lofted a 37-yard play-action TD pitch to Chandler—the fake handoff going to O.J. and Chandler outleaping cornerback George Hoey for a sensational grab in the end zone. Soon Leypoldt kicked his second of three field goals, a 34-yarder, and the gap was 27-6 after 6:22 of the third chapter. For all intents, the victory and a Bills' winning season were secure. But what about O.J.'s rushing yardage? With most of the game gone, he had only 78 yards in 12 runs.

There was no need for concern. After Plunkett slid—and the word is slid—five yards for a Patriot score, O.J. and his Electric Company took matters into their own hands. Simpson began doing what the snow removal equipment couldn't do—plow the field. With the score 27-13, O.J. began pelting the Patriots with everything but snowballs. To them, he looked like the abominable snowman in a helmet.

On first down from the Bills' 20, O.J. swept right on his favorite play, made a couple of sharp cuts and whoosh—he was gone. It was a Rembrandt of rushing. He broke free from safety Ralph Anderson along the right sideline and sprinted crossfield 71 yards before being snared by corner Ron Bolton at the Patriot nine.

"I was determined not to let him outrun me down the sideline," declared Anderson. "But he saw me coming and

O.J. leads Patriot linebackers on merry 71-yard chase. Juice is pursued
through snow by Edgar Chandler (50) and Ron Acks (51).
AP Wirephoto

slowed up just a little. I couldn't slow up on that slippery field
and he just slipped past me on the inside and bolted across the
field."

Pats' left end Ray "Sugar Bear" Hamilton offered his view.
"O.J. came around that corner and George Hoey turned the play
in, just like he's supposed to," Hamilton said. "The tackle
[Donnie Green] was blocking me and the tight end [Paul
Seymour] was blocking [linebacker] Steve Kiner. We both fought
off the blocks, but somehow I tripped over the end and O.J. just
made a move on Kiner. It was like he came around and I was in
front of him and he made a move and he was gone," Hamilton
ran on. "It was probably my fault."

Very suddenly, O.J. had exploded to a 149-yard rushing total.

He was assured of his 10th 100-yard game of the season, another NFL record. But he was far from finished.

Three plays later, Chandler beat Hoey again and caught his second TD pass of the day, a six-yarder which gave Buffalo a 34-13 margin and a 17-point third period.

The next time Buffalo took possession, O.J. swept for 28 yards and crashed the middle for 25—straight-arming Bolton en route. Just that quickly, off two carries to start a fourth-quarter series, O.J. surpassed 200 yards for the second time in his career, the second time in 1973, the second time against the Patriots . . . the only time at Rich Stadium. Some 75,841 fans rose to give the Juice and his team prolonged standing applause.

O.J. had 15 carries and 202 yards. Leypoldt soon followed with his third field goal, a 19-yarder to close the scoring of a 37-13 Buffalo rout. Before the game ended, O.J. carried seven times more, finishing with 22 attempts and a robust 219 yards—in snow!

En route to the dressing room, shivering all the way, O.J. thought about what he had done against the Patriots—469 yards rushing in two romps. Today, he had 176 yards in the second half alone. The Pats were thinking about it, too. All they could do was shake their heads.

"Whooooo-weee," shouted a voice from the Bills' shower room. "That man was running today like he had a bounty on his head!"

"Sure there's a way to stop Simpson," Patriot coach Chuck Fairbanks insisted in the New England room. "Of course, there is. You can stop him if you break both his ankles." Fairbanks had lost everything but his sense of humor.

In the Buffalo room, the crowd's frequent chants of "Juice . . . Juice . . .Juice" still rang in O.J.'s ears and he was happy. "These fans in Buffalo have been just great to us all year and I wanted to do something special for them in our last home game," O.J. explained. "I wanted to break Jim Brown's rushing record right here and the entire team wanted to do something special for our fans."

O.J. fell 61 yards shy of the mark, but the 219-yard show was special in itself.

"With good weather today, O.J. would have broken the rec-

Patriot linebacker Ron Acks (51) desperately hangs on to O.J. in Juice's
219-yard romp through Buffalo snow.
UPI Wirephoto

ord," McKenzie asserted. But O.J. disagreed that snow favored the defense. He explained why. "I knew where I was going. The Pats didn't. It's awfully tough for defensive backs to keep their feet on a slippery, icy field."

O.J. certainly didn't mind the snow or the bitter cold, though he couldn't stop shaking afterward. He couldn't have really minded because he wore short sleeves.

"I could feel them hitting me better that way and I could bounce away," O.J. explained, not too convincingly. "No, I didn't mind the snow. I had some of my best college days in the mud, but I never played well in snow until today. My feet were cold. It was tough keeping warm, and the snow hindered me turning the corner, but we did all right."

Only all right? Across the way, Patriot players would wince at that statement.

"While I was a mudder while running in San Francisco in my junior college days, this was nothing like that," O.J. went on. "Running on Astroturf in the snow is like nothing else I've done in my career. I was surprised I could make a couple of quick cuts on it in the second half, but once it started to melt, the footing wasn't all that bad. It was wet and cold, that's all. The thing that worried me most was keeping warm."

And yet, he wore short sleeves.

The snow provided a couple of other interesting stories. The Bills didn't have the proper equipment to remove it, and never attempted—except for several youngsters who shoveled along the yard-lines at halftime. Meanwhile, learning his team would be stuck in snow, Pats' business manager Herm Bruce went to downtown Buffalo during the first half, convinced a store owner to open up and purchased 29 pairs of shoes. They were the kind players wear on regular grass. The Pats changed at halftime and found these didn't work either. O.J. relied on his white "old faithfuls" and the Bills, as a team, wore six or seven different types. "I kept looking at O.J.'s feet," remarked Hamilton. "I wanted to see what he was wearing. I wanted to get me some."

O.J. was happy to show Hamilton his feet, especially the heels as he trotted away in the second half.

"I knew I was within striking distance of the records," O.J.

went on, referring to both his 250-yard single-game mark and Brown's 1,863-yard season. "All the guys kept saying, 'Let's get 280.' But the records can come next Sunday, though I wanted to set them here."

Saban, also shivering, explained how the Juice was able to break away with such rapidity in the second half. "They had to close inside the way Jim Braxton [15 carries, 70 yards] was running," he said. "That gave us certain outside advantages."

O.J. was more specific. "The Pats kept shifting to the strong side, and so we worked the weak side," he said. "You learn things over the years. The Pats have a fine offense, but are last in rushing defense. Running teams do well against 'em. They have a few weaknesses."

Weaknesses—such as the whole left side. It was enough to label them "Patsies," as some Bills' followers had happily done. But O.J. refrained. He was thankful Kiner and Co. existed.

"Give him a crack and he's gone," Kiner complained. "We have too many cracks in our defense, but the basic problem was him, O.J. Simpson."

"Our receivers couldn't make their cuts—it was a bad day for throwing," indicated Plunkett, inferring the Pats' offense was hurt worse by the snow. "And watching O.J. from the sideline wasn't much fun. It hasn't been much fun the last seven years [counting their Pac-8 days]. He's been doing the same thing all his life."

"We didn't expect to shut the door on Simpson—no one has," reviewed Fairbanks. "But they were able to do the things we hoped to avoid—make the long-gainer on a run, or pass."

And so, the Bills were 8-5 and O.J. at last had the feeling of a winner. He also had four NFL records: most rushing attempts (39) and yards (250) in a game, most consecutive 100-yard games (7) and most 100-yard games in a season (one more would make it 11). He was approaching 11 Bills' records. In flocking to see him, Bills' fans led the NFL in turnstile attendance with an average of 75,896 per home game. Simply put, everything was beautiful. Well, almost everything. They had only a remote chance for the playoffs.

O.J.'s teammates were clearly record-conscious after the Patriot encounter. "We've got it now," said McKenzie. "O.J. needs 61 yards and we need 176 to break the team [single-season] rushing record."

The Super Bowl champion Miami Dolphins had legged 2,960 yards a season earlier, and now the Bills threatened that approaching the season finale with the New York Jets at Shea Stadium. "Yeah, we'll get it," repeated McKenzie. "This opportunity comes once in a lifetime. No other team has come close. We'll get it. We'll get those 61 yards if we have to run Juice 61 times."

The Bills, seasonal winners for the first time since O.J. was a sophomore at the City College of San Francisco, joined into the spirit of the coming occasion.

"It's great, unbelievable," Joe D commented. "We've got to get the records next week."

"I get personal satisfaction out of keeping my man out of the play, but my ultimate satisfaction is going to come next week when O.J. gets his record and we break Miami's record," chimed in Donnie Green. "But it's not an individual thing. It's a team thing."

That was the whole point as far as O.J. was concerned. He never said "I" when talking of the record quest. The word was "we."

"If it was down to us and the Jets," the Bills' record runner declared, "then this game would be a big one. The big ones, as far as I'm concerned, are for the team. Sure, I would like to get the record. We'll still be trying for the win in the Jets game, but there's no doubt I'd like to get the record. Make that we."

The record quest was about to reach a climax.

"Sixty-one yards—that ain't nothin'," shouted linebacker Bo Cornell.

"Hell no," answered cornerback Dwight Harrison. "For the Juice, that's two runs!"

CHAPTER THIRTEEN

A Record Day At Chez Shea

It was Saturday night, the eve of the most memorable day in O.J. Simpson's fabulous football career. The Juice was restless and absolutely no one wondered why.

At practices during this final week of the 1973 season, his every move was monitored for posterity. Practically every question imaginable was asked and answered innumerable times. A virtual legion of reporters was following him now.

After the Saturday flight to New York, the interview crush happened all over again. O.J. was at center stage, where he belonged. And he loved it. He was about to cap his most fantastic season—the most fabled individual season in National Football League history—in the media capital of the world.

O.J. dined with ABC's Roone Arledge and Howard Cosell and returned to the Essex House Hotel across from Central Park to find the bar alive with reporters. Anticipation of the great event about to unfurl was mirrored all over the place.

Now he was upstairs in his room with Reggie. Two figures danced inside his whirling head—61 yards for him and 176 for the team.

"If I can break the individual record and if the team can beat Miami's record, tomorrow will the the biggest day of my life," the Juice told his No. 1 blocker. McKenzie nodded. It would be the greatest day for an entire Bills' offense.

The next morning, O.J. gazed out the window and knew immediately that snowy weather had followed him from Buffalo. High winds were whipping the white flakes furiously. He became prepared to do what he accomplished the previous week—to literally glide across frozen water—only this time into football immortality.

As was their custom before road encounters, the Juice and defensive line leader Earl Edwards left for the stadium two hours before the team bus, immediately after the pregame breakfast. Simpson's manager pulled up in a limousine to provide a personal escort service to Shea Stadium.

Along the route, O.J. couldn't help but reflect upon how great a distance he and the Bills had traveled in one season. A year earlier, upon winning his first NFL rushing title with those 1,251 yards, he was ecstatic after that upset of the Redskins. "The sky's the limit, there is no ceiling," O.J. declared that fateful day in Washington. "I'm not making any goals, but next year when we get all our guys back, who knows what can happen?"

Now, O.J. knew and the ramifications were staggering. Under Lou Saban's leadership, he could fulfill that boyhood boast—he could surpass Jim Brown's rushing records. And this day could be a milestone in that direction.

"O.J.'s got to be motivated," Saban had said in the RFK Stadium dressing room in 1972. "I told him I would stay with him. He had a rough three years, but I think he's found himself."

Was he ever motivated this day! Had he ever found himself—thanks to Saban!

O.J., highly nervous—some might call it natural stage fright before an actor's most famed performance—became ill in the Buffalo dressing room. But he didn't take long to compose himself. He really was ready. This was the day he had awaited all those years. Shea Stadium was his stage . . . 47,740 fans and millions watching via TV were his audience . . . the New York

Jets were his victims as kindly Weeb Ewbank closed his coaching career.

"When we took the field that day, we knew we were going to break Jim Brown's record and there was nothing that was going to stop us," O.J. later said. He was that confident, that sure. And there was that word "we" instead of "I" again.

The Jets realized the inevitable, too.

"I'd be proud to hold him to 61 yards," commented defensive tackle Richard Neal. "He has a way of getting 161 on you."

"With O.J., our job isn't to tackle him, but to catch up with him," quipped Ewbank. "I love O.J. Let him get his 61 yards, but spread 'em out. If he carried 61 times and made one yard a carry and didn't get a first down or touchdown, I'd be happy. But I'd like to see him break it. It couldn't happen to a nicer guy."

"He's so close," added linebacker Ralph Baker. "If he needed 100 yards, it would be different, but I think New England opened the door. The guy's a super runner. The biggest problem is getting him to the ground. You can't give him any room to operate. He can put five moves on you in three yards."

John Elliott, who tackled Simpson on the first carry of his initial pro game in 1969, even instilled O.J. favoritism over Brown into the picture. "He's a much better individual than Jimmy Brown," the large defensive end declared. "I'd rather see him have the record than Brown."

As they took the field, according to O.J., the Bills weren't even thinking of 2,000 yards, though McKenzie predicted it before the season. "Jim Brown's record was the most prevailing thought on our minds," the Juice said. "Two thousand just didn't come up."

The paper-thin possibility of a playoff berth also existed and the Bills were hopeful but not optimistic. They needed two smashing upsets in addition to their own success against the Jets. They needed a Houston surprise over Cincinnati—the Oilers won only once all season—and Cleveland had to upend Los Angeles. Neither would happen. The Bills almost knew it beforehand.

And so they dwelled upon the Juice's record chase, right from the opening kickoff. "When the game started, we went right after them," O.J. described. "On first down, I went over the middle for four and then we ran our favorite play—a '26'—and it broke beautifully for about 30 yards. It was me and Seymour, Reggie, DeLamielleure, everyone. It was like a convoy going downfield. I kicked the back of Seymour's leg and fell. I tried to get up and somebody [Baker] tackled me. Going back to the huddle, we all said to Seymour, 'Paul, we could have broken it on that one play.' "

Off just that play, the Buffalo offense indicated how easy this would be. Off that play, the hapless Jets knew how determined these Buffalo players were. Nothing would stop them from their goals. The Jets were getting O.J. Simpson rammed down their throats.

O.J. carried on seven of the first eight plays, becoming the 20th player to pass the 5,000-yard career rushing plateau with that 30-yard rip and amassing 57 of the 61 yards he needed before the Jets ever gained possession. Yes, it was a dark, frigid, snow-swept afternoon in Shea Stadium, but there was nothing dark or frigid or snow-conscious about this Buffalo attack. It was on fire, for the fourth straight week.

Simpson did everything but score on that opening 71-yard, 12-play march. Braxton handled that on a fourth down, one-yard plunge outside left tackle. The Bills had consumed the first 8:32 by going all the way on Simpson and Braxton carries, never thinking of a pass. Before the initial play of Buffalo's next possession, the offense realized O.J. needed only four yards to erase the Jimmy Brown record some had considered invincible. His next carry would also eclipse a Brown record for one-year attempts. "I didn't think I'd be that close until the third or fourth quarter, what with the conditions and all," O.J. said. "When we got that close so fast, it was kind of like, 'Oh, are we here that quick?' "

On first down from the Jet 49, O.J. took a handoff from Ferguson and headed left behind Braxton. The star guards, McKenzie and Joe D, blasted open a large hole and Braxton darted through to make it larger. Behind him whizzed O.J., who cut outside before bouncing off end Mark Lomas and down to earth. McKenzie instantly became the team yardage measurer. "Was the hole big enough?" Braxton asked O.J.

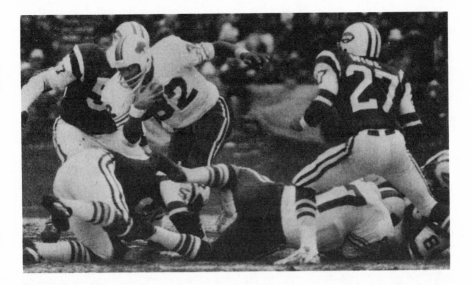

O.J. races through Jet line to break Jim Brown's record. Jets' safety Phil
Wise (27) looks on in vain.
AP Wirephoto

VOLUNTEERS. BUT YOU
DON'T HAVE TO BE A PRO
TO BE A VOLUNTEER. YOU
JUST HAVE TO BE YOURSELF.
FOR DETAILS-WRITE-VOLUNTEER
WASHINGTON-D.C. 20013.
THANK YOU

BALL ON 13 DOWN 3 TO GO 2 QTR. 2

		1	2	3	4	TOTAL
BUF BILLS		7	0			7
N.Y. JETS		7	0			7

2-TIME OUTS LEFT-N.Y. 3

O.J. heads for second-quarter TD on his record day in New York after
eluding Jets' Burgess Owens (22) and Ralph Baker (51).
AP Wirephoto

The Juice looked back toward McKenzie, his bodyguard. The crowd was quiet as Reggie peered to check the sideline marker. "He needed four yards," McKenzie thought. By gosh, he got six! McKenzie raised his arms skyward in triumph. The record was broken! O.J. had beaten Brown's record!

Now, O.J. looked to Braxton, smiling. He could answer the fullback's question. "The hole—it seems all right, I guess," he declared. Both grinned.

Immediately the public address announcer barked that O.J. was the new NFL single-season rushing yardage record-holder and the game was stopped. O.J.'s teammates mobbed him, slapping him wildly and happily. The officials presented the ball to O.J. and the Bills joined the Shea crowd in loud applause. The offense embraced him again and he came over to hug Saban and Ringo, depositing the ball which now rests at the Pro Football Hall of Fame in Canton, Ohio.

At this point, the Juice had severed Brown's two single-season NFL marks—most carries (305 in 1961) and most yards (1,863 in 1963)—but it was only the first quarter. He wasn't through by any means. But what followed immediately was hardly O.J.'s idea of how to react to a league record.

"The plan was to try and get me the record as quickly as possible so the pressure would be removed," O.J. explained. "With the record out of the way, it was thought I could relax and we could concentrate more on the game itself. But I relaxed so much, I fumbled on the next play."

Safety Burgess Owens recovered at the Jet 41. Just two plays later, Joe Namath fired a 48-yard touchdown pass to Jerome Barkum and the game was tied, 7-7, after a quarter.

Midway through the second quarter, the Bills' rushing offense began rolling again. Ferguson worked a fourth down sneak at the Jet 43, then passed 19 yards to Chandler along the right sideline.

On third down and two, O.J. bolted inside left tackle for his 12th touchdown of the season, a 13-yarder with 1:17 left in the half. The Bills seemed destined for a 14-7 halftime lead, but Namath fired two quick incompletions and Julian Fagan came in to punt with 39 seconds left.

Fagan kicked low and short to rookie Bill Cahill. The plan

O.J. takes handoff, uses block by Joe DeLamielleure (68) and hurtles_
forward for single-season rushing record in New York.
AP Wirephoto

called for a fair catch, but Saban noted how poor the punt was and yelled to Cahill, "Go with it!" He did—51 yards to paydirt behind a double block from Earl Edwards. The Bills were in control, 21-7, and never surrendered it.

O.J. had 19 carries and 108 yards at halftime, breaking his own NFL record with an 11th 100-yard game, almost twice the total of his first four seasons combined.

The Bills took possession only three times in the second half and batted 1.000 in efficiency, scoring each time. Ferguson found Chandler with a 36-yard pass at the Jet 16 and the Simpson-Braxton machine took over, Braxton scoring from the one. The gap was 28-7 after three quarters.

Three plays before that third round ended, O.J. burst off right tackle eight yards and just that quickly, the Bills had erased Miami's year-old league record for team rushing yards in one season. Only the players didn't know it yet. They were too committed to another goal.

On the very next play, O.J. swept right end for 25 yards, giving him 150 in 26 tries at the three-quarter mark and suggesting that the goal of another 200-yard game and a fantastic 2,000-yard season was within reach.

The fourth quarter was about to begin, and Ferguson came running into the huddle with big news from the Bills' bench. The rookie's eyes were bulging and he was breathing hard from sheer excitement. "I've got something to fire you guys up," he said. "Juice only needs 50 yards for 2,000."

McKenzie, recalling his summer prediction which seemed unbelievable, now knew it was there for the taking. "Let's get it," he yelled.

When Leypoldt's 12-yard field goal 4:02 into the fourth quarter stretched the margin to 31-7, O.J. had 158 yards. The game was long since cinched. Now only O.J.'s rushing yardage mattered. When Buffalo regained possession six plays later, O.J. took a first-down handoff and utilized that power sweep right for a 22-yard burst to the Jet 38. Now he was really in range of the magic number. He had 30 carries and 180 rushing yards.

A probe over left guard gained nothing on first down, but then the Juice swept left and netted nine. On third-and-one, Braxton

O.J. holds his arms high in victory as his teammates mob him after breaking 2,000-yard plateau in 1973 finale.
AP Wirephoto

Squeezing the Juice: O.J. takes the offense with him to postgame press conference. From left: Reggie McKenzie, J.D. Hill, Joe DeLamielleure, Paul Seymour, Bob Chandler, Donnie Green and Joe Ferguson.
AP Wirephoto

barreled four and got a first down at the Jet 25. Now, it was O.J.'s turn again and a sweep to the left produced five yards before safety Phil Wise forced him out of bounds. The Juice was told he needed six yards . . . just six yards and he would be football's first 2,000-yard man.

If ever an athletic achievement were surrounded by symbolism, this was it! Suddenly, as if to call attention to the historic event about to unfurl, the stadium lights flashed on—creating a spotlight effect. The crowd had dwindled below 20,000 because of the bitter cold and, to partisan Jet fans, the bitter score. But, small as the gathering was, all were excited. They sensed a never-to-be-forgotten moment was about to happen.

Finally, O.J. grasped Ferguson's handoff, cut behind left guard and followed big no. 67, his main man, on the record-breaking voyage both had dreamed about all season. O.J. sliced seven yards before Wise brought him to earth in roughhouse fashion at the Jet 13. "Any other time, I would have said something to the officials, because I thought he should have been called for a facemask penalty," O.J. said. "But as I was lying there on the ground, all the guys started congratulating me and I forgot what happened."

O.J. was mobbed and pummeled again by his teammates and chants of "Juice . . . Juice . . . Juice" could be heard most everywhere. There were five minutes, 56 seconds left to play, but this game for all intents was over. O.J.'s arms raised triumphantly, McKenzie and Ferguson carried Juice on their shoulders to the Buffalo bench, where the ecstatic pummeling scene started all over again. There were embraces, handshakes, back-slapping galore. All figured O.J. had amassed 198 yards for the game, 2,001 for the season—and O.J. sprinted off the field to a hero's sendoff from the New York crowd—kids tugging at his famed No. 32 jersey along the route to the dressing room entrance.

Actually, the figures were wrong. When the game tape was checked, statisticians learned O.J. had reached 200 yards exactly, giving him another NFL record of back-to-back 200-yard games. And his season rushing total was 2,003 yards off 332 carries—both league records.

The remaining 5:56 was played out, and after an 11-yard Leypoldt field goal, the Bills closed their finest season since 1966 with a 34-14 victory. And O.J., waiting below with a pulsating heartbeat, had eight NFL records in the 1973 satchel: most rushing yardage in a game (250) and season (2,003), most rushing attempts in a game (39) and season (332), most consecutive 100-yard (7) and 200-yard games (2), and most 100-yard (11) and 200-yard games (3) in one season. Beyond those, O.J. cracked 11 club standards and helped the Bills erase six others—all in one fantastic season.

And the main goal of the game just three hours earlier now was practically taken for granted. O.J. had smashed Jim Brown's one-year rushing record by 140 yards!

When the game ended and the Bills rushed toward their dressing room, they found O.J. waiting by the door. He shook everyone's hand, thanking all for their help, but for each member of the offense—regular or reserve—he had a special message. Just as each had accompanied him along his record run on the frozen tundra of Shea Stadium, he wanted each in the special interview room where a near-record 400 writers and broadcasters were waiting to see him.

He was football's first 2,000-yard rusher and the Bills were the game's first 3,000-yard rushing team (3,088). They had accomplished their dream together and that's how they would be interviewed—together. O.J. insisted on it and everyone knew this was no grandstand move. The Juice was sincere. "If I go in there, I want to bring the entire offensive team with me," he said.

And so in they went and the press gallery was amazed, but so very impressed, that O.J. would share his greatest moment with the whole offense.

"Gentlemen," O.J. smiled to the large press crunch, "I'd like you to meet some friends of mine. This is Joe Ferguson, our quarterback. He's a rookie and did he do a job!

"This is Jim Braxton, who missed the first half of the season due to an old problem, a birth defect in his back. When he got back in the lineup, he really opened things up for me.

"And, of course, this is my main man, Reg McKenzie," O.J.

went on with a special emphasis. Every offensive member was introduced and, in that way, shared in the moment of glory.

"I'm more impressed with O.J. Simpson as a man than as a player," remarked one member of the New York press.

"Yeah, you'd never see Joe Namath or Jim Brown do something like that—sharing the spotlight with his teammates," noted another scribe.

"I've never seen anything like this in 30 years of covering sports," remarked Milt Richman, United Press International sports editor. Other veteran reporters were similarly impressed. "Maybe it's my record, but I had a lot of help," O.J. reasoned. "These guys were just fantastic. They kept blasting holes open for me, and all I had to do was follow them through. That record was a team effort. No running back can get 2,000 yards without a lot of help."

Then O.J. turned toward Saban and paid him a matchless tribute.

"That man is a blessing for running backs," he declared. "He had Cookie Gilchrist at Buffalo and Floyd Little at Denver, and now this. Lou Saban saved my career. He told me he'd give me the football and an offensive line, and he's sure kept his word. I promised him I'd do the best I could, and I think I've kept mine."

The Juice reflected back to two seasons earlier, when Buffalo owned a 1-13 record. He thought of those three dark seasons during 1969–71. "Those first three years in Buffalo were living hell for me," O.J. admitted. "I had people booing me—not just once in awhile, but a lot, man. I had coaches who didn't like me and vice versa. The whole atmosphere was lousy—just one bad scene after another. I was turned off to football. We couldn't have been lower and I wanted out. I wanted to play somewhere else."

And then O.J. thought out loud about Jack Horrigan, the Bills' public relations director who died the previous June.

"Jack was my man," O.J. recalled with a smile. "He listened to my troubles and my complaints and he soothed me. He was a man you listened to. He told me then that Lou Saban was probably coming to Buffalo and that good times were ahead. He told me to be patient and wait, and I'm glad I did."

Again, O.J. glanced toward Saban and said: "I liked Lou Saban, believed in what he said and trusted him. I got my spirit back with the help of that man. And now, we've got some good, solid young players. That's why I want to help them win a Super Bowl. I want my teammates to be as successful as I've been."

O.J.'s teammates felt quite successful indeed just sharing in Simpson's record.

"It's a fantastic feeling knowing you're a part of sports history," beamed McKenzie. "Believe me, it took a lot of work. The next guy who comes along will know what we mean."

The star guard from Michigan said assistant coaches Bob Shaw and Billy Atkins were in telephone touch from the press box to alert the offense exactly how much yardage O.J. needed. "There was no way the Jets were going to stop us from getting it for the Juice," McKenzie said. "He's a helluva man. I mean, who else do you know who would take the entire line to a national press conference the way he did? He's just beautiful.

"I was visiting with him last summer and he told me, 'Wouldn't it be nice to get 1,700 yards?' I just told him let's get two grand instead and really set the world on fire. Now we have and it's beautiful."

DeLamielleure, the Bills' "other guard," listened nearby and agreed wholeheartedly. "We really wanted to get the record for him," the rookie said. "He's such a great guy. He's a star, yet he's one of us. He knows what it's like to be an offensive lineman."

Across the room, Ferguson was telling reporters he called his signals with O.J.'s rushing figures clearly in mind. "We knew what he needed, so I was very conscious of it in my play-calling," the Arkansas product acknowledged. "On the play where Juice got most of his yardage, we have an option where we can give it to the fullback instead. So I called that play to Braxton to keep the pressure off Juice."

Braxton kept the pressure off to the tune of 98 yards which gave the Bills a Simpson-Braxton combination worth 298 yards on a record afternoon. The Bills outrushed New York by an incredible 304-39 and amassed 18 first downs rushing to the Jets' two. Every time Ferguson handed off, the play averaged five yards.

"O.J. is surrounded by a young offensive line and he's young enough to be part of them," commented Saban upon seeing the figures and the togetherness of that offensive unit. "While they were learning, O.J. was carrying the burden. Now they work beautifully together."

Over in the Jets' dressing quarters, Dave Herman was presenting a watch to retiring Ewbank, who was in tears. "You have to take your hat off to a great halfback," Weeb said. "It's no disgrace not to stop him. We changed fronts constantly, we moved around and the guy still found daylight."

Linebacker Ralph Baker, a 10-year veteran who called the defensive signals, said he tried mixing them and nothing worked. "We tried them all and they didn't work. We even put in a couple of new wrinkles during the game and they didn't work, either," Baker complained. "They came here to get a record and they got it."

Baker said the Jets overshifted frequently to the strong side, moving strong safety Burgess Owens up to play almost as a linebacker because the Bills' tight end, Seymour, is not a pass-catching threat. "But then they crossed us up and went to the weak side time after time," Baker said. "That O.J., it seems like everything on him moves—arms, legs, head, elbows. His line provides tremendous blocking and he's got a 230-pound fullback to lead the way.

"What we hoped wouldn't happen to us, did happen," Baker went on. "We have no excuses. The field was ideal for football. A little snow doesn't hurt your footing. When Simpson has the ball, you know you can't leave your area. He bounces all over the place. You have to be under control at all times or he'll make a fool out of you."

Baker and Richard Neal couldn't single out any one of Simpson's blockers as a particular thorn. They all were. "Looking at films, we knew Reggie McKenzie was an outstanding blocker," Baker said. "Today, who could tell which guy was best?"

Neal observed how far the Bills' Big Ten-oriented front had developed in two years. "Individually, they don't have anybody who strikes you as great," the burly defensive tackle intoned. "But together, that whole line is great. They work a lot harder than they did last year. When I was with New Orleans, the Bills had some creampuffs. Not any more."

Wise, who tackled Simpson on his run past 2,000 yards, exchanged words with O.J. during the game following a couple of extra-hard hits. Wise heard that O.J. complained he reached inside his helmet on that record play. Afterward, one would never have known the exchanges had been made.

"I got tagged a few times and Wise did get me with a forearm, but it wasn't his fault," O.J. said. "I wear only two bars on the front of my helmet. The talk we had on the field was friendly. He came flying up a couple of times and caught me. I told him, 'Good play.' And he said, 'You're a good runner.' He's an excellent player. He didn't mean it."

Wise, meanwhile, had joined the O.J. Admiration Society. "Man, if I touched his eye with my finger or forearm, it was the only thing I touched on him all day," the safety said. "He just used me up. You know how a streetcar conductor punches your ticket? He just punched my ticket and waved to me in the end zone. He lets you stay with him awhile, then he cuts and he's gone. He's like a flim-flam man. All my life, I thought Jim Brown was the greatest runner, but O.J. broke his record. I don't see how anybody could be better. Even Jim Brown."

Delles Howell, a Jet cornerback, was another who witnessed plenty of No. 32 flying in his direction. "Simpson just has more of everything than anybody else—more acceleration, and more peripheral vision, which helps him see more of the field," Howell said.

Joe Namath, almost a forgotten man this day, also marveled at the rushing king from Buffalo. "I just like to watch him," Broadway Joe said. "Everything he does is great. I don't see any shortcomings in him. He runs the ball God knows how many times in a game and he never looks tired. He might walk back to the huddle slow, but when he has the ball, he's stepping."

And on the bouquets flew.

Someone asked O.J. if he minded that less than 20,000 were in Shea Stadium when his 2,000-yard run was completed? "I don't mind at all about the stands being near-empty," was the reply. "I knew a lot of people back in Buffalo were watching and they're the ones that count."

Someone else wanted to know how the record was possible with Bills' opponents playing for the run, keying on O.J., practically all the time. Here again, O.J. took special care to boost his line.

"Every team has been playing us for the run all season, but these guys have been knocking them out," O.J. answered. "My name is going into the record books, but it's as much their record as it is mine. I love these guys. These cats did it for me all year, and I'll be forever grateful to them for their work."

The Juice then addressed the inevitable question. After a season such as this, what could possibly be left in the way of goals? Immediately, the team-oriented O.J. surfaced.

"The Super Bowl!" he shouted. "That's what I want now. We're the youngest team in pro football. We average only 24 years. This is going to be a good team for a long time. Our goal is the Super Bowl and we're going to make it. Then there could be nothing else I could ask for in football. I won the Heisman Trophy and the rushing crown, but the Super Bowl is the ultimate goal.

"My only disappointment today comes from us not making the playoffs," O.J. continued before the huge audience of reporters. "We lost games this year we should have won, but we're the youngest team in the league, and we made mistakes you won't see us make next year. Inexperience cost us a playoff spot, especially in losses to San Diego and New Orleans, but also to Cincinnati. We're playing our best ball now, we won our last four and if we had made the playoffs, the way we are now, we'd have a 50-50 chance to win against any team in football."

The "Wait Till Next Year" fever spread throughout the dressing room. "We've done a helluva lot, we've come a long way and we'll do even more next year," McKenzie vowed.

"I'm thinking of next year right now," said tackle Donnie Green, the team's largest player at 6'8", 272. "I started thinking of next year as the final minute ticked off the clock. There's so much we can do. Everybody on this team knows this season is nothing compared to what we can do in the future. We know we're going to get better and we just can't wait."

Football was fun again for the Buffalo Bills and Joe De-Lamielleure indicated just how much fun this season had been for the usually unsung offensive linemen. "Nobody can take away from us what we did this year," he said. "There's not much glory in being an offensive lineman, but here's a record, some-thing we can identify with. We were counting yards on the field today, keeping track. Everybody wanted this."

O.J. nodded.

"All season long, people talked about the record, but I tried to keep it out of my mind so I could concentrate on playing football," he said. "I was able to do that pretty well until last week, when the record drew very near. Then, today, our game plan, as you could tell, was to go after the record from the beginning. Get it out of the way, then settle down and concen-trate on winning the game. I knew I gained a lot of yards on that first touchdown drive, but I didn't know how close I was to the record until Fergy came over to me on the sidelines and said we needed just four more yards."

Soon they were asking O.J. about his contract. Would Ralph Wilson tear it up with two years remaining and present him with a fat, new offer? "My contract is a personal thing," fenced O.J. "Ralph and I get along just fine. I like to think I've repaid him on the field."

Others wanted to know if O.J. had heard from Jim Brown. "No, I haven't heard from him about breaking his records, but I never hear from him until I see him," O.J. replied. "I can understand why he doesn't want to talk about it. I was very bugged about all the talk of me breaking his records. Knowing him, he wants his football left behind him. He has a whole new career [movie roles] to think about. I just hope my record lasts at least 10 years, like Jim's did."

Could O.J. beat the 2,003-plateau himself?

"It's not a once-in-a-lifetime achievement," answered the Juice. "I think I can gain more than 2,003 next year. In high school, junior college and even at Southern Cal, each year was better than the last. And the Bills' whole future is bright. We're so young."

Now the cash registers in some reporters' heads were clicking off. What could this record be worth financially? Certainly, the rush for endorsements from O.J. would be on again.

As tackle Dave Foley put it, "Everybody on the team would love to be in O.J.'s shoes right now."

O.J. knew he would be in business as never before, too.

"I haven't really speculated what running 2,003 yards will be worth," he said. "Chuck Barnes [his agent] is negotiating with three orange juice companies for a commercial contract and I already have other endorsement agreements."

In short order, O.J. Simpson was pushing sunglasses, athletic shoes, rent-a-cars and you name it. He was on television at ABC Sports and in the movies, entered in all-star casts, beginning with a $4-million-Paramount production "The Klansman," with Richard Burton and Lee Marvin.

O.J. was the "king of running backs," and the world was bowing before him. The list of awards was simply overwhelming. The Associated Press selected him "Male Athlete of the Year." The *Sporting News* declared him "Sports Man of the Year." He was everybody's MVP. He won the Maxwell Club of Philadelphia's Bert Bell Award as "Player of the Year," the Hickok Belt and Dunlop Pro-Am Awards as "Professional Athlete of the Year," and he headed all the all-star teams. He was "Lifesaver of the Year" and landslide recipient of every top-player award, from the Washington Touchdown Club to the Wisconsin Pro Football Writers Association.

The award crunch was nothing less than an avalanche.

From the evening of that never-to-be-forgotten game in New York, when many of the Bills flew back to Buffalo and a heroic airport welcome but O.J. flew directly home to California, the accolades poured in steadily. "Obviously, the record has made the off-season for me," beamed O.J. He compared this happy trip home with the sad occasions of previous Buffalo-to-LA trips. "I have a lot of fond memories of the year, which is kind of unusual since I went to Buffalo," he smiled.

"I won the rushing crown last year, but we only won four games. This season, I felt I really won the rushing crown. I didn't last year, because Larry Brown was hurt."

This time, the NFL rushing race was a shambles, the likes of which hasn't been seen before or since. Imagine, Simpson averaged six yards a carry and amassed 2,003 yards in 332 runs, while the runner-up, Green Bay's John Brockington, had "only" 1,144 yards and the American Conference's second best, Miami's Larry Csonka, was exactly 1,000 yards behind O.J.

As astonishing as that gap from No. 1 to No. 2 was, the irony of what O.J. accomplished that dark, bitterly cold Dec. 16—dashing through the snow in old New York—is what left a lasting impact on the Juice himself.

"All week long I was worried about 61 yards and I ended up with 2,000," O.J. observed, shaking his head. "Fantastic . . . Fantastic! . . . It's a fantastic feeling . . . It's really quite incredible!"

All of professional football agreed.

How They Compare

JIM BROWN - 1963

OPPONENTS	CARRIES	YARDS
Washington	15	162
Dallas	20	232
Los Angeles	22	95
Pittsburgh	21	175
New York Giants	23	123
Philadelphia	25	144
New York Giants	9	40
Philadelphia	28	223
Pittsburgh	19	99
St. Louis	22	154
Dallas	17	51
St. Louis	29	179
Detroit	13	61
Washington	28	125
TOTALS 14 Games	291	1863
Average Yards Per Carry - 6.4		

O. J. SIMPSON - 1973

OPPONENTS	CARRIES	YARDS
New England	29	250
San Diego	22	103
New York Jets	24	123
Philadelphia	27	171
Baltimore	22	166
Miami	14	55
Kansas City	39	157
New Orleans	20	79
Cincinnati	20	99
Miami	20	120
Baltimore	15	124
Atlanta	24	137
New England	22	219
New York Jets	34	200
TOTALS 14 Games	332	2,003
Average Yards Per Carry - 6		

CHAPTER FOURTEEN

Winning Without O.J.

The date was Sept. 16, 1974, and the Bills were ready to open with fanfare their most promising season in a decade. Howard Cosell and the ABC-TV cameras were back, and this time everyone knew what the attraction was months in advance.

The network which employed the Juice in the off-season was in Buffalo to beam nationally the continuing story of a legend, the superstar now referred to as "the Franchise" around Rich Stadium—O.J. Simpson.

O.J. had come full circle—from the most publicized player to enter the NFL after winning the Heisman Trophy, to the depths of three years in virtual no-man's land, to landslide recognition as football's greatest running back. That fabled 2,003-yard season represented instant immortality.

"Someone will break the record someday, but I'll always be the first to get 2,000 yards," O.J. declared with a satisfied smile. Of course, he knew that incomparable season is what made this opening game so attractive for the Monday night series. He knew the reporters would follow him in larger and larger groups now, that most every move he made and statement he uttered would be fodder for a writer's notebook. O.J. realized he would be the center of media attention and opponents' hit men, and he was ready.

"I suppose," he said candidly, "that everything I do for the rest of my career will be measured against that 2,000-yard season. From now on, I'll be marked as the guy who gained all those yards in one year."

And so this would be a nationally televised season opener with extraordinary appeal because of one man. So many wondered whether O.J. would embark upon another trip above the magical 2,000 barrier. Yet there was so much more to this inaugural. The Bills' opponent would be football's most winning team of the past decade, the Oakland Raiders. And another frenzied capacity crowd of 80,020 would pack every corner of Rich Stadium. To them, the Bills would receive the "acid" test immediately, opening the season at home against the AFC's best within a week—Oakland and then Super Bowl champion Miami.

The Bills, and indeed the entire NFL, had advanced a long distance just to reach this initial weekend. The entire season was threatened by a players' strike, which forced early exhibitions (including the Bills' Hall of Fame Game with St. Louis) into virtual rookie shows. Veterans didn't report until mid-August and some teams, including Buffalo, had to offer refunds for exhibitions played minus stars such as O.J. The Bills without O.J. were no Bills at all, many reasoned.

O.J. and most other veterans reported to the Buffalo area early, worked out in their own camp and stayed unified. Instead of straggling into the team camp individually, as happened with some teams, the Bills' veterans reported virtually as a team. It was a factor which boosted morale markedly in tough times. O.J., despite his new fame and wealth, was with his teammates as one of the guys.

There were other major events leading to this Oakland-Buffalo opener, which would become one of the most exciting of Monday night battles. Back in January, Reggie McKenzie was left off the Pro Bowl team (though he made the All-Pro squads) and O.J., as he had promised, threatened not to play. Then tackle Dave Foley was added to the AFC roster and O.J.'s quest for offensive line representation was satisfied. So O.J. played, though upset over McKenzie's absence.

Soon the fledgling World Football League was making overtures to the Juice, hoping to pry him loose from Buffalo and make him its feature attraction. But Wilson headed off this threat by signing O.J. to a five-year contract worth $200,000 annually.

The Big Question was answered. Yes, Wilson would reward O.J. for the most fantastic season any running back ever enjoyed and, just incidentally, for luring capacity crowds to nearly every home game. "This new agreement is insurance that there won't be a World Football League, just the Bills, for me," O.J. declared. "There was this possibility . . . Some people had mentioned the WFL to my manager."

It was soon learned that Ben Hatskin, who as owner of hockey's Winnipeg Jets lured Bobby Hull with a $2.75 million contract, was prepared to make a similar offer to O.J. to become the headline attraction of Hatskin's Hawaii franchise. Later, the Southern California *Sun* selected O.J. in the 39th round of the WFL draft, but that was merely a laugher. O.J. belonged to the Bills.

Saban also was busy in the off-season, pulling off probably his finest one-for-one trade. Bills' fans couldn't believe he was able to acquire classy wide receiver Ahmad Rashad from St. Louis for backup quarterback Dennis Shaw. The trade was widely viewed as an outright steal by Saban.

Rashad, who changed his name from Bobby Moore, would become an eye-catching figure immediately, electrifying his new following in this opening game with Oakland. He also became close friends with O.J. and McKenzie.

And so Rashad gave Buffalo a triple threat through the air. Ferguson had Hill, Chandler and now Ahmad as outstanding targets. Any team which isolated on O.J. would be burned. With Braxton's power running another feature, this seemed potentially the best offense in the NFL. One thing was for certain, it was no longer virtually a one-man show. This offense was balanced— with strength protruding everywhere.

Another capacity crowd of 80,020 and the ABC crew were on hand as the Bills and Raiders trotted out to open the 1974 season. Many were surprised when the first quarter between these explosive teams ended scoreless. But late in that period, the Bills began running from their 46.

It was Braxton on first down and Simpson on second as the Bills rolled to the Raider 31 in four plays. When the second quarter started, O.J. carried four successive times—gaining five off right tackle, two off right guard, three to the left and 13 through the middle to the Oakland eight.

On first down, Braxton slammed the middle for three yards, and on second down, Simpson cut inside for one more to the four. It was third-and-goal and the Bills had run either O.J. or Braxton for 10 straight plays. So Ferguson had the Raiders set up, and with the Raiders looking for one more rush, he passed to Hill for the touchdown.

The impressive march consumed seven minutes, six seconds and the Bills, returning to their bench to a standing ovation, had driven home their point. This offense could be overwhelming against football's best, and it could score in a variety of ways. Versatility was the new theme and a drive toward the Super Bowl had just been launched.

Later in the second quarter, the Raiders countered with a 24-yard George Blanda field goal and the Bills' lead was 7-3. Blanda kicked off and Ferguson started smartly with a 17-yard pass to Hill at midfield. On first down, he looked toward Seymour and threw incomplete. Second down brought the play O.J. and the Bills would remember all season—and longer.

Simpson took a handoff, bolted left, cut back right and into the clear! He darted 10, 15 and, with one defender in front and another with an angle on him, O.J. tried to cut again. Only this time, his right ankle gave way and he fell to the turf at the Raider 30. The gain was a robust 20 yards, but no one was thinking about yardage. O.J. was writhing in pain on the field and he wasn't getting up! Teammates rushed over and the referee signaled a time out. Suddenly, the whole season seemed dangling on a string. What would the Buffalo Bills be without O.J. Simpson?

O.J. finally scrambled to his feet, but he couldn't walk without aid. McKenzie and assistant trainer Bobby Reese helped him, his

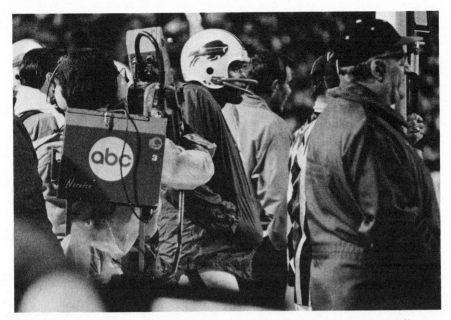

Injured O.J., forever on-camera, watches most of 1974 opener. Bills
won thriller over Oakland with O.J. on sideline.
Photo by Robert L. Smith,
Elma, N.Y.

Ecstatic Bills mob Ahmad Rashad (unseen) after late winning catch
against Oakland. It was one of the Bills' most exciting games ever.
Photo by Robert L. Smith,
Elma, N.Y.

arms draped over their shoulders, as he came off the field with the right leg bent backward. O.J. was done for the evening and many feared for much longer, perhaps even the season.

On the sideline, O.J. told his teammates what happened. He partially blamed the rise in the Astroturf field, a rise which creates an uphill effect when a player runs laterally from one side toward midfield.

"Skip Thomas [cornerback] was in front of me and someone was coming up on the right," O.J. explained. "I was in the middle and tried to cut left. I could feel the ankle twist and I sort of fell into Thomas' arms. No one hit me at all."

Back on the field, Buffalo's offense couldn't allow itself to think of O.J. now. But, to a man, everyone did. Only 48 seconds remained in the half, and thanks to O.J.'s 20-yard run (giving him 78 for the half-game), they were in scoring position at the 30.

Gary Hayman, a rookie from Penn State, went in for O.J. and barreled five yards. But Rashad nullified that by jumping offside. Ferguson's third-down pass for Rashad fell incomplete, and the Bills jogged sadly to the sideline. Leypoldt hoped to salvage at least three points for O.J.'s effort, but his 37-yard attempt sailed wide. The Bills, wasting the opportunity and with O.J. being helped to the dressing room, were ahead 7-3 at intermission and gloom appeared most everywhere in the packed stadium.

People who figured the Bills minus O.J. were a team minus offense were saying, "I told you so," after the second half began. Oakland marched 58 yards following the kickoff and forged ahead, 10-7, as Clarence Davis swept 15 yards to score.

The Bills couldn't move, Ferguson being thumped for a major loss by massive Art Thoms and Otis Sistrunk. Oakland marched back and Blanda booted a 41-yard field goal, creating a 13-7 spread. Leypoldt tried to counter but was wide again, this time from 36 yards.

The Buffalo machine, so awesome less than an hour earlier, was sputtering without Simpson and no one looked surprised.

In the fourth quarter, free safety Tony Greene intercepted a Ken Stabler pass at the Raider 36, giving Buffalo a chance and igniting an All-Pro season for Greene. Things looked beautiful as Hayman broke free on an eight-yard tear to the Oakland one. It was second down and the Bills had three cracks at the end zone. They never got there! And, even worse, they lost another running back, this one for the season.

On second down, Braxton tried the middle and found linebacker Gerald Irons waiting. On third, Ferguson threw incomplete toward Braxton. On fourth, Hayman was slammed to the turf by middle linebacker Dan Conners. Hayman suffered a broken fibular bone in his right leg and the Bills had that snake-bitten feeling. Here it was opening night and they had just lost O.J. Simpson and his rookie understudy. Now they had to go to Wayne Mosley, another rookie. This one had signed as a free agent while the veterans were striking. He finished the game.

Once again the Raiders couldn't stand prosperity and Marv Hubbard fumbled. Linebacker John Skorupan recovered at the Raider 33 and again the Bills were in business deep in Oakland terrain. This time, the opportunity was converted as Ferguson drilled a fourth down, eight-yard TD pass to Rashad with only 1:56 to play. Thanks to Oakland's bumbling, the Bills were ahead, 14-13, on Leypoldt's conversion and all they needed was defense to win. They got it, too, when Stabler missed three targets and Ray Guy punted with 1:33 remaining.

Now it seemed all the Bills needed was to run out the clock. Yet, on first down, Braxton stepped right and fumbled. Thoms picked it up and lumbered 31 yards to score. The stadium was in shock! Braxton had just handed Oakland the game. Only 1:14 remained and the Raiders, jumping for joy on their sideline, led 20-14.

Some fans, considerably more than a few, left early to escape the jammed parking lot. The Raiders had stolen this one, they figured. Few dreamed this offense without its main cog could zip downfield from its own 28 in one minute.

A few exiting the stadium turned around as Ferguson hit Braxton for 10 yards and a roughing-the-passer penalty added 15 to the Raider 47. The Raiders still weren't playing smart football! On second down, Ferguson passed 20 yards to Rashad and now fans were rushing back into their seats. Young fans were shreiking. Yes, a storybook comeback was possible! It was unfolding before their eyes!

The Bills used a time out with 48 seconds left. On first down, Ferguson passed to Hill for Buffalo's 20th first down and a 10-yard gain to the 17. Now, the stadium was alive. The din was tremendous and the Raiders were reeling. Ferguson tried another pass for Hill and it fell harmlessly, stopping the clock with 38 seconds showing. Next came another incompletion, but Thomas was called for interference with J.D., netting a first down at the 13.

On first down, Ferguson tried for Hill again and there were groans as the connection missed. Thirty-one seconds remained. Ferguson faded again, but this time looked for Rashad. Ahmad had faked toward the sideline, cut toward the middle and had a step on All-Pro corner Willie Brown. Ferguson, his eyes bulging, led him perfectly with a 13-yard pitch for a touchdown.

The crowd went wild! What a comeback! The Bills' bench emptied and all rushed out to mob Rashad and Ferguson and the entire offense. The Bills hadn't needed a minute to dash 72 yards. All they needed were 37 seconds—and without O.J. Simpson. Near-deafening cheers rolled up again as Leypoldt's PAT was good, giving Buffalo a 21-20 edge.

But wait! Now the Raiders weren't through. Maybe the Bills had scored too quickly. The southpaw Stabler passed to Cliff Branch at the Bills' 46 with 15 seconds remaining and then to Charlie Smith at the 33 with six seconds left. It was first down, but there was no time left for anything but a field goal. And here was Blanda, who had connected from 41 yards, trying from 40.

The crowd, still in a frenzy over Braxton's fumble for Thoms' TD and the comeback for Rashad's score, was on its feet. Here was the grand old man of football who, at the stroke of midnight just two minutes earlier had turned 47 years old. What a birthday present a field goal would be. What a disappointment it would be to the Bills and these fans.

The ball was centered, placed down and Blanda kicked. Some fans couldn't look. This game was just too much for them. Others screamed almost immediately. The kick was short! The

Bills had won—without O.J! Their fans began filing out, limp and hoarse. Indeed, their Bills had proved to the NFL and a national audience that this was a team which could beat the best, even with O.J. a spectator.

"They proved they could win without me," smiled O.J. in the celebrant dressing room scene. "We showed in this game how good a team we are [placing emphasis on the word team]. Even after I got hurt, the fans and everybody kept talking about O.J.— and while they were talking our guys went out and got 14 points. We've got a good, good football team.

"We've proved it with the two big steps we've taken," O.J. continued. "We took the first step last season when we beat Atlanta. We took the second step tonight when we beat the Raiders."

O.J. was still hurting, but he was determined to play the following Sunday in the second half of a jolting one-two season-opening punch, Oakland and Miami. "I've had this happen before and it usually took four or five days before I could run again," O.J. said. "But that can't happen this week. We have a big one coming up and I plan to be ready."

The spotlight this night belonged not to O.J. but Ferguson, incredibly poised for a kid 15 months out of college, and Rashad, the product of that Saban steal from St. Louis.

"I've never been so tired or excited in my life," smiled Ferguson. He was thoroughly drained from the ecstasy-agony-ecstasy of the final two minutes. The cool sophomore pro from Arkansas wasn't cool anymore. "Man, I'm tired," he repeated to reporters surrounding him.

"I'm just emotionally drained," declared Rashad to an equally large brigade of scribes less than 10 feet away. "We had to regroup twice—the first time after O.J. went out and the second after Oakland went ahead. Getting behind so late when we thought we had it won was a big letdown, but we came back. I'm tired, but I'm not going to quit smiling the rest of the night.

"Never in my life have I been so involved in a football game," the speedy receiver talked on. "I think the victory proved we're a definite contender in this league. I used to hear that Buffalo was just a running team, but since I've been here, I'm convinced we have a bona fide passing attack. After this, the rest of the league has to respect our passing game and it's on paper that they respect the run."

Rashad proceeded to explain the two touchdown passes from Ferguson which propelled Buffalo from behind twice in the final two minutes.

"My first was a quick post pattern on fourth-down-and-five from the eight. The cornerback [Skip Thomas] played inside. Joe laid the ball in perfectly and I kinda dove between Thomas and the safety [George Atkinson]. Coach Saban sent in the play during the two-minute warning. Joe had the choice of throwing to me or the tight end [Seymour]. There was only one place he could throw it and I knew it. I dove and we had a meeting of minds right there.

"When our defense held, I thought we had them," Rashad went on. "And when the fumble came, there was a big mental letdown. Some say there were tears on some players' faces, but I didn't see them. The game did have the most emotion I've seen, though. I saw that we had time for six or seven plays and knew we could still do it. The fact that we did is a mark of a good team. We all kept our poise."

Rashad told all about his 20-yard catch off a hook pattern, setting up the Bills at Oakland's 27. "I just happened to be wide open," he said. Then he told of being wide open on the first-down play from the 13, but Ferguson couldn't see him, throwing incomplete to Hill. "I came back to the huddle and didn't tell Joe anything," said Rashad, indicating both knew the next play could work like a charm.

"Our scouting report indicated they'd play man-to-man from the 30-yard line in," Rashad said. "And so we ran a '75' play, where I run downfield and flash across the center. The cornerback [Brown] got in front of me and played like he just knew I was going to the corner. When I stopped and spun at the two or three, I just knew I lost him. And Joe's pass was right on time."

Rashad was pretty explicit, but no Bill expressed the peaks and valleys of this emotionally bending game better than center Mike Montler. "Never in my life have I experienced such mental and physical highs and lows—such extremes—in such rapid succession," the Marine-type center from Colorado declared, perspiration dripping off him like a waterfall.

He mentioned Rashad's first touchdown catch, beating Thomas with a dramatic dive. "The play almost put me in heaven," Montler confessed. "It was as if I'd just found a $50,000 lottery ticket."

Then he described an incredible low—Braxton's fumble and Art Thoms' touchdown gallop. Montler thought the play had been blown dead and that Thoms was running "to try and get away with something."

"When I realized I was wrong and that it was an Oakland touchdown, I never in my life had such an overall mental and physical collapse. It was as if all the air had been taken out of the stadium. I couldn't breathe. I'd lost my lottery ticket."

Feeling utter despair, Montler admitted the tears began to flow. But then he took the field as determined as the other offensive members to get that giveaway touchdown back. And when they did, off that second Ferguson-to-Rashad scoring strike, Montler found his emotional mountain again.

"That touchdown gave me the greatest feeling I've ever had on a football field," exclaimed the strapping center. "It put me way, way up there—higher than I've ever been. It was as if I'd just found the $50,000 lottery ticket I'd lost."

The rest of the Bills felt similar emotion. It was mirrored, dramatically, on each of their perspiring faces.

The following Saturday, one day before the Miami game, O.J. stepped onto the Rich Stadium carpet and, for 45 minutes in a downpour, tested his right ankle for the first time from scrimmage since the Oakland game. He said he was ready to play, noting the importance of playing the perennial AFC Eastern champs, the Dolphins.

"The ankle didn't feel bad," he reported, unconvincingly. "It didn't hurt when I ran. I ran the plays I had to run. I plan to play all the way but once I get in the game, we'll see how it goes. The ankle feels much better than I thought it would."

Saban, ever hopeful his superstar could face the Bills' jinx foe, was a believer. "I gotta go with the Juice," he said. "He says he's ready."

Saban and his players realized that winning one game without their "main man" was one thing. Making it a habit was quite another.

CHAPTER FIFTEEN

Rallying 'Round the Juice

O.J. played in that second game of the 1974 season against Miami. He played every week all season long, but this was hardly the same O.J. Simpson who exploded for 2,003 yards the previous year.

This was a hurting O.J. He was a player with injuries which needed time to heal, but there was never enough time. The pain would begin to ease on Friday or Saturday, but after three hours of game warfare on Sunday, he was in discomfort all over again. And yet, he never asked for a weekend off.

"I've just got to admire the guy for being in the lineup," commented Dolphins' coach Don Shula after seeing O.J. put up a courageous front against his team. "I thought his ankle sprain was worse than the one he suffered against us last year. He's a real man."

Shula didn't realize the half of it. O.J. not only played with the right-ankle sprain, but twisted his left knee. "The ankle held up okay," he said. "I was taking a lot of shots because I couldn't push off and deliver the first hit at the point of contact. Then early in the game I twisted my knee a little, so I actually wound up favoring both sides of my body."

And that's the way Simpson played the 1974 season—hurt!

The effects were obvious in the Miami game. Fumbles by O.J. and Braxton deep in Buffalo's end (O.J.'s on the one) led to a pair of Miami touchdowns and a 24-16 defeat. He carried but 15 times for 63 yards, running just three times in the entire second half.

Yet, after being listed as "doubtful" to face the New York Jets, he carried 31 times for 117 yards and sparked a 16-12 victory over the Jets. The Juice was still in pain, and the following week's game in Green Bay was the only one he thought he might miss. But he played, and while the Packers overdefensed him, Ferguson picked them apart with a 13-for-16 afternoon in a 27-7 success. There was that balance again.

Those successes over the Jets and Green Bay marked the ignition of a six-game victory skein. The balanced Bills mowed over Baltimore (27-14), New England (30-28), Chicago (16-6) and New England again (29-28). They were 7-1 and life was beautiful—except that for O.J. it was beautiful and painful at the same time.

He was limited and everyone knew it. He didn't score a touchdown in the first five games of the season. "I like to score, sure, but we're winning and that's all I want," he reasoned. "I've had my individual goals—2,000 yards last season and the like—but we've never been to the Super Bowl and that's what we want this season. And how about that Joe Ferguson, isn't he something?"

Indeed, Ferguson was. He was the NFL's leading quarterback in pass efficiency ratings. No longer was he known simply as the fellow who hands off to O.J. Simpson. He was a premier quarterback and was proving it every Sunday.

"Ferguson hasn't been given the credit he deserves," noted Patriot cornerback Ron Bolton after the Bills' two high-scoring but airtight victories over their New England cousins. "He's a lot better than a lot of quarterbacks in this league with bigger names—a lot better."

Chuck Fairbanks, the Patriot coach, went even further in assessing the Buffalo team. "It's not a one-man team at all," he stated. "It's a fine offensive unit. Buffalo never used to throw on first down. In the past, they always ran. But in the two games against us this season and in every Buffalo game I've watched on film, Ferguson has done a heckuva job. The kid's a fine quarterback."

Meanwhile Simpson bore on and, despite the pain, he mustered four 100-yard games—117 against the Jets, 127 vs. Baltimore, 122 against New England and 115 against Cleveland.

The Cleveland game was something special.

After winning six consecutive games and flashing that 7-1 log, the Bills' attack stalled—badly. Lowly Houston, the biggest loser in pro football the previous season, came to Buffalo and, with Al Cowlings playing linebacker and dogging O.J. all afternoon, the Oilers sprang a 21-9 upset. Ferguson couldn't crack a four-linebacker defense and fired a club-record six interceptions, sending the moody Southerner into near-shock.

The following week, the Bills dropped a heartbreaking 35-28 verdict to the Dolphins in the Orange Bowl. Backup quarterback Gary Marangi, coming on after Ferguson was knocked out of the game by end Bill Stanfill's charge, rallied Buffalo from a 21-7 deficit to ties of 21-21 and 28-28 with a pair of impressive scoring passes. But with 51 seconds left, Bob Griese launched a 31-yard pass to Paul Warfield at midfield and, with Saban slamming his cap in disgust, diminutive Don Nottingham burst 23 yards through the middle on a draw play with 24 seconds left to win the game.

And so the Bills came to Cleveland reeling from two defeats and with their playoff quest threatened. They needed a "stopper," preferably a big game from the Juice.

On Sunday morning, O.J. felt up to anything but a big game. He was up all night with a case of influenza spiced generously with a gurgling stomach—thanks to a poor platter of fish for dinner. Then he glanced out the hotel window and realized he soon would be under the weather in a different way. It was raining, and knowing Cleveland Stadium, he realized he'd be romping through the mud.

O.J. didn't feel much better when the Bills had the ball just one series of downs in the first quarter. The Browns consumed 12 minutes, 58 seconds in a 24-play assault which churned away 85 yards and a penalty-aided 21-yard field goal by Don Cockroft. The Browns were not only on top, 3-0, one minute into the second period, but they were beating Buffalo at its own game—ball control. Again, the Bills needed a shot in the arm from Simpson.

One minute later, they got it.

Swift Wallace Francis bolted 46 yards with the kickoff, racing to Cleveland's 45. On first down, Braxton bulled four yards off right tackle. On second down, the handoff went to O.J.

Bob Babich, the Cleveland middle linebacker, shot the gap and was bumped aside just as he reached for O.J. and no one was left to pick up the Juice as he squirted through. Fullback Jim Braxton leveled strongside linebacker Charlie Hall with a crushing block, and O.J. sliced off right tackle 41 yards to paydirt. It was only his third touchdown of the season and, astonishingly, his last. But it did the trick—it lifted Buffalo from the doldrums.

"I was double-teamed with the slotman blocking down on me," claimed Browns' end Carl Barisich, switched from defensive tackle just that week. "All I saw was O.J. running downfield and I knew I sure wasn't going to catch him."

Babich mentioned he almost nailed Simpson for a loss when he blitzed. "I thought I'd get him in the backfield, and I did have a hand on him when somebody bumped me," the middle backer said. "He's so strong, though, that one hand doesn't do any good. He went outside tackle as I went inside, and he was gone."

The next time Buffalo had possession, O.J. picked on Barisich's side again, skirting right end for 18 yards to the Brown 41. Buffalo stayed on the ground and gained enough yardage to set up a 41-yard Leypoldt field goal for a 10-3 lead. Soon, quarterback Brian Sipe was dropped by tackle Mike Kadish for a safety and the Bills led at halftime, 12-3.

Late in the third period, the O.J.-Braxton express started up again. O.J. burst left for four and right for 12 at the Bills' 41. Braxton barreled 21 yards to the Brown 38 and was replaced by Larry Watkins. O.J. crashed right for six and Watkins followed McKenzie for five. The fourth quarter began with Watkins slashing seven yards, but delay-of-game forced Ferguson to the air for the seventh time in the game. He threw incomplete and Leypoldt kicked a 42-yard field goal for a 15-3 cushion.

Cleveland's only touchdown came with eight seconds left as Mike Phipps flipped three yards to Ken Brown and the Bills carted away a 15-10 triumph. A rushing assault—the success formula of previous days—had worked to revive the slumping Bills. Ferguson had only those seven aerial attempts and but one completion, a nine-yarder to Rashad in the third quarter.

The Bills had needed an awesome land machine in the mud and received it from Simpson, who carried 22 times for 115 yards and that decisive 41-yard touchdown. O.J. had proven again he loves an "off-track." This was for sure a "Juicey" victory.

"Simpson could play on ice," exclaimed Barisich. "He's sort of a flat-footed runner and gets good traction on any type of surface. He's just a super back."

Barisich noted that playing end was something new for him but that coach Nick Skorich moved him to instill a better pass rush. "I'm sure the Bills realized I'd never played there before and it was natural they picked on me," the former Princeton standout said. "They'd be crazy if they didn't."

The victory gave the Bills an 8-3 record and boosted them within a triumph of clinching a playoff berth, a coveted honor which had escaped O.J. throughout his pro career and which the Bills' team hadn't realized since their AFL days in 1966. They were even back in an AFC Eastern first-place tie with Miami—temporarily.

Once again, rushing had been the offensive vehicle. "Just stick with the Electric Company," declared Reggie McKenzie about the offensive front. "The Company's going to do it."

And yet there was no denying that defense had really been as major a factor as any. The Browns, not by any means a potent outfit, nevertheless were out to upend their Lake Erie rivals. And, after that impressive early march to three points, the Buffalo defense—using three "down" linemen and four linebackers—frustrated them repeatedly. But for Phipps' short toss in the waning seconds, they would have been held without a touchdown. And showing the way was free safety Tony Greene with two interceptions.

Defense was to emerge as even a larger factor the following

Sunday. Here were the Bills, regarded by many as potentially the most dangerous offensive team in football, actually being spearheaded into the playoffs on the strength of their defense. The fact was undeniable. The Bills edged the lowly Baltimore Colts, 6-0, off two Leypoldt goals and *defense*—replete with a game-saving goal-line stand in the climactic moments.

How ironic it was. A freezing, biting wind with gusts reaching 45 miles per hour reduced this game to off-tackle bursts and dashes around end. And there weren't many of those. It was like playing football in a wind tunnel, and Leypoldt handled the only scoring with three-pointers from 20 and 31 yards with a gale at his back.

O.J. carried 24 times for only 67 yards on this freezing Dec. 1 afternoon at Rich Stadium. He was clearly in the background on the day the Bills wrapped up a postseason spot for the first time in his six seasons with the club. Instead, the defensive stars were the targets of reporters' questions and they relished the unusual attention. They also deserved it.

To say the least, blanking the enemy has been a sometime thing for the Buffalo Bills. Until that windswept day, they had gone nine years or 124 games between shutouts and the occasions had spanned two Saban coaching eras. Their last previous shutout was in the 1965 American League title game when they pulverized San Diego, 23-0, to cap their second straight championship of Saban's first Buffalo tenure.

And the last time the Bills had whitewashed a foe in Buffalo was five games into the 1963 season, when they edged Oakland, 12-0, at old War Memorial Stadium. That was 82 home appearances earlier—when O.J. was a junior at Galileo High School in San Francisco.

The Colts launched only one major threat all afternoon, midway through the final period, going into the wind. Lydell Mitchell ripped off 23 yards for a first-down at the Buffalo eight. But on fourth-down from the four, Mitchell tried his pet play, sweeping right. "They try to overpower you," left end Walt Patulski said. "I slowed Mitchell down and Jim Cheyunski [middle linebacker] made the tackle at the two."

It was then that O.J. made his most important contribution,

converting a pair of third-down plays as the Bills spun the clock
from 7:45 left to 1:11 and escaped danger.

How strong a defensive effort was mustered this memorable
day? Well, the Colts failed to convert on all 13 first-down efforts.
The quarterback harassment was by far Buffalo's best of the year
with a robust eight sacks of Bert Jones totaling losses of 72 yards.
Further, the Colts found they couldn't run on a day when
rushing was mandatory. Their 21 attempts netted 46 yards,
compared to Buffalo's 138 in 46 thrusts.

"To give you an idea how difficult it was to run, Baltimore's
safeties were making tackles on one-yard dive plays," offered
tackle Dave Foley. "To give you an idea how cold it was, I was
the only player on the field in a short-sleeved jersey because I've
never worn long sleeves in a game in my life. But I almost went
to them today."

Bert Jones told of how difficult it was to pass.

"I had problems with and against the wind," the Colt quarterback said. "Twice in the first period, with the wind, I had
receivers open on 30-yard passes and the ball wound up going 60
yards downfield. I actually felt better throwing into the wind. But
even then, anytime the ball got more than 30 feet off the ground,
the wind played tricks."

Marv Bateman, the Bills' punter the players referred to as
Batman, explained what kind of tricks were played on him.
"From the time you'd drop it toward your foot, the ball would
move six inches because of the wind," said Bateman, who kicked
nine times. "When I dropped the ball, I had to really watch it to
see where it would go. I was just trying to kick it."

Almost overlooked because of this special day of defense and
O.J.'s 2,003-yard campaign a year earlier was his rise past the
1,000-plateau. Considering his weekly pain, this was quite an
achievement in itself.

"I'd like to do better," O.J. said when informed he had reached
1,004 yards after 12 games, "but the fact that we're 9-3 makes
me satisfied with the season. Overall, I'm happier this season
than I was at this time last year. Getting 2,000 yards satisfied my
ego and left me with only a few goals in football. In fact, getting
the 2,000 narrowed it down to one thing to attain in football—

playing on a championship team. I'd like to win the rushing championship this year, but it's a secondary goal. The first goal is the Super Bowl.

"I was aware before the game that I was close to 1,000 yards, but I was too intent on winning the game to even think about that," continued O.J., surpassing 1,000 for the third consecutive year. "Right now, the most important thing is making our playoff dream come true. Two years ago, we were 1-13 and now we're in the playoffs. A lot of teams get into the playoffs almost every year and it's old hat for them, but for us it's the realization of a dream. So that is more important to me than rushing yards. This win put us into a pretty elite group and I'm as happy as I can be."

Yet, even in the hour of rejoicing over reaching the playoffs, the Bills couldn't be completely happy. Tony Greene, the popular free safety who mushroomed to All-Pro status with nine interceptions, was injured in a freak accident. It happened as linebacker Dave Washington's interception smothered the Colts' last gasp.

"I was in the air and came down flat-footed," the star defensive back explained. "I heard something snap. I think I just hyperextended the left knee. I think it'll be all right."

It wasn't all right. There was ligament damage and Greene, the 5-9 live wire who made this defense go, was through for the year. He would see the playoffs only as a spectator.

The Bills, finishing their season with road losses to the New York Jets and Los Angeles Rams, felt the absence of Greene deeply in closing with a 9-5 record. They just weren't the same team, and even though those last two games were meaningless as far as the playoffs were concerned, they did cost Buffalo first place in the AFC East, Miami winning again. Buffalo was reduced to a "wild-card" entry. The losses also set a negative pattern.

The 1974 Bills never won another game without Tony Greene.

CHAPTER SIXTEEN

A Taste of the Playoff Life

The year 1974 will be remembered by O.J. for many things—
playing in pain, the promise of an improving, young team, the
advent of a more balanced offense, the manner in which defense
took over in two victories which cemented a playoff berth, and
for just plain stepping into the postseason picture.

The Juice followed that fabulous 2,003-yard season of 1973
with only 1,125 yards in 270 carries in 1974. The word "only"
couldn't apply to any other runner but Simpson. Others' standards just don't belong with him. He finished third in the NFL
rushing picture, behind Denver's Otis Armstrong (1,407) and San
Diego's Don Woods (1,162). And surely even Armstrong and
Woods realized they were not in the same class with a healthy
O.J.

Yet he was ebullient and so was Bills' owner Ralph Wilson,
who reaped the financial fruits of this march to the playoffs. The
Bills wound up 478 tickets shy of a perfect regular season of
home attendance—and those 478 came as the direct result of the
28-degree cold in swirling, biting wind gusts in that home finale
against the Colts. The Bills averaged 79,937 paid admissions per

game, best in the league. Their "no-show" total was 12,351, lowest in the league. Their average turnstile crowd was 78,187, best in the NFL for a second straight year.

Business was booming and the Bills were in the playoffs. Yet they were there with a turned-around format. At the time they had clinched their berth, the Buffalo offense was rated 11th in the 13-team American Conference. The defense was rated second best. Even as the Bills wrapped up that first postseason slot in nearly a decade, the offense was booed by the home folks. They found more interest in a fan in the stands taking off his shirt in the bitter cold.

Why? They were bored. And the offense seemed ill. In four weeks, it produced two touchdowns. It failed to score one against the Colts, whose defense was among the NFL's most generous. A week earlier, there was only O.J.'s 41-yard TD run in Cleveland—and the Browns were also weak. A Sunday before that, the offense was sagging badly in Miami until Marangi came off the bench. And on Nov. 10, the offense all but evaporated amidst six interceptions in that 21-9 flogging by Houston.

In short, a funny thing happened to the Bills' offense on the way to the playoffs. It all but died. Saban blamed the weather, heavy winds, mud, etc. But there was more. Where the previous year O.J. cracked eight NFL records and amassed 2,003 yards in a devastating show led by that power sweep right, this year defenses adjusted to shut off that maneuver.

Now the playoffs were coming and Saban needed more than a rather basic offense of Simpson sweeps and fullback thrusts. "It's been a tough year weather-wise. Under good conditions, we'll look like we did in the first half of the season," Saban promised.

What the coach really needed were a few new wrinkles, even the element of surprise. He also needed a return of confidence to Ferguson, who never quite recovered from that six-interception holocaust against Houston. Saban needed all of this badly, for his Bills were no longer facing losing teams such as the Browns, Colts and Jets. They would open the playoffs against the fast-rising Pittsburgh Steelers in Three Rivers Stadium. Saban had to solve the problem of his team's turnabout—long on defense, short on offense. He had to remedy the attack's ills immediately.

O.J. attends Tennessee banquet honoring teammate Robert James.
Bespectacled Bill was All-Pro cornerback.
AP Wirephoto

The Steelers boasted the toughest defense in pro football and, led by Mean Joe Greene, the most menacing front four. And here were the Bills, venturing into the NFL playoffs for the first time and having lost four of their past six encounters.

Saban was hopeful a more wide-open attack—placing O.J. on a wing, and using three wide receivers in one formation—would shake loose his offense. The coach realized his underdog team needed a quick jump against the powerful Steelers. Otherwise playing catchup against Greene and Co. was virtually an impossible assignment.

O.J. was confident the Bills could forget their slow finish and regard the playoffs as a new season. He also was encouraged by his previous success against Pittsburgh. In two games since 1970, he gained 249 yards in 36 carries against the Steelers—a heaping 6.9 average. Included was the club-record 94-yard run in 1972, the third longest dash from scrimmage in NFL history.

"Pittsburgh plays reckless on defense," O.J. observed. "They were reckless four years ago and they're still that way. Against them, because of the way they stunt around, they can either burn you badly on a play or be burned themselves."

There was reason for Ferguson to be aroused, too—reason other than just making his initial playoff trip. Both he and Steeler quarterback Terry Bradshaw were products of the same high school, both raised in the Southern Hills section of Shreveport, La. They lived less than two miles apart. "Everybody down here is excited about the game because we've watched Bradshaw and Ferguson grow up," reported Jerry Robichaux of the Shreveport *Times.*

"This is the first time we've gone against each other," commented Ferguson, "but it's not a personal thing. We're both trying to do a job and we'll both be giving it our best shot."

Ferguson was more occupied with trying to sharpen his aerial game. He admitted thoughts of the Houston nightmare still haunted him. "Yeah, I think about it now and then," he said. "It's hard to get something like that out of your mind when you're playing such an individual position as quarterback. But I know I can't think about it now. I feel very fortunate being in the playoffs in only my second year. It's just the beginning, really. I hope to go a long way with this team. Right now, it's kind of scary being just two games from the Super Bowl. But really, can you think of a better time to start a three-game winning streak?"

O.J., Ferguson and the other Bills realized the odds were stacked against them. Pittsburgh had the experience of being in the two previous playoffs and Chuck Noll, their coach, claimed they had learned from those games. "We're wiser in all departments," Noll said. "My players know what to expect."

Saban was hoping Noll would think just that way—thus, the revised offense. "We're as well prepared to play this one as any game we've been in," Saban declared. "Whether the Steelers permit us to do what we want is the big factor."

Saban chose to start Rex Kern, the former Ohio State star, in the free safety slot filled so splendidly for 12 games by Tony Greene. Sophomore pro Donnie Walker had operated in the slot the two games since Greene incurred torn knee ligaments, but was whipped in the season-ending losses to the Jets and Rams.

Tempers raged in the Bills' practices as game day neared—and that's often an encouraging sign. Linebacker Dave Washington and rookie tight end Reuben Gant exchanged blows after an unusually hard-hitting midweek drill.

O.J. avoided that type of thing and chose lighter thoughts to occupy his mind. For instance, both he and Saban were thinking of Lynn Swann, but in far different ways. Saban was fretting over Swann's 577 yards in 41 punt-returns, the second best total of all time in the NFL. Simpson laughed as he thought of Swann as his family's occasional baby-sitter.

"Lynn babysits for me back in Los Angeles," O.J. smiled. "He's among several good friends I have on the Steelers . . . along with Andy Russell, Dwight White and Joe Greene. If I had to cover Lynn as a pass receiver, he'd be shut out. I'd work on his mind."

O.J. was grinning broadly as he cracked the shutout statement.

Finally, it was game day. The Bills were worried about slick conditions (following heavy rain) on the tartan turf, but the Steelers themselves formed a far greater worry. How would they penetrate this defense with that ferocious front four and All-Pro outside linebackers? Could the defense neutralize unpredictable Terry Bradshaw and silence "Franco's Army," the legion of support for star running back Franco Harris?

The answers would soon be obvious. The Bills would demonstrate that they were even more unpredictable than Bradshaw. They would perform another turnabout and revert to form. Though O.J. was clearly in the background in his only playoff venture, the offense would surface. But the defense? Well, a baseball term applied. The playoff Bills were strictly good-hit, no-field.

The first quarter went decently, as far as the Bills were concerned. Roy Gerela kicked a 21-yard field goal for a 3-0 Pittsburgh edge at 6:09, but two possessions later, Ferguson moved the Bills. He flipped eight yards to Braxton for a first down at the Steeler 24 and then spotted Seymour slipping free in a zone past safety Glen Edwards. Ferguson drilled a 22-yard pass and Seymour scored. The Bills had moved smartly 56 yards in six plays and led, 7-3, after a period.

Then the second quarter started and the Bills virtually went south. For 15 minutes, any semblance of defense all but disappeared.

Bradshaw scrambled for a pair of first downs, and with time seemingly sufficient to read a newspaper, he drilled a 27-yard touchdown pass to Rocky Bleier for a 9-7 Steeler lead, the conversion try blocked. A bomb went through Rashad's hands and Glen Edwards blitzed to nail O.J. for a four-yard loss on third down. Marv Bateman followed with a 28-yard punt and the Bills began coming apart at the seams.

Swann went to the end-around, his pet maneuver, and the Bills reacted as if they'd never seen it before. "We practiced it all week," Saban later said. Swann circled left for 25 yards after Bradshaw faked a handoff to Harris. The Steelers never saw second down again as Swann caught a 12-yard pass at the Bills' 26, Harris swept left end for 11 and Bradshaw hit Swann again for 13. Pittsburgh was at the two and two carries later, Harris was in the end zone. The score was 16-7.

On first down, Braxton ripped off 30 yards, but cornerback Mel Blount yanked the fullback's arm and forced a fumble, linebacker Jack Ham recovering at the Pitt 42.

Bradshaw was smoking now. He found Bleier for 19 and Swann, beating All-Pro corner Robert James, dived for a magnificent 35-yard catch at the four. On second down, Harris burst four yards over right tackle to score and, with another Gerela PAT blocked, the difference was 22-7.

O.J. was thrown for another loss on a draw attempt, this time a five-yard setback by Ham, and the Steelers soon were in business again. The Bills couldn't do anything right. Bleier burst 10 yards to the Bills' 44, and James was nabbed holding Swann on a pass pattern. Bradshaw found tight end Larry Brown behind linebacker Bo Cornell and, with 18 seconds left in the half, fired a 28-yard strike to the one. Harris scored his third touchdown standing up. Gerela converted and the Bills were dead, 29-7.

Just like that—without the second half even starting—this game was over and all 48,321 in attendance realized it. In the second quarter, Pittsburgh had blitzed the Bills, 26-0. "It was our best offensive showing of the year," Noll beamed.

O.J., who had but 28 yards off nine carries at intermission, scored in the third quarter on a three-yard pitch from Ferguson. It was absolutely no consolation. He finished with 15 carries for 49 yards and three receptions for 37, and his team was soundly beaten. The Steelers had contained him and his Super Bowl dream was shattered, 32-14.

This was a playoff in which game statistics meant nothing. Halftime figures told the tale of a rout. In amassing that 29-7 spread, the Steelers rolled up 295 yards to Buffalo's 146 and built a first down advantage of 20-7. Swann had three receptions for 60 yards, Bleier three for 59. Harris was a virtual workhorse, carrying 18 times for 56 yards. And Bradshaw, whom some had labeled a "dumb" quarterback, was absolutely brilliant with 166 passing yards and a TD, completing 10 of 14, and keeping three times for 22 more yards.

When all was finished, the Steelers had accumulated an AFC playoff record 29 first downs. The 26-point second-quarter explosion was the largest since the present NFL playoff format was established in 1970. And Harris established an AFC playoff mark for most rushing TDs in a game with three. He had all three in the second quarter.

O.J. tried to rationalize the shocking one-sided nature of the outcome in the tomblike Buffalo dressing room. "Everybody set their goal at wanting to make the playoffs and it's possible that once we made it, we may have become a little satisfied at doing that and lost some of our edge," he said softly.

"Next year, we're all coming back with the goal of making it to the Super Bowl, and maybe that idea will carry us all the way. It's hard to single out any one thing as being the turning point. The entire second period was the turning point. When a good team gets as hot as they were that period, they can put a lot of points on the board. We outscored them 14-6 in the other three periods, but they scored 26 points in the second."

O.J., despite his difficulty working the draw and a small-yardage afternoon, felt the Buffalo offense moved effectively. "We were able to do most of the things we wanted to do on offense, but so did they," he noted. "It seemed they were on the field offensively most of the time. They just happened to play 15 minutes of perfect football."

Noll enthusiastically agreed with the Bills' superstar. "It's no deep, dark mystery why we scored a lot of points in the second period," he said. "We made a couple of minor adjustments in the first period, but that's all. Our offense just did some super executing. I'd like to take credit for masterminding what happened in the second quarter, but I can't. The men just executed."

Bills' strong safety Neal Craig explained what happened from a defensive viewpoint in a remarkably candid interview. "We folded or tightened up," the bald defender said. "We made a lot of mistakes. Nothing they did surprised us, but we just couldn't handle them. They kept calling the right play at the right time in the second period. They had a super game plan, but we made two or three mistakes that really hurt us. You can't let a quarterback run around for 10 or 15 yards when you have him hemmed into his own end. Maturity might be the best choice of words to describe the difference today. This was our first trip to the playoffs. The Steelers had been there before."

Craig also pointed out that first-down plays crushed the Bills throughout that second quarter. "First down is so important and it killed us," he said. "If you can hold a team to two or three yards on first down, you can stop it. But when you give up seven yards and more like we were, second down is a joke."

Defensive tackle Earl Edwards, nicknamed the "Secretary of

Steeler lineman Dwight White reaches out for O.J. in Bills' bitter 1974 playoff defeat at Three Rivers Stadium.
Photo by Robert L. Smith,
Elma, N.Y.

Defense," was at a loss to explain the 26-point crush. "After the first quarter, I thought we'd win," he said. "Then all hell broke loose. Whatever defense we came out with, they were expecting it. Whether it's a case of their being smarter, I don't know. But Terry Bradshaw is no genius."

And yet he certainly looked like one in that second quarter. "I think his running hurt us more than his passing," Saban complained. "He got himself out of jams every time. I think the most telling factor was they just handled us offensively. They did a great job. I'm not sure how they did what they did against us, but they blew us out. It was quite a struggle getting to the playoffs, but now that we're here, I can't say that I like the final result. We just suffered a defensive breakdown in the second period. There are words to describe how we played on defense, but I don't intend to use them here. I can't find fault with our offense. We moved the ball. But the defense . . ."

Saban was shocked by the porous defensive show. He realized middle linebacker Jim Cheyunski had a dozen tackles and six assists and Rex Kern was a super surprise with eight tackles, five assists, two TD "saves," a recovered fumble and a near-interception—but what about the others?

Where were his four linebackers when Bradshaw took off five times for 48 yards, Saban wondered. Where were they on passes over the middle? Where were they on all those wide runs by Franco Harris? Apparently Bradshaw ecstatically was wondering the same thing. "I've never felt in such control of a game," Terry boasted. "I felt I could do anything I wanted."

In the second quarter, he certainly did.

J.D. Hill, the speedy wide receiver, explained the bitter pill which was this playoff embarrassment most explicitly—as far as the team's rank-and-file was concerned. "We lost a chance at a lot of money today," he said. "I'm not an O.J. Simpson where I play good football and people come after me with offers to do this and that for money. If it takes looks to get into the movies, I'll never make it. My chance at making extra money comes from playing football. I make my money on the field. It may sound like I'm feeling sorry for myself, but I'm not. I could get in a car wreck or something where I couldn't play again, so I've got to make it while I can. And we had the chance today. Man, here was a chance to make some extra money, up to 25 grand, and we blew it."

Hill pounded his heavily taped right fist into his left palm for emphasis. "Do you know how much 25 grand is?" he asked. "Very few people on this team make that much. There are lots of players begging, just begging, to be in our position in the playoffs. We got there and what did we do? Nothing!"

Then the Bills' No. 1 free spirit thought of a defensive player who could have made a difference. "If there was one thing about this season I would change," he said, "I would bring back the little guy, Tony Greene. His injury was the worst thing that happened to us all year. The little guy understands this game, what it's all about. He meant so much to us. That's the kind of compliment I want some day."

Over in the Pittsburgh boudoir, the Steelers were pointing out

O.J. is a picture of dejection after playoff defeat in Pittsburgh. The
message on the blackboard indicates Bills' mood.
Photo by Robert L. Smith,
Elma, N.Y.

that O.J.'s babysitter had grown up. "I'd have to say it was my best game as a pro," smiled Swann, echoing Bradshaw's self-assessment and savoring his big second-quarter plays and his contribution to the Steelers' 438-yard foray. "I was in the locker room before practice Saturday talking with O.J. and he yelled over to Robert James, their cornerback, 'Eat him alive, Robert.' I just laughed and went about my business."

Business such as destroying Buffalo with that end-around.

"With three down linemen, they've got to penetrate to stop the pass," Swann explained. "If you can get them hooked, the reverse will work well. Once I saw Earl Edwards had penetrated, I just went around and turned it up."

In the process, Swann opened the second-quarter floodgates and 26 points ensued. "Damn, damn, damn," repeated J.D. Hill as he thought of that quarter and the wasted opportunity which this game represented.

The Steelers were just beginning to roll and the Bills were all done. Pittsburgh went on to Super Bowl IX and won, 16-6, over Minnesota in New Orleans. Even that was of small consolation to O.J. and the Bills. Their Cinderella season was gone. The ball was long since over and the glass slipper was too tight. The flowers had faded, the music had stopped and the Steelers had let the air out of the Bills' balloons.

O.J. only hoped that next fall, when they were pumping those balloons again, he would get one more crack at the Steelers. They had made a shambles of his only playoff venture and he would never forget it.

CHAPTER SEVENTEEN

A Return to Three Rivers

As irony would have it, the Bills' initial road game of the 1975 season was in none other than Three Rivers Stadium. The Super Bowl champion Pittsburgh Steelers would open their home season against the very team they conquered in their last Three Rivers appearance.

O.J. was presented his chance for revenge—before a national television audience.

But before that chance came there were all kinds of explosive developments. There was a wildcat players' strike in the NFL, with the New England Patriots refusing to play an exhibition with the New York Jets, and smaller walkouts (including a two-day affair by the Jets before the opener with Buffalo) joined in threatening the season itself.

While some teams seemed to be torn asunder, the Bills remained a unit, voting 43-0 not to strike. They followed O.J., having seen him play the previous season in pain, thus boosting their tremendous respect for him. "I don't like politics, but I've been forced to get involved," said Simpson, blaming the NFL Players Association director, Ed Garvey, for the strike. "I once thought I could be an athlete and not worry about all the other stuff, but I now know that every one of us has to face our problems and figure out just how much we're willing to put on the line."

The preseason was costly—painfully costly. The Bills lost Ahmad Rashad, their leading receiver of 1974, All-Pro cornerback Robert James and new strong safety Doug Jones for the season via injuries. These were tremendous blows. Bob Chandler, his knee injury corrected by surgery, could step into Rashad's spot. But who could replace James? The answer was no one. And, with Neal Craig traded to Cleveland and Jones hurt, the strong safety slot was similarly weak.

Then there were other, more subtle kinds of adjustments—such as attitude. "We set our standards too low last year," O.J. declared. "We had won the last four games of the 1973 season and it was new to us to finish a winner. I really don't think we knew how good we were. All of us kept talking about how our goal was to make the playoffs. At the time, it seemed far away for us. But then we made it with a couple of weeks still to play in the season.

"Everything after just making the playoffs seemed beyond us," O.J. elaborated. "Maybe we were satisfied with going just that far. At any rate, we couldn't beat the Steelers."

O.J. vowed that, even with the loss of Rashad and James, this 1975 season could be different.

"Our target is the Super Bowl," he said. "It won't be easy. The schedule, for one thing, is harder than those of the last two years. Five games are against playoff teams—Miami twice, Pittsburgh, St. Louis and Minnesota. Denver and Cincinnati are other opponents. And the Patriots and Jets from our own division are improving.

"I've heard a lot of talk about how difficult our schedule is, but people forget we played our best against the better teams the last few years. Last year, we upset Oakland and the year before Atlanta was on a seven-game winning streak and the hottest team in the league when we beat them. The year before [1972], we won only four games, but two were against playoff teams, Washington and San Francisco. The only times we've looked really bad were against 'down' teams—like when New Orleans shut us out in '73 and Houston upset us last year."

There was one notable exception—the playoff embarrassment by Pittsburgh. O.J. hadn't forgotten, he simply chose not to mention it. He intended to do something about that in game two of the season.

Yet there was one phase of the game O.J. couldn't affect— Buffalo's defense. The Steelers had exposed the weaknesses for the entire NFL to see—and exploit. The Bills used the "Oklahoma" defense (three down linemen and four linebackers) to conceal shortcomings and failed.

In the off-season, Saban moved to bolster that defense by acquiring end Pat Toomay, a strong pass rusher, who played out his option with Dallas. But he also traded away linebackers Jim Cheyunski (Baltimore) and Dave Washington (San Francisco) for draft choices, and their absence would be felt. So would the losses of James and Jones, the latter being hurt just after being obtained from Kansas City. Saban would use a variety of left cornerbacks (James's post) and rookie safeties. The defense, obviously, was one gigantic question mark—at best.

The season opened on an emotional level against the Jets at Rich Stadium. Several Jets had vowed a "blood bath," calling the Bills "a lousy bunch" for not taking an active role in the strike. The Bills responded by humbling them, 42-14, as O.J. carried 32 times for 173 yards and two touchdowns—his 39th and 40th as a Bill, breaking the club record. "You fellows played pretty well for a lousy bunch," Ralph Wilson told his players.

O.J. might have surpassed his NFL-record 250-yard game and surely would have enjoyed a fourth 200-yarder, but two dashes of 31 and 49 yards were nullified by penalties and he left the game with half the fourth quarter still to play.

"Buffalo just kicked hell out of us in every phase of the game," losing coach Charley Winner admitted. That rout set the stage for the return of O.J. and the Bills to Pittsburgh. This one, for obvious reasons, was something special.

"I'm 28 now," O.J. had stated before the season, remembering the average life of a running back in pro football is five years. "I'd like to blow everybody's mind before my career is finished.

When Gale Sayers was 28, his career was just about over."

Here was the game in which O.J. could "blow everybody's mind." This time things would be different against the Steelers, he vowed. This time he was not in pain. "There were times last year when I thought I was going to break all the way," O.J. recalled about the 1974 season. "I'd just have to get past one guy or cut a little sharper. But someone always seemed to be sticking out an arm or catching me just as I cut at the last minute."

John Leypoldt asked me two days before the game who I was picking. "Pittsburgh," was the quick reply. "After last year, I'd have to go with the Steelers."

"Whatever you do, don't do that," Leypoldt responded, shaking his head. "We're going to take this one. You can just feel it."

The first quarter was strikingly similar to the opening period of that lopsided playoff game. In fact, it was better for Pittsburgh. Instead of trailing by four points, the Steelers were even in a scoreless battle. Yet it was soon obvious that Bradshaw wasn't sharp. He fumbled away a threat at the Bills' 26 and, on the Steelers' next possession, fired badly over the middle for Frank Lewis. Middle linebacker Merv Krakau intercepted at the Steeler 24, setting up Leypoldt's 37-yard field goal.

Soon Bradshaw made another blunder—a real laugher. With Earl Edwards descending quickly, he cocked his arm, but the ball flipped up behind him. The surprised Edwards caught it, darted five yards until Bradshaw grabbed his waist and then lateraled to burly tackle Mike Kadish. Big Mike lumbered 26 yards to score his first touchdown ever. The score was 10-0 and the Three Rivers partisans were hooting the world champion Steelers. How quickly they forget!

Steeler fans couldn't believe their eyes. The Bills, beaten so badly in the playoffs, now were dominating their team. Pittsburgh allowed 18 sacks, least in the NFL, in 1974. And here was Buffalo chasing Bradshaw all over the field—dropping him four times! The Steelers had led the league with an awesome 52 sacks of opposing quarterbacks. And here was Ferguson—not being touched. He never was dropped.

In the third quarter, Ferguson hit Seymour for 17 yards and the diving Chandler for 11, handed off to O.J. and Braxton for

Bearded O.J. shows
determined expression
in 1975 opener. His
return to Three Rivers
marked a sensational
227-yard show.
AP Wirephoto

O.J. begins 88-yard run during 227-yard game in Pittsburgh as tackle
Donnie Green blocks L.C. Greenwood (68).
Photo by Robert L. Smith,
Elma, N.Y.

seven and eight, and then lofted a seven-yard TD spiral to Reuben Gant, who beat linebacker Jack Ham in the deep right corner. It was Gant's second pro reception and his first pro TD. The score was 17-0 and now the natives were really howling. Noll pulled Bradshaw out of the game, inserting Joe Gilliam at quarterback. But Gilliam couldn't solve the revitalized Buffalo defense, either.

At least, Noll thought on the Pittsburgh sideline, the Bills were pinned in their end at last, as he watched Bobby Walden's punt bounce out at the three.

Three plays later, O.J. delivered the coup de grace. With the "Steel Curtain" looking for a short plunge on third-and-inches, O.J. swept right and was freed by a crushing Braxton block of Ham. O.J. turned and whoosh—off he sped, 88 yards down the right sideline for the second-longest touchdown of his pro career and longest in the NFL since he sped 94 against Pittsburgh in 1972. Now the Steeler fans were cheering. They appreciated greatness, and even with their champion team being embarrassed 23-0, they cheered O.J.

"It was our 46-play," the Juice later explained. "Joe called something else in the huddle—either a sneak or Braxton straight ahead. They were looking for it, too, on third and inches. Jim made the big block and soon I realized it was a footrace."

Nobody beats O.J. in a footrace.

"I couldn't tell where their secondary was playing, but they had everyone else in tight," O.J. said. "After I got around end, I saw that even their backs were in close. I changed from my football stride to my track stride and could only think about the 100-yard dash I won in the Superstars competition [in 0:09.6]. A Steeler dove at me around midfield and when he missed, I realized the play would go all the way."

Ferguson described his checkoff thinking which freed O.J. for the 88-yard trip.

"I called for a quarterback sneak, but when we got to the line of scrimmage, I saw Pittsburgh was in a goal-line defense," Ferguson drawled. "With a good charge, they may have stopped the sneak, so I checked off and called O.J.'s play. That was one of the few checked plays I called all game. After Juice got the ball and turned the corner, all I could do was stand back on the 10-yard line and cheer. Checking off and seeing that play turn into a touchdown made the day for me."

The Bills were in ecstasy, mobbing O.J., where they had been so downtrodden the previous December. They were annihilating the world champs in their own backyard and O.J. suddenly was on the threshold of a fourth 200-yard game, which would tie another Jim Brown record. O.J. had 162 yards in 19 carries. The Bills hardly noticed when Leypoldt's conversion kick sailed wide.

Late in the third quarter, with Buffalo obviously in charge and the only major question being whether O.J. would crack the 200 plateau, Marv Kellum provided a distraction by blocking Marv Bateman's punt. Loren Toews recovered and raced 30 yards to the Bills' six, setting up Pittsburgh's first touchdown—a two-yard pop over the middle by Franco Harris. The third quarter ended with the score, 23-7, and O.J. with 174 yards in 23 trips.

Some Steeler fans hadn't given up and, as the fourth quarter started, the Bills were hemmed in at their 10 on third down and 11. Ferguson faded and fired a 16-yard dart to the kneeling Seymour, silencing the partisans. Ferguson then found Gant for 18 and, just like that, the Steelers couldn't concentrate on O.J. anymore.

Then on first down, it happened. Ferguson handed off to O.J., who cut over right tackle and exploded for 28 yards to the Steeler 28. The fourth quarter had only just begun and O.J. just soared past the 200-yard barrier. He had 24 carries, 202 yards. And he had thundered this damage against the finest team in pro football.

The Steelers seemed in shock. Two plays later, Ferguson fired a 28-yard touchdown pass to Chandler, who speared the ball over his head. The score was 30-7. The Steelers were thoroughly whipped.

Pittsburgh struck for two touchdowns—Gilliam's 20-yard pass to Randy Grossman and Harris' yard plunge—which made the final score appear respectable, 30-21. But there was no question the Bills had stunned the champions soundly.

Many witnesses thought O.J. could have beaten his 250-yard NFL single-game rushing record that day, but he came out after picking up 25 more yards. Leaving with almost five minutes left, he finished with 227 yards in 29 attempts.

It was the most yardage ever accumulated in one game against Pittsburgh, breaking a record held by Steve Van Buren. O.J.'s rushing total also broke the Three Rivers Stadium standard. Yes, he could have toppled his own league mark, but he was weary and Saban did not wish to risk injury to "the Franchise."

O.J. was absolutely aglow in the Bills' electric dressing room atmosphere, a study in contrast to the scene in that same room after that December playoff tilt. This was his finest 200-yard game, even though the total indicated it was his second best. It was his greatest performance because it came against the best—and conquered the best.

"There were two great things about this game," beamed O.J. "First of all, it came against the Steelers. I regard them as the best defensive team in football, by far. Secondly, I got a chance to do something I've never done before. I won what amounted to a 100-yard dash on a football field. Once I turned the corner on that 88-yard touchdown, it was nothing but a sprint.

"My teammates keep telling me they can beat me in a sprint like 100 yards," O.J. grinned. "No way. Even McKenzie thinks he can beat me, but he's slow. Nobody can beat me if I'm healthy and fresh. Nobody outran me today, did they?"

O.J. was comparing as he talked. He was drawing for reporters an analogy of the slowed, hurting Simpson they saw throughout 1974 and in that sorry playoff game at Three Rivers and the healthy, uncatchable, matchless Juice. There really was no comparison.

It was obvious that O.J., off to the fastest rushing start in his or any running back's pro career (400 yards in two games), was bursting with happiness. The Bills were walloping their opponents, a trend which would continue two more weeks. They were scoring freely. And this upset marked the first time since 1965 that the Bills opened a season with two victories.

Yet, as happy as he was and his teammates were, O.J. realized this was only a regular season game. There was no way it could really compensate for the despair which comes from being walloped from the playoffs—as the Steelers had done to them.

"As much as we wanted this win, as great a win as it was, I'd swap it for a win here last December in the playoffs," O.J. declared pensively. "But we'll be back in the playoffs. We know now we can beat anybody. When you beat the Super Bowl champs, you can beat anybody."

Somebody asked O.J. what the difference was, other than his healed leg injuries, which enabled him to rise so far beyond that 49-yard performance of his playoff game. "We honestly stuck to the game plan we had here last time," O.J. replied. "The difference was we grabbed the lead and held the ball, not them."

Nearby, Reggie McKenzie was nodding his head.

"We moved the ball well here last year," the muscular guard remembered. "But we just didn't have the ball often enough. So the coaches decided not to panic, not to change, but to stick with what they felt would work best. It worked, too. When you stop to think about it, O.J. is our game plan. And why shouldn't he be?"

The Steelers were simply overwhelmed by Simpson's magnificence.

"Most backs wouldn't have gained a yard on the play he gained 88," remarked Noll. "They talk about Pittsburgh being someplace special. Well, O.J. is something special. An ordinary back would have been caught for a loss. The only thing we caught was the No. 32 on the back of his jersey."

Dwight White, the front four's vaunted right end, echoed his coach's sentiments. "I never played against Jim Brown," he said. "I'm sure he was great. But if there was ever a better back than O.J. . . ." White let out a loud whistle.

"They talk a lot about Buffalo's offensive line," Mean Joe Greene commented, "and they can keep on talkin' about the line. But it's the Juice who makes the difference, not the line. The Juice!"

Back in the Bills' quarters, Ferguson was talking in superlatives, Edwards and Kadish were talking on and on about their touchdown and Saban countered Greene's assessment by stating the game was won where most games are decided—in the trenches.

"This was the greatest thrill of my life—beating the world champs," exclaimed Ferguson, who set some sort of record by going a second game against the Steelers without being sacked.

Edwards, who sacked Bradshaw twice, recovered two Bradshaw fumbles and had four unaided stops, talked of the game's first touchdown—the weird play in which Bradshaw lost control and let the ball pop into the air as he tried to throw.

"He has lost control of the ball in situations like that before," Edwards noted. "I only dreamed he'd do that with me around. He did and when he grabbed me at the waist, I heard Kadish yelling, 'Earl, Earl.' So I lateraled him the ball and he looked like a sprinter."

"I didn't know if I could make it all the way [26 yards]," Kadish admitted with a grin. "I never scored a touchdown before in my life—high school, college or pro. When I got there, I thought of the spike I worked on in practice during the week. But I never spiked it!"

He was too stunned.

Saban remembered sitting in that dressing room amidst black thoughts, really despair, the previous December. "I sat in this stadium after that playoff loss and thought we weren't all that bad," the coach declared. "You have to keep them from that basic pressure. The control of both lines has to be there and it was today. It was a big game."

For Saban, never one for punchy quotes, that was saying a mouthful.

The statistics backed him up. O.J.'s rushing feats were but one facet of this stunning show. The Bills had possession for 34 of the game's 60 minutes, a complete turnabout from the playoff meeting. And Bradshaw, who never felt so fully in control back in December, completed but three of eight passes, was sacked four times, fumbled for a touchdown, threw an interception which led to a field goal and was driven to the sidelines early in the second half. What a contrast! What a difference one year can make!

Joe DeLamielleure, the Bills' "other" guard who actually outshined McKenzie in 1974, minced no words in placing the credit for the Bills' amazing form reversal. "I attribute this showing to Jim Ringo—he's the best line coach in football," Joe D announced. "The Juice made many great plays, but I feel the entire offensive line enjoyed its best day. And I'd say this was our most important victory since I joined the team in 1973 because we beat the champs and we beat them in Pittsburgh."

And all Joe DeLamielleure did was neutralize Joe Greene, perhaps the game's finest defensive tackle.

The Steelers were so aroused by this humiliating loss, they won their next 11 games, finished 12-2 for the season and went on to a second straight Super Bowl success. For the Bills, this was their finest show of the season. There would be other triumphs, but nothing like this and no postseason play. Months later, there was simply the remembrance of O.J.'s greatest game.

Breaking the 200-yard barrier against the Patriots and Jets, as O.J. had done in 1973, was one thing. Doing it against the Super Bowl champions is quite another. O.J. had run not only around but through the Steelers this day. And the Bills had outrushed the Steelers, 310 yards to 122. They had totaled 434 yards!

The Denver Broncos, Buffalo's next opponent, watched films of the Juice's performance and couldn't believe their eyes. "The Juice is a once-in-a-lifetime back," star defensive end Lyle Alzado said. "He's got the right instinct for everything, and he can see and pick out a hole faster than anybody I've ever played against. I don't see how any running back can do some of the things he does. He's simply incredible."

As well put as Alzado's description was, Bronco coach John Ralston was even more precise. Hardly anyone was more aware of Simpson's overall ability sooner than Ralston, who as Stanford coach scouted the San Francisco area and saw O.J. in high school and junior college. He also saw O.J. beat his Stanford team twice.

"When O.J. was a junior at USC, he broke loose on a long run against us," Ralston recalled. "As he passed me on the sidelines, I turned to an assistant and said, 'There goes the greatest running back ever to play this game.' That was a pretty strong statement to make, but you could see his ability then, and he hasn't done anything since then to make me change my mind."

Back in Buffalo, sportswriters and Bills' teammates were heaping the verbal bouquets on O.J. for his greatest individual showing. However, Reggie McKenzie didn't join them. He was holding out for a greater day. "Was it his best game?" Reggie asked himself. "I'm not sure," he answered.

"O.J. always amazes me. I can see a day when he gains over

300 yards in a game, and when that happens, then I'll say that's the greatest game he's ever played."

"I'd like to be the first guy to get 300 yards in pro ball," O.J. smiled. "I remember getting 304 yards on 17 carries in junior college and not too many guys—high school or college—can say that."

And no one else can say he ran for 227 yards against the Pittsburgh Steelers, either.

CHAPTER EIGHTEEN

O.J. the Super Receiver

The seventh game of the 1975 National Football League season holds a special niche among O.J.'s finest games, but hardly because of his rushing exploits. In fact, when the New York Jets "held" him to 94 yards by land that Nov. 2 afternoon in Shea Stadium, that was his second lowest total for a half-season.

This was the day O.J. passed Leroy Kelly and became the fourth leading all-time rusher in NFL history. This was the day he reached 1,005 rushing yards at mid-season, prompting many to predict another venture above 2,000. Yet he was toasted for a different quality and no one who witnessed the game wondered why.

This, for all intents, was O.J.'s coming-out party as a first-class receiving threat.

O.J., through most of his six and a half seasons as a pro, heard and read stories about his supposed "bad hands"—a penchant for dropping passes within his range. He even joked about the reputation. One day, O.J. told an acquaintance: "I could set scoring records, too, if they passed to me more often."

The Juice was reminded that, according to some reports, he doesn't catch very proficiently.

"I forgot about that," O.J. chuckled. "That's right, there were two small flaws in John Rauch's plan to make me a great rookie receiver—my hands."

Indeed, there was statistical evidence to support allegations that Simpson wasn't exactly setting the world afire via the airwaves. Before this game, he had caught only four passes all season. He had scored only four pro touchdowns as a receiver in those six and a half seasons—and three came during his 1969 rookie year. He never scored through the air from 1970 to 1973 and did so only once in 1974.

One might conclude that O.J. was due.

And yet he performed so tremendously as football's finest active rusher that hardly anyone noticed he wasn't a threatening receiver. He had set the football world on its heels with that 2,003-yard trip in 1973, led the Bills into the playoffs when hurt in 1974 and was traveling a record course through the first half of 1975.

After that overwhelming 227-yard show in Pittsburgh, O.J. followed with 138 (in 26 carries) against Denver, 159 (in 32 runs) against Baltimore and 126 (in 34 tries) opposite the New York Giants. The previous Sunday, in realizing 88 yards in 19 thrusts against Miami, marked his first 1975 day under 100.

Yet, despite all these explosions, the Bills needed even more from O.J. in New York. He had romped 697 yards to power the high-scoring Bills to victory in their initial four games of the season, even departing early with lopsided scores in three. But in the two previous games, his team had found difficult times.

The lowly Giants came to Rich Stadium, prompting some to predict a 300-yard game for O.J. and as lopsided a triumph as 63-0 for the Bills. Instead, the Bills faded after taking a quick 14-0 lead and were shocked, 17-14, in one of the greatest upsets the Monday night television audience has seen.

The Bills had looked past the Giants toward Miami and paid the price. The following Sunday, they seemed about to atone by outscoring Miami, but free safety Jake Scott intercepted a foolish pass deep in Buffalo's territory late in the game and rallied the Dolphins to a 35-30 victory.

So now the Bills, who scored 148 points in assembling those

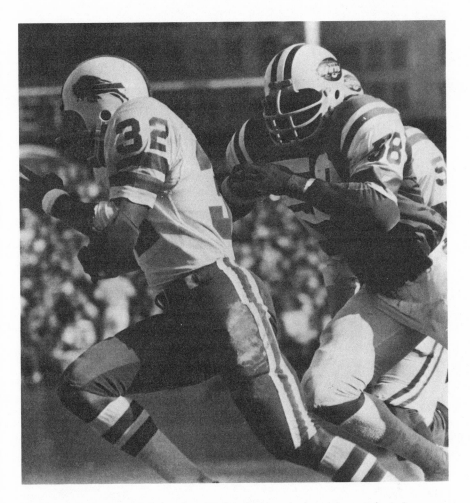

O.J. breaks past Jet linebacker Richard Wood after big catch. Juice completed 64-yard touchdown for 24-23 Bills' victory.
Photo by Robert L. Smith,
Elma, N.Y.

initial four victories, were skidding at 4-2. They had dropped two games they should have won. They needed someone to inspire them out of the slide and, naturally, they turned to O.J.

Sometimes inspiration comes slowly, and this was such a game. And sometimes that inspiration requires an assist from dame fortune. This also was the case.

After 37 minutes, or midway through the third quarter, the Bills trailed by the heaping score of 23-7 and were staggering badly before a sad-sack Jets' outfit which was routed in its three previous encounters. It was becoming a downright humiliating scene for O.J. and his teammates, who were the talk of the league the first four weeks of the season.

The Bills had scored first, as usual, on an 11-yard pass play from Ferguson to Braxton. But then came 23 uninterrupted Jets' points. Pat Leahy clicked on three field goals—measuring 42, 41 and 31 yards—and Joe Namath fired touchdown strikes of 16 yards to Emerson Boozer and 31 to Eddie "The Flea" Bell.

Meanwhile the Bills were doing just about everything wrong.

Ferguson was seeing perfectly thrown passes being dropped. Vic Washington fumbled away a kickoff return, setting up a Jet touchdown. There was one penalty after another, including four holding infractions. Tight end Reuben Gant drew the first two, nullifying a Braxton TD. McKenzie was nabbed and that stunted a scoring threat. Then DeLamielleure was caught clutching and that wiped out Ferguson's apparent 16-yard touchdown pass to Chandler.

On the very next play, Ferguson fired to Braxton for another apparent score, but this time Ferguson stepped three yards over the line of scrimmage before firing, a violation. The Bills, seeming snake-bitten, had scored twice on successive plays and neither touchdown counted. They settled for a 40-yard Leypoldt field goal.

Those three points seemed small consolation with the score 23-10, but they proved so major. New York went immediately for a killer score, but after Namath found tight end Rich Caster for 29 yards at the Bills' 33, the Bills finally received a positive break.

Linebacker John Skorupan pursued Namath vigorously, and the legendary quarterback threw wildly toward Bell. Tony Greene intercepted, falling into his end zone. Now Ferguson warmed up, hitting Chandler with a pair of passes and then switching to J.D. Hill for a 28-yard touchdown. Now the Bills were within range, trailing 23-17 after three quarters.

The Jets, however, could have put this game away so easily. Greene's interception had saved one touchdown, but Namath came back twice more. Pat Toomay's third-down sack thwarted one advance and an incredible decision by Jets' coach Charley Winner stopped the second try. With 5:55 to play, John Riggins was stopped cold by tackle Earl Edwards on third-and-one at the Bills' 20. Winner could have sealed almost certain victory by sending in Leahy for a 37-yard field goal.

Leahy had connected on all three of his attempts, two of which were from longer distances. Another three-pointer would have netted a 26-17 cushion, meaning the Bills would face the unlikely prospect of scoring twice in little over five minutes to win.

The correct decision seemed obvious to most of the 58,343 in Shea. Winner should go for the field goal. But there were the Jets' players over on the sideline trying to talk Winner into gambling. And he was listening.

Riggins, a horse of a running back, shredded the generous Buffalo defense all afternoon, gaining 108 yards in 24 thrusts, mostly up the gut. Winner thought about this success on play after play, ignored his no-gain of the previous play and gave Namath the okay to gamble on fourth-and-one. Most onlookers couldn't believe it. The red-hot Leahy wasn't being used with the game in the balance.

There were the Bills, on the ropes with their chins exposed, all set up for Leahy's kayo punch and Winner, anything but that this day, wouldn't allow Leahy to deliver it. Winner was playing Santa Claus and Christmas was coming seven weeks early to the Bills.

So Namath handed the ball to Riggins and the fullback slammed into the middle of the line. Again, he was stopped cold by Edwards, who nearly knocked himself out making the tackle. There was no gain, the Bills took over and Jets' fans were furious. Understandably furious.

"Everybody on the line felt I could make a yard," Riggins later explained. "Hell, I wanted to go for it. If I can't get a yard when I need one . . ." The fullback's voice trailed off.

Stan Jones, the Bills' defensive line coach, couldn't heap enough praise on Edwards. "It was a great effort by Earl," Jones beamed. "It was just unbelievable how he went underneath [guard Randy Rasmussen] and came up to make the tackle. The situation called for a great play and Earl came through."

Winner claimed he was a victim of bad information. "They [his players] told me it was this much," the coach said, holding his hands as far apart as the length of a loaf of bread. He was indicating how far he thought the Jets had to advance for a first down. "I guess it was longer than that," Winner concluded.

Here was the New York Jets' version of "The Longest Yard." That yard and Winner's failure to make the obvious decision gave the Bills a new life.

Four plays later, O.J. made the Jets pay for Winner's mistake.

Ferguson started from his 20 and passed nine yards over the middle to Braxton. With time slipping away, he sneaked on second-and-one and reaped a surprising seven yards. On first down, he fired incomplete toward Seymour. Now it was second-and-10 from the Buffalo 36.

Ferguson dropped back and drilled a short, quick pass over the middle to Simpson, who hardly ever was on the receiving end of aerials in that danger zone. O.J. made the reception at the 50 and juked linebacker Richard Wood, who lunged to come up with two handfuls of air.

The Juice also faked John Ebersole, another linebacker, and darted left. Suddenly he turned on that tremendous speed and was off to the races. O.J. outlegged free safety Delles Howell to the goal line, scoring a spectacular 64-yard touchdown—as a receiver! In all, he eluded four Jets in scoring the tying touchdown. O.J. was mobbed by his ecstatic teammates. Seconds later, he looked on happily as Leypoldt kicked the decisive conversion with 3:46 to play, giving the Bills a 24-23 triumph.

No one would ever lay the "bad hands" rap on O.J. again. He had beaten the Jets by air and land, and the dramatic 64-yard score was the longest touchdown pass reception of his pro career.

"Their linebackers were helping cover our wide receivers," O.J. explained to a swarm of reporters. "I gave 'em an outside move and the middle was wide open. After I caught the pass, I felt somebody right there on me. The field was pretty wide to the left and once I got past No. 20 [Howell], I knew I was in."

O.J. realized his touchdown might not have emerged a game-turner without Winner's losing decision. "I was happy to see them go for the first down," the Juice acknowledged with a broad smile. "That was the game-winning play. I was looking for their field goal unit. The way the Jets were moving the ball, it would have been tough for us to score twice."

The Jets' brass knew it, too. The unfortunate decision plummeted Winner toward the exit ramp as Jets' coach. For Buffalo, it was a fantastic stroke of good fortune. Thanks to the opening Winner provided and O.J.'s ability to convert it, the Bills recovered for a 5-2 record and trailed Miami by only a game in the AFC East.

Further, the Bills' offense was recovered from its mysterious malady. Ferguson, completing 15 of 29 passes for 296 yards and three touchdowns against New York, now had a whopping 14 touchdown aerials in a half-season. And O.J., scoreless the first five games of the previous season and realizing only a trio of TDs all year, now had eight in 1975. He had scored in every game and, ironically, this game in which he was even more than usual the leader was the first all season in which he hadn't managed a rushing TD. But that 64-yard jaunt with a Ferguson pitch was pretty close to one. And yes, it would suffice.

"We went out there with the idea of taking away the outside from O.J.," defensive end Richard Neal said. "We did it, too, kept him bottled up all day except for that long pass play. But that's O.J. He'll beat you if it takes him all day to do it. He's the greatest athlete I've ever seen in my life."

Neal mentioned the Jets were doubling Buffalo's wide receivers. Since Simpson ran outside patterns the few times he went out for passes, the Jets had their outside linebackers watching for him and middle backer John Ebersole looking for Braxton over the middle.

"Yes, Ebersole was watching for Braxton," O.J. affirmed. "I

caught him leaning that way and then looked for J.D. to block for me. He just said, 'Take it yourself, you're on your own,' and that was it. The play was the first over the middle to me in the game and was the same one Braxton runs."

The play was called by Saban, who noticed the Jets were playing minus a true middle linebacker. Starter Steve Reese was injured early in the third quarter and Ebersole, a substitute outside backer, was moved to the middle.

As a result, O.J. not only received a chance to show why he's the best, but got an opportunity to kid about his pass catching. "The guys call me knuckles," he smiled. "People say I can't catch, but I was always a good receiver in college. I've been grounded a few years and complaining about it didn't do me any good, either."

Soon O.J. was posing for a postgame picture with Namath. "We had a local photographer do it—we thought we'd have it done in case we don't play each other again," O.J. explained.

Nearby, Ferguson was still marveling over what O.J. had done with his short toss over the middle. "It's a play set up to make a first down," the soft-spoken quarterback declared. "But whenever you give the Juice room, he can do anything. I never saw him run so fast."

Ferguson was still wide-eyed in admiration. He had thrown for a first down and wound up with a 64-yard winner which signaled a new era—the coming of age of O.J. Simpson as a first-rate receiving threat.

CHAPTER NINETEEN

O.J. vs. Ken Anderson

Just one week later, the Bills learned how it felt to watch a sizable lead vanish as the Baltimore Colts, trailing by 21 points, reeled off five uninterrupted touchdowns to deliver a 42-35 shocker.

The second time O.J. touched the ball, he darted 44 yards for a touchdown. He scored the game's first three TDs, following the quick dash with six-point passes of 22 and 32 yards from Ferguson. And yet that wasn't enough. Colt quarterback Bert Jones riddled the Buffalo defense for 306 aerial yards and ran for 59 more, including a 19-yard go-ahead touchdown.

The Bills had played eight games and their record was 5-3. Some of their supporters felt that, with the proper breaks, they could be 8-0. They had lost to the Giants, clearly an inferior team. They had led Miami for 58 minutes, then threw away the game in the final two, bowing to the Dolphins an 11th straight time. And then they blew a three-touchdown cushion over the Colts—at home.

A pattern was becoming painfully clear to O.J. He realized that, despite some fans' thinking this team could be undefeated, that the defense couldn't hold an opponent. The offense could and did score against anyone, rolling up big numbers each week and threatening several NFL records. But the defense was porous, and when powerhouses meet, it's defense which determines a champion.

The Bills' explosiveness on offense and vulnerability on defense was illustrated dramatically in the ninth game of the season, another Monday night extravaganza on ABC-TV. The Bills were up against the Cincinnati Bengals and Ken Anderson, the AFC's leading career passer, in Cincinnati's Riverfront Stadium.

Saban attempted to inject some semblance of stability into his defense by reverting to the 3-4-4 or "Oklahoma" he employed the last half of the 1974 season. He used three "down" linemen, benching Pat Toomay except for third-down pass situations, and had four linebackers. One of them, Mark Johnson, played on the line of scrimmage, and another, John Skorupan, played just off it.

The revised setup bothered Ken Anderson not at all. The Bengals never punted all night.

Anderson marched the Bengals downfield immediately, a demoralizing 80-yard march consuming 15 plays in 8:36 and rattling off seven first downs. Anderson capped it with a five-yard TD pass to Lenvil Elliott and, after the point was missed, Cincinnati led, 6-0.

O.J. gave quick indication of the individual battle with Anderson about to unfold by darting left and speeding 59 yards to the Bengal 13, falling at the 20, getting up and averting two Bengals to muster seven yards more. But the Bills realized only a 28-yard Leypoldt field goal and trailed, 6-3, after a quarter.

In the second period, O.J. broke loose again, dashing 44 yards before Tommy Casanova, Cincinnati's brilliant safety, corralled him. After four carries, O.J. had an astonishing 113 yards. A Braxton fumble killed the drive, however.

Now it was Anderson's turn. He hit Isaac Curtis for 13 yards and then spotted him all alone for 47, Isaac racing to the Bills' nine. Cornerback Dwight Harrison became flustered and was

O.J. ties his cleated shoes for more action in Cincinnati as frustrated Al Beauchamp, Sherman White and Ken Johnson walk away.
Photo by Robert L. Smith,
Elma, N.Y.

nailed interfering with Curtis on an end zone pattern, and Stan Fritts' one-yard TD gave the Bengals a 13-3 lead.

Then the spotlight fell on O.J.—after Vic Washington raced 42 yards with the kickoff. O.J. hauled in a sideline pass and gained 13. He took a handoff and, trapped, reversed his field brilliantly for 17 tough yards. After a 12-yard pass to Hill, O.J. swept for nine. Ferguson sneaked five, and O.J. fought two yards for his 12th score of the season. He had 152 yards on eight carries and at halftime he had 154 in nine. A fifth 200-yard game seemed certain, and he was on course for professional football's first 300-yard rushing show.

O.J. was to realize neither.

Before halftime, Anderson found Charley Joiner for a 20-yard touchdown pass and a 20-10 cushion. In the second half, Tony Greene's interception and 32-yard return set up O.J.'s 13th touchdown, a one-yard plunge. Now, the Juice had 170 yards in 13 trips and the Bills trailed, 20-17.

The breaks seemed to be turning Buffalo's way. Elliott raced 101 yards with the kickoff, but a clip nullified the score. Dave Green's 37-yard field goal hit the left upright. Soon, however, Anderson hit Chip Myers for 30 and 14 yards, setting up Green's 28-yard field goal. He followed that with an 80-yard, seven-play drive leading to Fritts' one-yard TD and a 30-17 cushion. Buffalo replied with Ferguson's 10-yard TD pass to Hill.

The Bills had committed themselves to a passing attack on that march and, forced to play catchup, O.J.'s rushing yardage became of secondary importance. In fact, it was all but abandoned. After three periods, O.J. had traveled 184 yards. He never reached 200.

Cornerback Dwight Harrison had a golden opportunity to turn around this offensive show, but dropped what seemed a sure interception at the Bengal 30. Anderson then found Boobie Clark for a 27-yard pass play along the sideline and, on third-and-11, hit Myers for 12 yards at the nine. Those plays set up Green's 18-yard field goal with 1:57 left, cementing a 33-24 Bengal victory.

O.J., who for a half seemed destined to soar above 300 yards, finished with 197 on only 17 carries. It was a phenomenal display, to be sure, but tarnished by defeat and capped with a

O.J. hurtles over Reggie McKenzie in duel with Ken Anderson.
Pursuing Bengals are Tom Casanova (37), Ron Carpenter (70) and Ron
Pritchard (60).
Photo by Robert L. Smith,
Elma, N.Y.

huge letdown. O.J. needed but three yards for 200, yet never
carried on the Bills' last six plays. Under the guise of playing
catchup, the Bills all but ignored their most devastating weapon
for virtually the entire fourth quarter.

So outstanding was this Simpson running show that he approached 200 yards despite being on the field for only 25
minutes. He gave the Bills eight yards a minute, but the defense
couldn't get the ball back for him without surrendering points.
Anderson was simply devastating, converting 10 of 15 third-
down plays as Cincinnati controlled the ball—running 84 plays to
Buffalo's 47.

The Bengal quarterback finished with a team-record 447 aerial
yards, completing a fantastic 30 of 46 attempts and netting 22
first downs and two touchdowns. Cincinnati retied Pittsburgh for

the AFC Central lead with 8-1 records and Buffalo dropped to 5-4, virtually out of the playoff picture.

Fans filed out of Riverfront buzzing over the fantastic two-man exhibition they had witnessed. Anderson, passing seven times to Curtis for 139 yards, also hit Myers seven times for, 108, Clark six for 64 and Joiner five for 90. He passed the Bills, whose secondary was riddled by injuries, into the NFL basement as far as aerial defense was concerned. Meanwhile, O.J.'s 197 yards were the most against the Bengals in their eight-year history. O.J. had averaged 11.6 yards per carry.

As awesome as Anderson's 447-yard display was, it failed to topple the NFL record—Norm Van Brocklin's 554-yard show for Los Angeles against the New York Yankees 24 years earlier. But it did hike Buffalo's total for aerial yardage permitted to an embarrassing 2,061 for nine games.

"I've never seen a game when a guy was so precise," declared Chip Myers of Anderson. "He's by far the best quarterback in the game. Every pass he had time to throw was perfect."

The Bills were quite subdued afterward, except for Braxton vowing to get even with Bengal linebacker Al Beauchamp for a postgame spitting incident. O.J., knowing defense was his team's Achilles' heel, waxed philosophical.

"If anything can be salvaged from this season, I would like for it to be a winning record and to be the best team in the league in total offense," he said. "No matter what goes on out there, the offense has made up its mind to be the best at what it does."

O.J. was still ahead of his record 1973 pace, having traveled 1,325 yards with five games to play. But he could sense that, unlike 1973, this season would not finish on the upbeat. Anderson had exposed and exploited the defense's numerous weaknesses and all the other NFL teams were watching via national TV.

The Bills had nearly reached the extremes of offense and defense—leading in scoring, total offense and rushing, last in pass defense and second-last in total defense. And the 3-4-4 defense, called the "30" by Saban, appeared to emulate what "30" means in journalistic circles—the end.

"It was the same old story passing," Saban mourned. "It was

obvious what they were going to do to us. We tried at least five different fronts—overshifting, undershifting and with four men on the line. Our young players in the secondary just aren't ready for all the tactics they saw.''

Indeed, they weren't. Cincinnati finished with a team-record 33 first downs and Anderson, tying his own Bengal record of 30 completions, attempted one less pass than Buffalo's total of offensive plays.

Saban was hot at the officials' apparently errant placing of the ball (once robbing Chandler of four yards), the absence of interference calls when Hill and Gant were thumped on pass routes and inconsistent interpretation of pass possession. "The officiating has been just terrible in five of our games," Saban fumed.

These were upsetting times for the Bills' coach and he was fast becoming involved in a more important dispute. Upon the Bills' return to Buffalo, Saban and Wilson were huddled in closed-door meetings, Saban emerging with a long face. The coach indicated he was not in control of his team's destiny as one with the title "vice-president in charge of football" should be. There were charges of front-office interference, later challenged by Wilson. Saban was particularly discouraged by the draft situation, feeling his powers eroded and seeing a pronounced dip in the quality of draft choices.

It was a decaying situation confronting the Bills, despite tremendous offensive statistics, and there was no end in sight. O.J.'s playoff dream had all but mathematically slipped away.

CHAPTER TWENTY

A Quartet of Touchdowns

By the normal measure used to gauge O.J.'s greatest games, his appearance Nov. 23, 1975, against the New England Patriots at Rich Stadium was sub-par. He averaged only 2.6 yards per carry and finished with just 69 yards in 27 trips, his lowest average and rushing total of the season.

Yet this was truly a special game for the Juice—and for evidence all one needed was a glance at the scoring statistics when the game was done.

This was another scoring fest—neither defense able to mount a semblance of stubbornness until Buffalo's came to life in the waning minutes. It was also an unusual game in that Lou Saban, amidst growing reports he would soon resign, appeared on the field late and unusually dressed—formally—in a blue suit, tie and topcoat.

Saban usually wore a red Bills' windbreaker and, on a chilly afternoon such as this, a stocking cap. He shook hands with two assistant coaches upon entering the field, another unusual happening. At halftime, he changed into the windbreaker and stocking cap, stating he was cold. Later, reports revealed Saban seriously considered resigning before the game, thus the formal attire. And had the Bills bowed for the fifth time in six weeks, he just might have stepped down.

At any rate, there he was in front of the Buffalo bench, and the Bills responded with two touchdowns in the opening 10 minutes as Ferguson found Gant and Hill for touchdown pass plays of 19 and 77 yards.

Yet, Sam "Bam" Cunningham matched those scores on a 10-yard run and 10-yard pass from Steve Grogan. O.J.'s two-yard rip for a touchdown and Leypoldt's 28-yard field goal boosted Buffalo ahead again, but Grogan hit tight end Russ Francis for a 21-yard TD. Then, early in the third quarter, Cunningham's third TD (a one-yarder) gave New England a 28-24 edge. O.J. and Braxton took command.

The Bills' magnificent one-two rushing punch carried eight times in a 12-play march and O.J. scored from three yards late in the third frame. Still, the Bills' defense couldn't hold, and Englishman John Smith tied at 31-31 with a 34-yard field goal.

Now the Bills were really determined to down their "cousins" an eighth straight time. Vic Washington sped 56 yards with the kickoff, and Ferguson followed with a 44-yard pass to Hill. O.J. bounced off a stack for the final yard and the Bills led for good, 38-31. Finally, a 58-yard interception return by veteran Ike Thomas, a newly acquired free safety, set up another Simpson score—a three-yard pitch from Ferguson—and the Bills prevailed, 45-31.

When all was settled, Saban was smiling again and O.J. had realized his only four-touchdown game as a pro. The Juice's scores were from short-distance—two, three, one and three yards—but there were four of them and now he owned a resounding 17 for the season. He needed just six in the remaining four games to set an NFL record for most touchdowns in a single season.

The Bills' offense—again—was next to unstoppable. Not only did O.J. have four touchdowns, but Ferguson had four touchdown passes, two to the Juice. Ferguson's four tied a Bills' record and extended his total of scoring passes for the season to 22, another club mark.

As for O.J., while a stunting Patriot defense held him to 69 yards, four receptions upped his season total to 15, a third of which went for touchdowns. The aerial success was particularly pleasing to O.J., who remembered the "knuckles" tag out loud again.

"My teammates started calling me Knuckles late last year because I never was a big part of our passing attack," O.J. smiled. "But there's more to it than that. It was so cold during some of our practices last year and my fingers often were stiff, so I would try to catch the practice passes with my palms. You know you can't catch too many of them that way."

The Bills' version of the Six Million Dollar Man broke into a broad grin. "I'm more into our passing attack this year and now I don't think I'll be hearing them call me Knuckles anymore."

Someone told Ferguson that O.J.'s 17 touchdowns enabled him to break the Bills' single-season record of 15, established in 1962 by Cookie Gilchrist. Immediately, Ferguson turned to O.J.'s receiving abilities as the difference in 1975 and he, too, mentioned the nickname Knuckles.

"Juice is now a very important part of our passing offense," Ferguson said. "There's no question about that. I guess we should have used him more in the past. If we call him Knuckles now, he can throw it right back into our faces with statistics."

Ferguson and his teammates recalled how the Patriot linebackers blitzed on nearly every play, often stopping thrusts as they just got under way. But they couldn't halt Ferguson, who completed half of 32 passes for 263 yards and the four TDs. Their keying on O.J. left them vulnerable to the pass.

"Their defense was designed to fill gaps and they did a good job of it," commented Reggie McKenzie. "We changed up a little, going man-to-man drive blocking on every play."

The Bills also went to Braxton, who responded with 84 yards in 13 carries. All but one carry and four yards came in the second half.

"It was hard to get our blocking keys the way they were

moving around," declared O.J. "But then I haven't run well against New England in the last three games. Our offense can do many things, though, and we made some adjustments and gained some yards today."

O.J. also talked of the Wilson-Saban friction, but was not at ease doing so. "I consider Ralph a friend of mine and you know how I love coach Saban," he said. "A little communication was all that was needed. Lou told us he wouldn't let us down, that he would give us everything he had, and I don't think he would leave us now.

"Lou has meant a lot to me," the Juice went on, deep in thought as he spoke. "He understands me more than any coach I ever played for. He's done a lot for my career, and I respect him. I never believed for a minute that he would leave us."

Nearby, Saban was fielding questions about his reported exit had the Bills lost—and he was defending them well. His team's defense should have operated so well, observers opined. Saban glanced at the statistics sheet, saw Grogan's 25 completions of 46 passes for 360 yards and shook his head. He glanced at New England's total yardage of 498 (compared to Buffalo's 416) and shook it again.

"I looked up, saw we had 45 points and still wasn't sure we would win," Saban smiled. "The defense is still struggling and it's a trying time for them."

Saban realized that his defense was nowhere near adequate to defeat the better teams. And his players realized it, too. "I knew we didn't have enough defensive talent to go all the way when we were 4-0," outspoken defensive end Pat Toomay declared. "I knew there were problems when the trade deadline went and no help came."

Saban had wanted former All-Pro middle linebacker Mike Curtis from Baltimore and looked longingly toward Ted Hendricks before Oakland acquired the high-priced, classy backer. The Bills wound up not making a positive defensive move after the acquisition of Toomay in summer and the void would prove fatal to the team's quest for a return to the playoffs.

This victory over New England provided a temporary lift as Miami lost quarterback Bob Griese for the season and bowed to the Colts, 33-17. The Bills (6-4) trailed Miami by only a game in the AFC East title race, but they wouldn't be that close for long. And defense, or the lack of it, was the reason.

CHAPTER TWENTY-ONE

O.J. the Record Scorer

O.J.'s bid to better his record 2,003-yard season of 1973 fell by the wayside the following two weeks, and after a 32-14 victory in St. Louis on Thanksgiving Day, so did the Bills' playoff aspirations.

The Bills followed Jim Braxton's greatest day as a pro, 160 rushing yards and three touchdowns against the Cardinals, with a controversial 31-21 defeat in Miami and the 7-5 won-lost record left them back in the familiar pre-1974 position of being on the outside of the playoffs looking in.

And yet a case could be made for including all three last games of the 1975 season among O.J.'s most memorable appearances.

In the Orange Bowl, O.J. rallied the Bills from a 21-0 halftime deficit with a 14-yard touchdown jaunt. After Ferguson fired a 31-yard scoring pass to J.D. Hill, O.J. was on the receiving end of a gorgeous 62-yard pass-run play from the Arkansas rifle and the Bills trailed by only 24-21 with 10 minutes to play.

But on the following series, head linesman Jerry Bergman made a double interpretation rabid Bills' fans will never forget. Linebacker Doug Allen smashed Miami's Mercury Morris, divorcing the flashy runner from the ball at the Dolphin 28. John Skorupan, another Bills' linebacker, dived upon the apparent fumble for what seemed Buffalo's big break. Instead, Bergman ruled there was no fumble, that Morris hit the turf before the ball popped loose. And further, he ruled Pat Toomay elbowed him (Bergman) intentionally. Instead of third-down and seven, that "personal foul" interpretation gave Miami a first down. The Bills were furious, especially Saban. Several had to be restrained along the Buffalo sideline. And on the field, the Bills' concentration was lost.

On the very next play, Don Nottingham rolled 56 yards to the Bills' one, setting up Norm Bulaich's killer touchdown on the ensuing play. The Dolphins won, 31-21, and the Bills went wild verbally. Wilson vowed never to allow the Bills on the same field with Bergman, prompting a $5,000 fine from Commissioner Pete Rozelle.

And O.J. was disconsolate. "This is the biggest series of the season and the officials decided it," he complained. Wasted was O.J.'s 14-yard TD in which he bounced off linebacker Bob Matheson. Wasted was his brilliant 50-yard touchdown dash after taking a 12-yard pitch from Ferguson and shaking off a forearm smash from safety Charlie Babb. Momentum after that sensational score had clearly belonged to the Bills and a playoff berth was still possible, but the officiating decision turned all that around.

Still, it was and remains a memorable game for O.J. He amassed 213 yards that afternoon, 117 through the air off eight receptions and 96 by land via 18 carries. Yes, there were 213 yards and two touchdowns, but the end result was disappointment.

The season's semifinal Sunday brought a memorable game, as well. O.J. broke loose against his New England cousins for 185 yards in 21 carries, he scored his 21st touchdown of the year on a 63-yard burst and the Bill's 26 first downs gave them 298 for the season, an NFL record. Further, the 34-14 victory in Foxboro, Mass., assured the Bills of a third consecutive winning season.

O.J., upping his season rushing total to 1,760 yards, could

easily have realized a record fifth 200-yard game and perhaps would have exceeded his record 250-yard effort against the Pats at Foxboro two years earlier. However, he was removed with more than nine minutes remaining.

"We went into the game hoping to get 200 yards for O.J.," Saban remarked. "I talked to him early in the fourth quarter when he needed 15 more yards, but I didn't want to risk an injury at that time. The score was 34-7 and we were in control. I said it was up to him whether to stay in and he told me to do what I felt was best."

So out came the Juice, and for the second time in 1975 (the Cincinnati game being the other), a seemingly certain 200-yard show never came off. In Cincinnati, he just wasn't handed the ball as the Bills played catchup by air. In Foxboro, he simply sat down and watched most of the fourth quarter. As things materialized, O.J. and Braxton both surpassed 100 yards (Braxton gaining 101 yards in 23 trips) and the Bills amassed 349 yards and 19 first downs by land while conquering the Patriots for the ninth straight time. This marked the fourth time in three years the Bills featured two runners over the century mark (100 yards) in one contest.

"I said to Braxton as we were waiting around the locker room before the game playing music, what a strange feeling it was to be going into a game that doesn't mean anything," O.J. said. "I told him we should just go out and have some fun. I was loose."

The Juice was loose, indeed. He overcame two early fumbles to wind up eclipsing the 8,000-yard plateau for seven NFL campaigns. He reached 32 games of 100-yards or better, matching his uniform number. He had 1,760 yards and 21 TDs in 317 carries and could have owned so much more were it not for being yanked early in two early games and this one.

More importantly, O.J. was one touchdown shy of the NFL single-season record established by Chicago Bears' great Gale Sayers a decade earlier (1965) in his rookie season. That quest is what made O.J.'s final game of 1975 extra-meaningful, even though the game meant nothing in the standings and despite O.J.'s meager 57 yards in 12 carries.

This final game came against the NFC Central champion

Minnesota Vikings. The 54,993 hardy souls who turned out at snow-capped Rich Stadium on a frigid Dec. 20 afternoon saw not only O.J. but the Vikings' Chuck Foreman battle for Sayers' record, and they also witnessed Viking quarterback Fran Tarkenton erase John Unitas' NFL record for career touchdown passes.

It wasn't much of a game, Minnesota romping, 35-13. Practically all the attention focused on O.J., Foreman and Tarkenton as the shivering fans unleashed a torrent of icy snowballs at the players.

Tarkenton, picking apart the Bills' 3-4-4 defense with frequent passes to his backs, broke Unitas' record with pitches of one and six yards to Foreman, closing the Viking point parade. Tarkenton dodged snowballs more often than pass rushers and raised his 15-year career touchdown pass total to 291, one more than Unitas compiled from 1956 to 1972. Tarkenton already had erased Unitas' pro records for pass attempts and completions and sailed merrily along by hitting on 25 of 36 for 216 yards before Bob Lee replaced him with 35 seconds left in the third quarter and Minnesota in command, 35-7.

Foreman rolled up four touchdowns—a four-yard burst and one-yard plunge in addition to his pair of receiving scores—and would have had five but for a fumble near the goal line, recovered for a Viking touchdown by wide receiver Jim Lash.

The quartet of touchdowns gave Foreman 22 for the season, tying Sayers' mark along with O.J., who darted 24 yards on a second-quarter quick opener for his 22nd score. The goal-line fumble and a snowball from the stands, forcing him out early with blurred vision, prevented Foreman from breaking Sayers' mark and opened the door for O.J.

After Foreman's fourth TD enabled him to catch O.J. at 22 seasonal scores, O.J. lost no time replying in record style. On the first play after the kickoff, backup quarterback Gary Marangi spotted O.J. all alone along the left sideline and fed him a perfect pass.

"It was a play similar to a touchdown Jim Braxton scored against Denver [in the season's third game]," Marangi commented. "Juice said he was open the whole game over there. Sure enough, he was. They [the Vikings] read the quarterback's

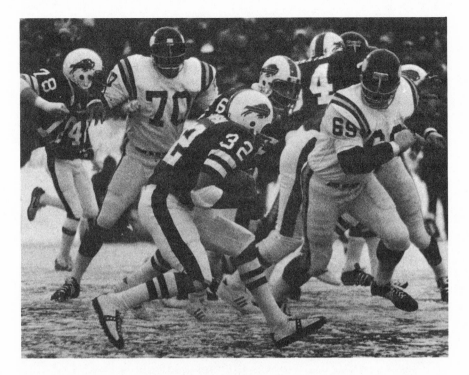

O.J. breaks loose in snowy 1975 finale with Minnesota. Bills' Dave Foley (78) and Vikings' Jim Marshall (70) and Doug Sutherland (69) watch the Juice on record scoring day.
Photo by Robert L. Smith,
Elma, N.Y.

eyes so much. J.D. ran to the strongside post and I looked that way first. Then I turned my body and Juice was alone."

O.J. snared Marangi's pass at the Viking 40 and had two men to beat. He took care of both, safety Paul Krause and cornerback Joe Blahak, with one deft hesitation at the 20. Then he sped into the end zone to break Sayers' record with 47 seconds left in the third quarter. O.J.'s 62-yard pass-run play from Marangi had produced a 23rd touchdown and, on a day in which he scored both Buffalo touchdowns, he tied Leypoldt for the Bills' career scoring mark with 366 points. O.J. also eclipsed club records with 16 rushing TDs and 138 points.

And, because mainly of O.J., the Bills established an NFL record for most first downs in one season, 318. No team had ever eclipsed 300 before. The 57 touchdowns were the fourth highest total in league history, among a host of new club records. Others included the 5,467 total yards, 162 rushing first downs, 28 aerial TDs (25 by Ferguson), 51 PAT and a resounding 420 points.

The last figure astounded O.J. most of all. Here the Bills had mustered an incredible 420 points in 14 games—30 points a game—and did no better than an 8-6 record. They boasted the finest offensive team in football, broke an all-time record for first downs and were out of playoff contention two weeks before the season ended.

After the final game, O.J. talked not about the touchdown record, but about whether he would return for another season—a subject which would create national controversy a half-year later. Yet this day most of the postgame noise was generated by the Vikings, who cleared their bench toward the dressing room early because of the snowball barrage from the stands. They were particularly upset over Foreman's eye injury, feeling the icy missile which cut him, forcing blurred vision, might prevent him from opposing Dallas in the playoffs a week later. It didn't.

"That snowball barrage was the most ridiculous thing I've seen in 19 years of football," fumed Tarkenton. "The people of Buffalo ought not to be very proud of what happened here today."

Tarkenton said he saw fathers making snowballs for their children and encouraging them to throw at the players. He even claimed one of his 11 incompletions actually was deflected by a snowball. And on another attempt, he said he was belted with a snowball, causing a third-down pass to go awry. "Some guy hit me with a snowball just before I threw," Tarkenton said. "Whoever he is, he's got the damndest arm I ever did see. I thought it was a defensive end's hand hitting me in the head."

Just as O.J. spoke hardly at all about his touchdown mark, Tarkenton soft-pedaled his career touchdown pass mark. "I was really more concerned with Chuck breaking Sayers' record," Francis said. "Not many realized how close Chuck was to that mark, and it was an interesting highlight to me to watch O.J. and Chuck battle it out in the second half. I'm glad my record is done and behind me. Now I won't have to live the whole offseason answering questions about whether I'll break it. I'm proud of it, but we have other things to do."

O.J. only wished he could say that.

Off in another corner of the Viking room, usually placid (stonefaced, many NFL observers call him) coach Bud Grant was very loquacious about the snow barrage. "All of us got hit in the head," he said. "I got it four or five times in the face and about 100 times in the back. I told our players to keep their hoods up, heads down and not to turn around. There were no police—no one was there to stop it. That's why our bench left early."

Over in the quiet Bills' quarters, O.J. was talking about his future.

"I'm planning on playing next year—I'm really going to try and work it out," he said sincerely. "If a good acting opportunity comes up, I'll have to grab it, but I have reason to believe I can work both careers together again next year."

The Juice indicated he wanted more money—more than any other NFL player, more than Joe Namath's $450,000 annual salary. "If you feel you are the top player, naturally you want to be paid the top salary," O.J. reasoned. That was another storm warning in the increasingly turbulent Bills' world.

O.J., actively campaigning for a major role in the movie "Ragtime," pointed out that football soon would beccme his past occupation. His future was clearly in celluloid, he said. "Acting is what I want to do. It's where my future is, but I also want to play some more football," O.J. said. "I won't place any odds on it, but I think I'll be back next year."

And so, off O.J. flew toward his Los Angeles home. He had eclipsed yet another NFL milestone, the touchdown record with 23. He had averaged 5.52 yards per carry, best in the league. He had recaptured the NFL rushing crown with 1,817 yards in 329 carries. The title was his third in four years, and the 1,817 yards were the third best aggregate in NFL history—behind his own 2,003 of 1973 and Jim Brown's 1,863 in 1963.

O.J. had won the NFL scoring title with 138 points and he had realized what most experts considered his finest game, the 227-yard show in Pittsburgh. O.J. had even enjoyed a banner season as a pass receiver, gaining 426 yards and seven TDs (including the record breaker) off 28 catches. His combined yardage, rushing and receiving, was 2,243—higher than the 2,073 of his most celebrated season, 1973.

Yet the big question was unanswered and would remain so longer than anyone dreamed the day frozen snowballs applied an icy finish to a once-promising Bills' season. Would O.J. return? Even he wouldn't wager.

CHAPTER TWENTY-TWO

Booed in Buffalo

The Super Bowl hadn't even started when turbulence began swirling about O.J. in 1976. Two seasons remained on his contract with the Bills, but he wasn't satisfied. He was clearly out to renegotiate.

"I plan to talk to Mr. Wilson next week," O.J. declared as the Steelers and Cowboys were preparing in Miami for the NFL championship. "I have to talk to him about my security. We always have had a very good relationship. I would like to play another year or two of football, but I want to quit on top. I also want to get paid what I'm worth.

"Joe Namath has set the standard in football from the time he signed that first $400,000 bonus contract," O.J. went on. "He makes $450,000 a year and that's six figures more than I make. I tell myself, 'Joe can't be that much better a football player or that much bigger a gate attraction than I am.' So this is a big factor when I sit down with Mr. Wilson."

It wasn't the money which motivated O.J.'s quest. It was pride. Intense pride. As football's best running back, he felt he should be paid not $300,000 annually but at least what Namath was receiving and preferably more. Money was hardly a problem, however.

He enjoyed a lucrative contract with ABC-TV. He was doing high-profit commercials for Hertz, Hyde SpotBilt shoes and others. He had a Hollywood agent who landed him movie parts in the best company of screen stars. "I love acting," O.J. declared. "I have made four movies and have two others in the works. I am really interested in playing the part of Coalhouse Walker in E.L. Doctorow's *Ragtime*. It is the one picture for which I would give up my football career."

Well, the *Ragtime* part wasn't offered and the tête-à-tête with the Bills' owner never came off. O.J. went on to Rome, where he played (of all things) a priest in the movie *The Cassandra Crossing*, with Sophia Loren and Ava Gardner.

Even from Rome, he applied the pressure for a better contract. "I'm getting old," O.J. said. "I realize I don't have many more years for football. When I retire, I want to say I was the best and was paid the best."

Here was O.J., only 28, telling people he was getting old. Yet, as running backs go, he was correct. And this was a running back who had rushed 8,123 yards in seven seasons and set the league single-season record with 2,003 in 1973. He was 475 yards from second place among NFL all-time rushers.

However, a thespian career was quickly consuming as many of his thoughts as football. "I remember as a boy growing up in the San Francisco Bay area and sitting in Kezar Stadium dreaming of being a great football player," O.J. said. "I hope I can do the same thing in acting."

Wilson declared himself unwilling to meet any O.J. price tag approaching a half-million dollars per season. And so, an uneasy aura prevailed right into June, with O.J. returning to Buffalo to be best man at Reggie McKenzie's wedding and declaring retirement from football was a "possibility."

Then on June 12, the bombshell dropped. Mel Durslag, sports columnist for the Los Angeles *Herald-Examiner* and a close friend of Wilson, broke the story. O.J. told Wilson he would never again play for the Bills and asked to be traded to a West Coast team, preferably the Rams. If a trade could not be worked out, O.J. said he would retire from football.

O.J. cited as his reason not monetary dissatisfaction, but family unity. "This is something I have to do to keep my family together," he said. "I just can't bear to be away from home for six months at a time anymore."

O.J.'s wife, Marguerite, had not been with him in Buffalo the previous season. She didn't relish living there, even for a half-year, and stayed with their two children in Los Angeles. Divorce rumors ensued, but they were groundless. Still, O.J. was unhappy over the long separation from his family. He also felt the Bills' management was not making the moves to field a title team.

Wilson stated he would try to accommodate O.J.'s trade request, but with one stipulation. "I promised to trade him to a West Coast club, but only if I received fair value," Wilson said. "I made it absolutely clear that I would not let someone take advantage of a distress situation and try to steal him. I told O.J. he could just retire quietly from football. I said I was not going to be anyone's pigeon. We agreed to those terms."

In subsequent weeks, O.J. learned how stubborn Ralph Wilson can be. Three West Coast teams—Oakland, San Francisco and San Diego—were hardly in the picture, although the Raiders were mentioned often. The Rams drew most of the attention, and practically a third of the LA roster was mentioned in connection with a possible O.J. trade at varying times and in varying combinations.

The most persistent report had running back Lawrence Mc-Cutcheon, middle linebacker Jack Reynolds and defensive tackle Mike Fanning Buffalo-bound for the Juice. Wilson reportedly insisted on the Rams' star defensive end, Jack Youngblood, and Rams' owner Carroll Rosenbloom labeled him an "untouchable."

So, nothing happened. O.J. became increasingly uneasy, and while the Bills went to training camp, he went to Montreal to describe the Olympics for ABC-TV. Howard Cosell interviewed him one night and O.J. said he couldn't understand the lack of progress. Many, including Wilson, got the impression O.J. was trying to negotiate his own trade on national television, and the Bills' boss absolutely boiled over the interview's content.

Other names entered the picture, but no trade came off. Rosenbloom suggested Wilson wasn't serious and declared the talks dead. "It was Wilson who stopped the trade," Rosenbloom said. Wilson countered by saying he would have okayed the trade if the Rams had offered either of two defensive line starters, Youngblood or Larry Brooks. He said LA's final offer was Mc-Cutcheon, Fanning and draft choices. The Rams even offered their entire 1977 draft for Simpson, and Wilson quickly rejected that.

"I just couldn't trade a player of O.J.'s great quality for Fanning," Wilson said. "In effect, that's what the deal would have been. I'm not downgrading Fanning, but I couldn't trade O.J. for him. And I couldn't tell our players I got draft choices for O.J. Simpson, either."

(Ironically, two years later, that's all the Bills would get for O.J.—five draft choices from the San Francisco 49ers.)

Wilson charged that Rosenbloom "never came up with a definite deal." He wondered how serious the Rams were. "They tried to steal O.J., that's all," he asserted. He said Youngblood and Brooks were mentioned, but neither was offered outright. "What they'd do is dangle a player like a puppet on a string and when you'd reach out, they'd pull up the puppet," Wilson quipped.

And so the trade deadline passed without a deal. Back in Buffalo, Saban was preparing to build his running attack around Jim Braxton, with a couple of rookies bidding for O.J.'s old slot. Saban went the entire preseason with this plan and was assuming O.J. was gone from the Bills.

Inside, Saban also was most distressed that he was being kept out of trade negotiations for O.J. The "control of the team's destiny" issue still was festering. Suddenly, a few days before the season opener, Saban was informed following practice that Wilson had flown to Los Angeles to meet with O.J. Saban was furious. Now he wasn't even being kept informed by Wilson, he thought. "Why didn't he tell me he was going to do this?" Saban exploded to a Bills' aide.

Wilson had called O.J. and told him he wanted to fly in and discuss his football future. "It's not a good idea," O.J. told him. "Don't bother." They said goodbye. But the ever-persistent Wilson called O.J. later in the afternoon and told him the number of his flight. And out he flew, meeting two hours with his superstar

After trade request, O.J. rejoins his teammates for 1976 opener. Gary Marangi (jacket), Joe Ferguson (12), Joe DeLamielleure (68) and Reggie McKenzie (67) take the field.
Photo by Robert L. Smith,
Elma, N.Y.

and two hours with O.J.'s wife, Marquerite. Wilson made O.J. an offer he couldn't refuse, but Marquerite wasn't so sure.

"She was the tougher one to deal with," Wilson later related. "When I left them, I'd say I was losing 28-0 late in the fourth quarter. I didn't see any chance of winning."

But the next morning, O.J. called and they met for breakfast. "I thought it was his way of letting me down easy," Wilson said. "But he told me he agreed to come back to Buffalo and we ironed out the contract. He changed his mind overnight. Marquerite knew how bad he wanted to play."

The contract called for approximately $2.2 million spanning three seasons—making O.J. easily the best paid player in professional football. Yes, it was an offer he couldn't refuse.

"Considering all our conversations and looking over what Ralph had in mind and what we want to secure for the future of the family, Marquerite and I decided it would be best for us if I went back to football," O.J. explained. "I never wanted to leave the game, and I felt bad about not being able to play with the fellows."

It was clear O.J. returned to Buffalo for one reason—money. It was as impressionist Rich Little kidded him after they flew in on the same plane: "O.J., your greatness is equaled only by your lack of taste. Once again you succumbed to the almighty buck."

No one laughed louder than O.J. at Little's crack.

"I was very close to retiring," O.J. declared. "I can be very stubborn, but the Bills made me an offer I couldn't pass up. There was just too much security."

O.J. also knew that his endorsement agreements—lucrative arrangements with Tree-Sweet orange juice, Hyde SpotBilt Shoes and Hertz among others—wouldn't be attractive to the companies unless he played football. Hertz, for example, paid him $150,000 to do four commercials which, as a Hertz spokesman put it, "combine the speed of O.J. with the speed of Hertz service."

And so O.J. returned to Buffalo on the eve of the season-opening game with Miami on Monday night television. He was not accorded a hero's welcome. To the contrary, the initial reaction was coolness, especially from Braxton, who was to be the offense's main cog, but suddenly was O.J.'s blocking back again.

Braxton and his teammates had sweated through the long, hot summer with six exhibition games while O.J. said, in effect, "Trade me or else." Yet there was something deeper bothering Braxton and other veterans. While O.J.'s absence was rewarded with a record contract, their presence drew only token recognition. And their renegotiation requests were rejected.

Braxton confronted Wilson near midfield on the evening of the "dress rehearsal" practice, O.J.'s first with the team. The fullback asked Wilson to renegotiate and the owner refused. Braxton responded by threatening not to play the following evening. It took considerable talking by Saban and others to convince him otherwise.

Saban recognized the unmistakable signs of deterioration, however. There was no getting around it: O.J.'s return had touched off bitterness within the squad, bitterness not so much at O.J. as with the way Bills' management handled the situation, affording the Juice special treatment. Jealousies were inevitable

The camera focuses on the Juice after he returned to Bills for reported
$2.5 million.
Photo by Robert L. Smith,
Elma, N.Y.

and so was disgust. It was bound to affect the team's performance and Saban knew it.

Without question, his squad was distracted from the opener by
all the commotion surrounding O.J.'s return. All his careful
preparation was going down the drain. Only a day earlier, Saban
had remarked: "Never have I had a better training camp. Never
has one of my teams worked harder than this one. We are as
ready as any team could be."

Now all that was a shambles. Saban insisted he would not start
O.J. even as Wilson and Pat McGroder, a club vice-president,
tried to persuade him in a closed-door meeting after the final
practice. And he stayed with that stand, although he knew he
would have to play O.J., who was not in shape for the season.

Further, Saban was boiling about being left out in the cold for
one of the most crucial decisions in Bills' history. A proud coach,
he was reduced to asking reporters after practices, "Well, what
do you hear?" when the Simpson trade talks were brewing. It
hurt him to be excluded when he was convinced he could make a
deal for O.J. which would greatly help the Bills, especially on
defense.

Suddenly, in the span of 48 hours, Saban's team had declined
from a spirited, young outfit bent on proving itself to a confused,
sullen and even rebellious group.

Sherman White, a veteran defensive end acquired from Cincinnati, talked openly about the transformation. "I hate all this
controversy beginning a season," he said. "Too many players are
thinking about money instead of playing tomorrow night."

Asked if O.J. being wooed while others' financial requests were
rejected had the players upset, White nodded. "Some feel that
way," he said. "I felt enthusiastic when I heard O.J. was coming
back. It gave me a big lift, but some guys are pretty down
because someone turned against them. I can see the problem in
some guys' eyes. But then O.J. is not the average player. O.J. is a
box-office attraction. The owner stood to lose $4 million [in
unsold tickets] and I can understand him giving O.J. $1 to 2
million, or whatever he got."

White's point was well made. For the past three seasons, the
Bills had led the NFL in attendance and they grossed over $10

million in 1975. But in 1976, with Simpson saying he'd never
return, season sales lagged by 10,000, and five days before the
Miami opener, there were 26,000 unsold tickets. Now, with O.J.
back, there were just over 2,000 unpeddled.

O.J., feeling he was in shape to play, said he was eager. "The
reality of the matter is I know I can play, but for how long I
don't know," he said. "I hope to get in. I felt good running a
couple of plays in practice."

O.J. virtually committed himself to the Bills for the rest of his
career. "All along, the people and my teammates have supported
me and I plan to play in Buffalo two or three more years," he
said. "Right now, I feel if I leave here, it's going to be strictly to
retire and not to play for any other team. I'll never ask to be
traded again."

On opening night, O.J. soon learned the Bills' fans were no
longer with him, as he indicated. When he was introduced, most
in the crowd of 77,683 responded with loud boos. The fans in
this largely blue-collar town jeered O.J. and cheered Braxton as
never before. They felt rejected, betrayed by O.J., and the
working men related to Braxton, who had labored all preseason
and stood up to Wilson the night before.

Then, on only the second play after kickoff, Braxton took a
handoff, thundered into the Miami line and tore right knee
ligaments. Just like that, he was lost for the season. Only one
night earlier, he had threatened not to play, but relented and
wound up injured on the season's initial series. The Bills' already
low morale was crushed.

"Bubby [Braxton] is the best blocking fullback I've ever seen,"
O.J. lamented. "Now we'll have to adjust our offense, using less
power plays and more swing passes, trap plays and counters."

But the damage was done. The Bills were stunned. Three
penalties against defensive tackle Jeff Yeates set up speedy Benny
Malone's five-yard touchdown sweep which enabled Miami to
break on top, 7-0. Ferguson countered with a strange TD pass,
aiming for tight end Paul Seymour. The big receiver reached in
vain for the ball, but behind him John Holland had a step on
cornerback Jeris White. Holland hauled in the pass at the 30 and
raced to a 53-yard score. Don Nottingham's yard burst pushed

Miami ahead again, 14-7, but once more Ferguson found Holland. This time, the connection clicked for a 58-yard score, tying at 14-14, and the young Holland added insult by taunting Jeris White. He waved the ball in the defender's face as he crossed the goal-line, then threw the ball at White's feet.

O.J. was disgusted at his teammate's move, recognizing yet another problem. "I know it's only my first week back with the team and I shouldn't say too much, but that crap can come back to hurt you," he said. The action was an affront to the Dolphins, but also to the classy style O.J. and his teammates had cultivated through the good years. This was a team which picked up hopeful tacklers after they had been whipped. This was a team which didn't spike the ball. Suddenly, Holland was showboating and he was told never to do it again.

The affront to White seemed to stir the Dolphins. Garo Yepremian kicked a 25-yard field goal for a 17-14 halftime edge. Bob Griese fired a 30-yard TD pass to Nat Moore, who stole the ball from rookie cornerback Mario Clark in the end zone. Then another Yepremian three-pointer made it a 27-14 game.

Ferguson rallied the Bills within 27-21 with his third scoring toss, a 12-yarder to Chandler with better than 10 minutes to play. But Yepremian booted his third field goal, a 30-yarder with 5:07 left, and the Dolphins were in command, 30-21.

That was the final score, but only after O.J.'s best play was wasted. Saban avoided overusing him, and he ran just five times for 28 yards. The boos were ringing, but in the final quarter O.J. caught a short pass over the middle and flashed those familiar moves, darting 43 yards to the Miami 11. Suddenly, the home folks were cheering O.J. again.

"Those boos just went in one ear and out the other," O.J. later confided. "People are fickle, but they have a right to be. I was fickle when I tried to get traded, so how could I blame them? It was up to me to win them back."

O.J. tried, but three incomplete passes followed and Leypoldt missed a 27-yard field goal, which could have left the Bills within striking distance. Actually, field goals were the difference in this game with a nine-point margin. Yepremian converted all three of his attempts and Leypoldt came up empty on his three, sealing his fate. Saban soon overreacted, placing the usually steady kicker on waivers.

Saban was disconsolate after the defeat, sounding as if he were about to resign during a radio interview. "This has been the worst week I've ever spent," the coach admitted. "After all that's happened, I have to wonder if it's all worth it."

Deterioration continued. Classy receivers Ahmad Rashad and J.D. Hill were already gone, Rashad being allowed to play out his option in a development that infuriated Saban. Hill refused to report to camp and was traded to Detroit. Pat Toomay had been left available to Tampa in the expansion draft, a move Bills' fans couldn't understand. Earl Edwards, a controversial defensive line leader, was peddled to Cleveland. Braxton was hurt. And now Leypoldt was on waivers.

They were breaking up that old gang of O.J.'s and the roller-coaster ride downhill had commenced. The Bills were big losers again. O.J. had his money, but was clearly unready for the season. The defense was a shambles, Miami's 48 carries for 204 yards setting the tone for the entire Bicentennial season. Norm Bulaich enjoyed his first 100-yard game in five years. Thanks to the absence of a trade, the defense was not rebuilt and the quality of the line was not major league material.

Miami, the opponent Saban had pointed toward all summer, left Buffalo with its 13th straight conquest of the Bills. Saban's players were distracted, demoralized, he felt left on the outside of off-field action, and his fullback was out for the season. The superstar he thought was gone had returned, but the turbulence had torn his team asunder. And O.J. was weeks from being ready. Saban knew the Bills were in deep trouble.

CHAPTER TWENTY-THREE

Banned near Boston

For the first three weeks of the 1976 season, O.J. underwent what is supposed to be done during the exhibition campaign—training. Signs such as one which greeted him for the opener—"Miami Needs the Oranges but Buffalo Don't Need the Juice"—disappeared. But O.J. was far from peak form.

"I should have been able to get away from that last guy," O.J. said on several occasions. "But I was tired. I didn't have the overdrive."

With an under-par Simpson and sundry other problems, the Bills were dragging. Houston followed Miami into Rich Stadium, and with O.J. managing only 38 yards off 16 carries, the Oilers became the first team in two years to hold Buffalo without a touchdown, winning 13-3.

The Bills were 0-2 and the following week nearly lost to fledgling Tampa Bay, which never did win a game in 1976. If quarterback Steve Spurrier had been able to capitalize with a touchdown on just one of many glowing chances, the Bills would have been 0-3 and embarrassed by the Buccaneers. Instead, Ferguson fired a pair of touchdown aerials and the Bills escaped with a 14-9 triumph. "We won—beyond that I have nothing to say," a disgusted Saban quipped.

O.J. managed only 39 yards off 20 carries and nearly fumbled away the game in the waning minutes, the Bills holding after he lost possession at the Buffalo 26. The Bills showed only 109 yards rushing, often a sub-par afternoon for O.J. alone. And these were the lowly Buccaneers doing this to a once-vaunted rushing attack.

The following week, Kansas City riddled the Bills' defense for 502 yards, but turned the ball over six times. The Bills capitalized for a touchdown on each occasion and, despite being outgained, walloped the Chiefs, 50-17. O.J. scored the last two touchdowns, and after managing just 105 rushing yards in the first three games combined, totaled 130 in 24 carries against KC.

The Bills reached a 2-2 record with that rout of the Chiefs, but Saban and his players still weren't optimistic. They realized the defense was virtually composed of jelly. And the offense, despite that 50-point explosion, still wasn't operating smoothly. KC gifts had led to the high aggregate.

Soon disaster developed. Pat Leahy's 38-yard field goal enabled the lowly New York Jets to topple the Bills, 17-14, in Shea Stadium and, five days later, Saban stepped down as the Bills' head coach.

The friction with Wilson and the turbulent inner-squad situation since O.J.'s return had taken their toll. And how ironic it was that O.J., however innocently, should have a hand in Saban's departure. They respect each other greatly. It was Saban who was responsible for turning O.J.'s career around and it was Simpson who was the catalyst of the Bills' success under Saban. Yet O.J. had wanted to be traded and Saban, knowing that, preferred him traded for needed defensive help. But he was left on the outside of negotiations which were never consummated, and O.J.'s return wound up disrupting the team.

"I've been thinking about this decision for a long time," the 55-year-old coach declared. "The team's performance last Sunday was a big factor. There was too much talk about our problems and I wanted to put it to rest. I felt I had carried this club as far as I could. A change was necessary in the best interest of the ball club and organization. It's a decision I and no one else made. I'm history now and that's the way I want to let it be."

Saban's decision wasn't totally unexpected, and O.J. tried to carry on as usual, but became caught up in the emotion of the moment. "We're in the middle of the season and it's tough," he said. "Lou came here when we were just a rag-tag team and he salvaged my career. We've had some super times, done a lot of things and gone a long way. I didn't think this would happen until the season was over. But I guess Lou reached a point, as I will with my career, where the end has to come sometime. Maybe we can get a new start now."

That new start never had a chance.

Jim Ringo, the eight-time All-Pro center and a star of the great Green Bay era, was appointed Saban's successor and the sixth head coach in the Bills' 17-year history. The Bills never won a game under his direction in 1976.

The Baltimore Colts spoiled his debut, 31-13, and the following week, the Bills not only lost a game to New England, 26-22, but Joe Ferguson for the rest of the season. The quarterback, scrambling loose, was seemingly the victim of a late hit and suffered four fractured transverse processes in his lower back.

So now the Bills were minus their fullback, quarterback and coach. What else could happen? They found out a week later. Few figured the punchless Jets could muster a repeat victory over the Bills in Buffalo, but they did, 19-14, despite O.J.'s 166 yards on 29 rushes and despite Joe Namath's new role as a super-paid spectator.

The Bills were 2-6 and saddled with a four-game losing streak, but fans seeking a ray of sunshine figured O.J. at least was coming around. And right around the corner was a Nov. 7 game with his old cousins, the Patriots, in Foxboro, Mass. It was O.J.'s 100th pro game in eight years.

A chance for recovery, many in Buffalo figured. Little did they realize an unforgettable O.J. game was about to unfold for a vastly different—and bizarre—reason.

The Patriots were leading, 3-0, nine minutes into the first quarter on John Smith's 46-yard field goal. O.J. had carried five times for a paltry eight yards. He was getting practically nowhere against a swarming Patriot defense. He was frustrated, but a third Buffalo series was about to start from the Bills' 32.

O.J. took a first-down handoff from quarterback Gary Marangi and tried to sweep. Again, he was "greeted" by three defenders. Two let go of the Juice as his forward progress was halted and he was held to no gain. But defensive end Mel Lunsford hung on and slammed O.J. to the turf. O.J. was furious.

He came up swinging at the burly Lunsford. Only a couple of punches were thrown, but then Reggie McKenzie jumped on Lunsford's back and scratched the Patriot's eyes. Finally, cooler heads prevailed.

Yet, soon after calm was restored, the officials went into a huddle. When they broke up, O.J. couldn't believe what he was hearing. He was ejected from the game!

Here he had been roughed up after the play was dead. Lunsford not only wasn't penalized, but was allowed to stay in the game while O.J. was banished. And McKenzie, who had jumped on Lunsford's back, was permitted to remain as well.

The 61,157 fans in Schaefer Stadium, many of whom had come to see O.J. play, were denied the opportunity—except for those meager nine minutes. Officially, O.J. was banished for fighting. He couldn't believe it and neither could most witnesses—Bills' and Patriots' fans alike.

Simpson said the referee, Gordon McCarter, was the one who broke the incredible news. "He came over to the huddle and said I was out of the game," O.J. declared. "Before I knew what happened, I was the only one out."

And so he left the game with a grand total of six carries for eight yards!

"I watched the rest of the half from the bench," O.J. related, leading to another unexpected discussion. "Then at halftime one of the officials informed me I couldn't stay on the field. I spent the second half in the dressing room."

This was the first athletic event—football, basketball, track, baseball—that he had been ejected from in high school, college or the pro ranks. He was just stunned. And so were the Bills, who suffered a fifth straight defeat, 20-10. Their attack without O.J. was next to nil.

In the Buffalo dressing room afterward, O.J. voiced his displeasure candidly. "I've taken a lot of clean shots in football and I often compliment the guy afterward," he said. "But this one. I let up when two of the three guys who were holding me let up. Then this other guy [Lunsford] flung me around over on my head. I'm sure it was overexuberance. I didn't say anything and neither did he. It was a sorry fight and I was surprised at two things. One, that there was no flag on him for a personal foul and, two, that I was thrown out of the game.''

Linebacker Bo Cornell had an excellent view of the proceedings from in front of the Buffalo bench. He couldn't understand the officials' interpretation, either. "The ref said O.J. started the fight,'' Cornell stated, incredulously. "I think it was a terrible call. O.J. was pulled down after the whistle.''

McKenzie was particularly upset. "When you're a losing team, you always get the dirty end of the stick,'' the star guard commented. "Lunsford knew who he had in his hands. Maybe he was overemotional, but he put a little something extra into it.''

McKenzie then explained why he jumped on Lunsford's back. "If the Juice and I were in a barroom brawl, I would expect him to come to my aid,'' McKenzie said. "I looked at the matchup and I didn't wait a little bit.''

Of course, the Patriots were ecstatic at their sensational fortune—O.J. Simpson being ejected early without even one of their players exiting with him. They were ready and waiting with the witty quotes in the postgame scene.

"It's reassuring to know there's no favoritism to superstars in this league,'' quipped defensive end Tony McGee.

Ray "Sugar Bear'' Hamilton, the Pats' nose tackle, was even happier. "The whole idea of our game plan was to hold O.J. under 100 yards,'' he smiled. "We had a great game plan.''

CHAPTER TWENTY-FOUR

A Record Turkey Run

"When I got kicked out of the New England game for fighting, I figured I'd be damn lucky just to get a thousand yards. What I didn't figure was what the linemen would do for me."

O.J. was talking about a goal the offense set with the Bills deep in misery. After the New England defeat, there was another in Dallas, 17-10, on a Monday night TV appearance. O.J. rushed for only 78 yards and, after 10 games, had but 738. The goal was declared and the chant was picked up in huddles and on the sideline: "Let's give the ball to the Juice."

The Bills wanted to get O.J. his fourth rushing title in five years.

As Joe DeLamielleure put it, the offensive line wanted to demonstrate: "Nobody ever kicks our ass on the line." O.J. began running with the abandon one sees in those Hertz commercials of his in airport scenes. Clearly, he was now in A-1 condition and he was the only positive feature the downtrodden Bills had to showcase.

"For the first half of the season, I was in shape to run with the ball, but I wasn't in good enough shape to improvise," O.J.

admitted. "If there was no hole, I couldn't shimmy or bounce out of trouble the way I wanted. Some of the guys told me that I was getting sharper, and they'd get the rushing title for me."

Game 11 was the Bills' home finale and the story was familiar—even the low-voltage Chargers romped against an already poor defense missing four regulars. Quarterback Dan Fouts completed his first eight passes, San Diego scored on three of its first four possessions and breezed, 34-13. The Chargers rolled up 255 yards in the first half alone.

But O.J. began to rev up his engine—rushing 118 yards in 25 attempts. That was the Bills' highlight as they bid farewell to their disappointed home fans for 1976. They said goodbye with a seventh straight setback. No one was sorry they would close this maddening season with three road encounters.

O.J. and the rest of the offense decided they would use those three final games to demonstrate that the Buffalo rushing game, at least, was as potent as ever. "Football is basically a numbers game at the point of attack," O.J. stressed. "The ideal situation is to get four men blocking only three tacklers. But if we at least clear enough of their guys out to leave me one-on-one with the last tackler, that's cool, because one-on-one is my game."

In one breath, O.J. was (understandably) super-disappointed: "I'm depressed and frustrated. It took a long time to build ourselves up to a playoff team, and now we're right back in the old situation again. I look around the locker room and I wonder where all the talent went, all the guys who got us into the playoffs two years ago. We are not the team we used to be."

In another breath, he was philosophical: "I certainly don't want to play through another season like this. I want to play for a team that I know has a chance to win. I still stand by my thoughts that the Bills would be a better team if they traded me and brought in a few good players. I knew back in May this team was going to have problems and I'd be lying if I said I was optimistic."

Then O.J. took a quick glance backward: "After a season is over, the players go home and read the newspapers to see what trades are being made to help the team. When J.D. Hill and Earl Edwards were traded, I felt that other deals were going to be

The number's the same, but that's all: O.J. is taking aim on Jimmy Brown's career rushing mark. The Cleveland star of nine seasons amassed 12,312 yards.
AP Wirephoto

made to help the team, but that never happened. I'm not trying to run the organization, but the guys on this team know the true situation. We knew whether the talent was here or not. And then there was that situation over who was really running the team. We heard all about that for over a year."

Finally, O.J. searched mightily for that ray of sunshine amidst all the nimbus clouds: "Right now I just want to finish the season as positively as possible. Mike Montler was saying the other day that the only thing the offensive line had left to shoot for were positive statistics. The offense wants to go out in style."

The Bills had only three practice days between games, playing Thanksgiving Day against the Detroit Lions at the Pontiac Silverdome. It was a nationally televised game, and O.J. is always at peak readiness and raring to muster the spectacular when the coast-to-coast cameras are upon him.

This day was no different—only O.J. would offer a special edition of the spectacular.

The game pattern was familiar. Soon after a scoreless first quarter, there wasn't much question as to which team would win. Lions' quarterback Greg Landry fired touchdown passes of 21 and 24 yards to rookie tight end David Hill, and in between Benny Ricardo (waived by the Bills weeks earlier) kicked 22- and 35-yard field goals. Detroit was in charge, 20-0, late in the third quarter.

But by that time, O.J. had given fair warning he would stage a show to be remembered. On his third carry, he cut inside right end, turned left and barreled 36 yards to the Lion 21. The eruption boosted him past the 9,000-yard plateau for career rushing production.

When the first quarter ended, O.J. had 66 yards in eight carries. At halftime, his figures were 15 carries, 111 yards. And the Bills hadn't scored a point. They fashioned plenty of running but no passing attack, and everyone knew it.

The Lions were especially aware, stacking eight defenders on or near the line of scrimmage, hoping to stop Simpson and daring Gary Marangi to throw. This was no ordinary defense, either, but one rated statistically the best in the league. And yet, even with that stacked arrangement, it couldn't contain the Juice.

After the score reached 20-0, the Bills had a second-and-10 at the Lion 48. O.J. took a handoff and exploded over right guard, cut left quickly and, behind a diving block by wide receiver Bob Chandler on cornerback Levi Johnson at the 10, O.J. raced to paydirt for a 48-yard score.

"I was looking around for the block, the one that J.D. used to make," O.J. explained. "Bobby has been blocking for me since our days at USC, but I think that was the best he ever threw."

Coach Jim Ringo explained the play in detail. "We knew the Lions were stacking their line to stop the run, so in certain instances we used the T-formation with Chandler lined up in the [full-house] backfield," Ringo said. "Reggie McKenzie and Joe D opened the hole on the right side and Bobby threw a tremendous block."

After three quarters, O.J.'s rushing total was 181 yards. The

O.J. breezes to 48-yard touchdown in record 273-yard game. Detroit's Lem Barney (20) reaches for Juice in vain.
AP Wirephoto

score was 20-7, but after Dexter Bussey dived in for a four-yard TD, giving Detroit a 27-7 cushion, hardly anyone concentrated on the score anymore. The spotlight was on O.J., and even the partisan Lion crowd of 66,875 joined into the spirit. They were cheering on O.J. against their team. They appreciated class and were seeing a performance they would never forget. And the Bills were dedicating the rest of this game to O.J.

On the very first carry after Bussey's touchdown and on his initial rush of the final quarter, O.J. raced over left tackle for 19 yards. He had reached 200 yards exactly—and the NFL record of four 200-yard games within one career was eclipsed at last. This was O.J.'s fifth venture above 200.

Now the next target was O.J.'s single-game record of 250 yards. Unlike several previous occasions, he would not be yanked early this day. And, despite the 20-point margin, the Bills would not play catchup through the air. They would continue to hand off. They were clearly after Simpson yardage, not necessarily points.

With 11:23 left in the game, O.J. ran inside left end for 18 yards. That series fizzled but, with 7:35 to play, O.J. needed only 33 yards to erase his single-game mark. Marangi handed him the ball six consecutive times and, on the sixth, O.J. cut left behind Joe D and dashed 16 yards to the Lion 15. The record was broken. O.J. had cruised 261 yards in 28 trips against a stacked, top-rated defense.

The large Pontiac crowd was on its feet, giving O.J. a standing ov tion, chanting, "Juice, Juice, Juice."

But O.J. wasn't through. He wanted this memorable drive to be rewarded on the scoreboard. Suddenly, though, he wasn't getting the handoff. He had drawn the standing ovation when his record was flashed on the Silverdome scoreboard. He had gone to the Bills' bench and hugged Ringo, architect of the offensive line which turned his career around. He had shaken hands with his teammates as the partisan Lions' crowd went wild, but he stayed in the game.

He watched Jeff Kinney lose two yards. And he saw Marangi fire incomplete to Chandler three times, including a fourth-down toss which nearly beheaded the classy catcher. The drive seemed ended, but an offside infraction gave Buffalo a second fourth-down chance. Now it was O.J.'s turn.

Marangi called O.J.'s number and the play fooled the Lions completely. On the previous three plays, O.J. had seen the defenders come at him and he quipped, "Hey man, I don't have the ball." This time, they weren't looking for him at all. "I guess they finally felt I wasn't going to get the ball," smiled O.J.

A switch at the last moment threw them off. Jeff Kinney yelled, "Far right, O.J." The play was a draw, and the Juice bolted 12 yards for the touchdown which capped his most productive performance. He had traveled the entire 58 yards of the series in seven plays, scoring his and the team's second touchdown and capping a record 29-carry, 273-yard Turkey Day display.

His sense of the dramatic, even in this "down" season, hadn't left the Juice. Always "up" on the national tube games, he

O.J. embraces Coach Jim Ringo after breaking single-game rushing record. Juice exploded for 273 yards on Thanksgiving Day.
Photo by Robert L. Smith,
Elma, N.Y.

treated Thanksgiving viewers around the country and he treated
Ralph Wilson in his home town to something very special.

It was so special that the Lions' Bussey amassed 137 yards in
27 carries and hardly anyone noticed. Landry, the NFL's top-
rated quarterback by statistics, had flipped those two scoring
tosses to Hill and these, too, were greatly overshadowed. O.J. was
at center stage and the Lions' fans were giving him more
standing applause as he came to the sideline to stay with 3:40
remaining.

The game ended 27-14 and the Lions had evened their record
at 6-6, but the conversation piece was O.J.'s record show. Never
had a team been so deliriously happy in defeat, mobbing O.J. and
backslapping him. They were literally jumping in ecstasy and
had just incurred an eighth straight defeat.

Truly, this was a one-man show. O.J. had broken his single-
game rushing record with 273 yards. He had become the first
player to attain five 200-yard games. He had passed the 9,000-
yard career rushing mark (reaching 9,252) and now was the
NFL's second all-time runner behind Jimmy Brown. He had
reached 1,129 yards for the season, eclipsing 1,000 for the fifth
straight year. And he scored both Buffalo touchdowns, measuring
48 and 12 yards.

"The first score was a 26-play which broke beautifully," O.J.
said. "Joe D hooked the outside linebacker and Reggie kicked out
the cornerback. I broke right, cut back and beat the safety.
Bobby's best block knocked off the one man I had to beat and I
just cruised in. It was easy!

"Before my second touchdown, I heard the coaches calling
'Draw!' from the sidelines. I lined up on the wrong side, but I
jumped over to the left in time. Both off-tackle holes were cleared
out and Mike Montler [center] took his man clean out of the
middle. There was a huge hole and I just cruised straight up the
middle to score. This whole thing was one super job of blocking
by our offense. You don't break records like this without that
kind of blocking."

O.J. wound up with 66 yards in the first quarter, 45 in the
second, 70 and a touchdown in the third and 92 plus another TD
in the final 15 minutes. "We were really surprised we were able

Bills' famed No. 32 slices between Lions on record day. Defensive back
Charlie West (40), two others stop him only temporarily.
Photo by Robert L. Smith,
Elma, N.Y.

to run the ball against this team, especially without an effective
passing game," O.J. commented. He was happy about the record,
but he was keenly aware of one difference which separated this
game from his earlier four 200-yard efforts. This time the Bills
had lost.

"This record is something that, when your career is over, you
can look back on with fond memories," O.J. said. "But our
objective coming in here was to win and we didn't do that."

Tommy Hudspeth, the Lions' coach, made reference to that
fact in his post-game remarks. "O.J. is one hellatious football
player," he marveled. "There's just one O.J. But I'd take a win
over a record any day. O.J.'s in a class by himself. No doubt
about it. He has tremendous acceleration, great balance and a
great field of vision. What makes him especially good is great
lateral movement."

Other Lions heaped praise on O.J.'s performance. "I grew up watching O.J.—he's an unbelievable back," said Bussey.

"If he really slams into you, he's easy to handle—but you can't get him to slam into you," remarked linebacker Jim Laslavic. "The man has a thousand moves."

Over in the Bills' quarters, the usually quiet Ringo also was spouting superlatives. "Fantastic," he declared. "I've never seen a halfback run like that. He deserves the record for what he's put into the game."

Marangi, down because of his passing failures and the losing skein, nevertheless joined the tributes. "Our offense is built around Juice," he said. "So we might as well go with him until he gets tired—then call time out so he can rest."

O.J. was asked the inevitable question, was this his best game or was the 227-yard effort against Pittsburgh in 1975 still the peak, as most experts feel?

"It's hard to rate which of the 200-yard games is the best achievement," he replied. "But coming at this time in a disappointing season, I'm proud of this one. It happened on national TV and I like that, but I'm sorry we didn't win. The 227-yard game in Pittsburgh was big because the Steelers are defending champions. But this was a record. The Lions were the No. 1 defensive team in the league and we were all kind of up for the game. Obviously, it will go down as one of my favorite days. We were going inside. We wanted to run straight at them. They were blitzing linebackers, but we had a few tricks to pull on them, too."

The Bills were 2-10 and losers of eight straight, and Ringo was winless at 0-7. They had lost three games in 11 days. But there were broad smiles in the Bills' dressing room. It was an unusual sight, to say the least.

The difference was the electricity generated by the Juice. O.J. had salvaged the spectacular in the most dismal of seasons. He had realized every individual feat within reach but a 300-yard game, and that could have been his if the Bills had gained possession again after his 12-yard TD. They never did. Detroit ran out the final 3½ minutes. Once again, the Bills' defense couldn't hold.

Besides the two NFL records, most single-game rushing yardage and most career 200-yard games, O.J. reveled in the knowledge that he was breezing along in peak form again. The San Diego game was an indication, but this 273-yard explosion was an outright declaration.

"Going into the game, I felt I hadn't been able to help the team like I can," O.J. acknowledged. "I was just not doing the things I'd like to do. This was the first week I was able to do things downfield that I wanted. Even in practice, I could feel it. Abe, our trainer [Ed Abramoski], told me: 'Juice, maybe you'll go 200 yards this week.' I guess he knew it, too.

"By 100 per cent, I mean this was the first time I could get into the secondary and juke a guy. Once I made the initial move, I could make another one. I was delivering the blow instead of taking it."

Someone asked O.J. what he said to Ringo when he came over to the Bills' sideline to embrace the coach after breaking his record. "I just thanked him," O.J. responded. "Jim has been part of every huge success I've had in pro football. Ringo has been as responsible as anyone I've known. He coached the offensive line which did the great blocking for me. He put in the game plans and said, 'This stuff will go.' I told him I'll finish with him and I also said that to the guys in the huddle."

O.J. had reached four figures in rushing (1,129) through virtually eight games, owning but 105 yards after three and being ejected nine minutes into the Patriot affair, emerging with eight yards. He was riding high now and he was in a talking mood about his future. He decided to announce eclipsing Jim Brown's record of 12,312 career yards in nine Cleveland seasons was his goal. He was 3,060 yards away.

"Like everyone else, I'd like to be No. 1," O.J. declared. "Jimmy Brown set the standard. If I stay in football long enough, I'd like the chance to pass Brown. It's incentive for me, as for all runners.

"Last year, I came into training camp in the best shape of my life," O.J. went on. "This year, I missed camp and this was the first week I felt in 100 per cent shape. Next year, I'll be in camp in the best shape of my life again. And that will be with the Bills, unless Ralph trades me."

Wilson lost no time declaring he had no intention of peddling the superstar widely recognized as "The Franchise." "No one is in a class with O.J. Simpson," Wilson stated. "And I have no intention of trading him. Watching him run on Thanksgiving, wouldn't that have been wonderful—trading him to Los Angeles for Mike Fanning? The Rams' Lawrence McCutcheon [who reportedly would have come to Buffalo in the deal] is a fine young man, but he's not the leader O.J. is. O.J. has been a positive influence on the whole organization and not just on the football field. I really admire him for what he's done."

That was the owner of a declining 2-10 team talking, the owner of a team which smiled broadly in taking an eighth straight loss. Clearly, he was looking ahead to a fresh beginning in 1977, but two weeks remained in the Bicentennial season. And O.J. was just beginning to hit his stride.

CHAPTER TWENTY-FIVE

Rushing Past the Dolphins

Of all the Bills' opponents, the one which has easily been the most troublesome in the O.J. Simpson era is Miami. And troublesome is hardly the word. To the Bills, the Miami Dolphins are almost unconquerable.

Entering the semifinal game of the 1976 season, the Bills had defeated Miami only once in O.J.'s reign—and that was in 1969, the Juice's rookie season. The Bills rolled that day, 28-3. But now, as they escaped the Buffalo snow for the sunshine by Biscayne Bay, they had lost 13 straight games to Miami, never beaten coach Don Shula and were winless in the Orange Bowl for a decade.

O.J. and his teammates, given three days off following the Thanksgiving Day affair in Detroit, vowed to end the season on the upbeat. He went home to see his family in California for the first time in three months and returned determined. "I want to lead the league in rushing and win," O.J. announced. "But we're playing two pretty good teams, Miami and Baltimore."

Winning was becoming a pipe dream among the Bills, and O.J. knew it. But the rushing title? Yes, it was possible, but it would take a torrent of yardage, perhaps another trip beyond 200 yards. Chicago's Walter Payton had been a big leader, but O.J. was closing the gap quickly.

The game started promisingly. The Bills jumped ahead and had the advantage of opposing little-used Don Strock at quarterback instead of star Bob Griese. Shula wanted to review his younger players in this game which meant nothing in the standings.

It became immediately apparent that this was going to be a wild, offense-minded afternoon, the kind of game in which O.J. excels. The Bills' Roland Hooks took the opening kickoff and raced 79 yards to the Miami 18, setting up George Jakowenko's 28-yard field goal.

The Bills kicked off and rookie Duriel Harris sped 63 yards to the Buffalo 37, leading to Garo Yepremian's 53-yard three-pointer, just one yard shy of his peak.

Quickly, there was another kickoff, but there were no fireworks on this one. Yet on first down, and just 23 seconds after Yepremian's boomer, O.J. turned left end and raced 75 yards down the sideline to electrify the Miami crowd. He was uncatchable, and the touchdown gave Buffalo a 10-3 lead. It also left safety Ken Ellis and cornerback Jeris White, Simpson's pursuers, slightly winded.

"That was the 27-play we put in during the 1972 season," O.J. explained. "That's the one I told Jim Ringo would never work and the first time we used it, I went 94 yards for a touchdown against Pittsburgh. On this play, both guards pull. Joe D took good care of one guy, but it was Bobby Chandler who really made the play go. He stayed with his man [cornerback Curtis Johnson] and I got inside and accelerated.

"Had I been forced outside, the pursuit probably would have caught me and I would have gone out of bounds instead of being able to run up the sideline."

The 75-yard jaunt was the longest against Miami in eight years.

When the first quarter ended, the Bills still held that 10-3 lead, and O.J. already had amassed 110 yards in eight carries. Yes, O.J. was penetrating the Dolphins at last. He needed only nine minutes, the same length of time before he was ejected in New England, to surpass 100 yards for the 38th time in his pro career. O.J. had never gone past the century mark and did so only once against Miami (1973), but needed just nine minutes this day. The Orange Bowl PA announcer quipped, "That's the first 100-yard quarter ever run against the Dolphins."

The Bills' success, except for O.J.'s yardage, hit the skids once the second quarter began. The score was respectable at halftime, the Dolphins leading by just 17-13, but it was a sharp downhill slide thereafter. Fred Solomon staged a spectacular three-touchdown performance, racing 79 yards with a punt, hauling in a 53-yard scoring pass from Strock and dashing 59 yards for his third score. Solomon reaped 191 yards off the three TDs and finished with 114 aerial yards off five receptions.

Harris set up Yepremian's 53-yard field goal with that 63-yard kickoff dash and later hauled in a 37-yard TD pass from Strock. And Strock figured in three TDs. It didn't matter who was the quarterback against the Bills. Whoever it was made like a superstar for at least one Sunday.

For Buffalo, there was only O.J. Oh, Marangi fired a pair of touchdown aerials, but couldn't complete a pass until three minutes remained in the first half. By then, the tide had turned. Miami rolled on to a 45-27 cakewalk, mustering the largest point total of a comedown year (six wins) for Shula and Co. The second best, 30, also was mustered against Buffalo in the season opener.

The Bills enjoyed a 125-8 yard rushing bulge, thanks to O.J., in that first quarter. But then they collapsed in a flood of penalties, lapses and assorted other mistakes. Shula notched his 154th career victory, elevating him to fourth place among the NFL's all-time winningest coaches. Ringo became 0-8 as a head coach, and the Bills' debit skein rested at nine.

But then there was O.J. What a game this was for him! After that 110-yard first quarter, he quieted for a spell and finished the half with "only" 121 yards off 13 carries. That's a 9.3-yard average. In the third quarter, while Strock passed 53 yards to Solomon and ran a two-yard bootleg for TDs and a 31-13 margin, O.J. rolled his yardage to 173 in 19 thrusts.

When Don Nottingham's one-yard plunge closed the scoring (45-27), O.J. still needed 14 yards to reach the 200-plateau for the sixth time. There was no way he was going to miss it. Though exhausted, he burst the middle for eight yards on first down. On second down, Marangi handed off to him again and once more he sliced eight yards, this time around right end. The 200-yard level was his again! He had reached 202 yards against his most pesky opponent over the years. He carried once more, reaching 203 yards in 24 carries. Yes, the Bills lost to Miami a 14th straight time, but O.J. had once more exceeded 200 yards despite the lack of a passing game to shift some of the defense's attention from him.

"The only thing left for me is yardage," observed O.J., who tied his own NFL record with back-to-back 200-yard games. "I thought I'd be doing well to gain 900 yards, when you consider that I didn't report until the night before our opening game; when you consider we've spent over half the season without a fullback who can block like Jim Braxton; when you consider the absence of a passing game since Joe Ferguson got hurt; and when you consider I got thrown out of the New England game after nine minutes."

O.J. talked about beating not only Dolphin defenders but intense heat to reach 203 yards on the Orange Bowl polyturf. "I really got tired in the fourth quarter and had to come out for awhile," he said. "But I've always been able to recuperate when weary. It's why I run sprints instead of long-distance when training. I knew I needed 14 yards for 200 in that last drive and it's the only reason I came back in.

"I had to work and pick a lot," the Juice went on. "I was tired because I'm not used to running in this Miami heat. We had difficulty practicing during the week with the Buffalo snow and we practiced there in long johns. We weren't really running up there."

But how he ran in the Orange Bowl!

"I'd much rather win football games than set rushing records, but I'm a realist, too," O.J. said. "We know we're playing against defenses with eight guys stacked to stop the run. But we have an offensive unit with a lot of pride and our running game will not go down. Our record is 2-11 and we've lost nine straight, but I think we'd have a winning record with just two injured players back—Ferguson and Braxton. We'll get them back next year."

The 203 yards enabled O.J. to assume firm command of the American Conference rushing race with 1,332 yards in 262 carries. Now with 476 yards in his last two outings, O.J. was only nine yards behind Walter Payton's pace atop the NFL. He was within easy striking distance of the Bears' star with one game remaining, but he was second-guessing himself, too.

"I wasn't as mad about getting thrown out of the New England game at the time it happened as I am now when I realize how much it might cost me," O.J. declared. He realized Payton, who would close the season at home against Denver, could outlast his bid for a fourth rushing crown in five years.

"Payton is a genuine star," O.J. commented. "He's not one of those young guys who will make people say, 'Hey, remember Payton, he had that one big year.' He's what I call one of the insane runners—the kind who can make the moves without having to stop and think."

Reggie McKenzie feels that's precisely the type of runner O.J. is as well. "And as long as Payton's gonna be around so long, we figure we ought to get this year's title for our man," the large guard intoned.

"We won't exactly be distracted by any playoff plans," O.J. laughed. He was amazed to be vying for the league rushing title again, but thankful the team had at least that highlight to seek. "I felt I was having one of the worst years of my career until a few weeks ago," O.J. said. "It surprised me that one good game could put me ahead of most of the guys and move me so close to Payton. I'd been reading what a super year Walter is having while I'd been depressed about my season."

The following Sunday, in the season finale at Baltimore, the Bills suffered one of the most embarrassing defeats in their 17-year history, 58-20. It was the most points ever accumulated by a Colt team and the most ever allowed by the Bills in one game. Yet it was on such a dismal afternoon that O.J. carried 29 times for 171 yards and captured the NFL rushing crown. Payton, coming out of the Bears-Broncos game with a third-quarter ankle injury, mustered just 49.

So O.J. embraced his fourth rushing title with 113 yards more than Payton. O.J. had accumulated an incredible 647 yards in the last three games to finish with 1,503 yards in 290 rushes. In his first seven games of the season, he managed only two 100-yard games. In the last seven, he had only two games in which he gained less than 100.

In the first 10 games, O.J. ran for 738 yards. In the last four, he ran for 765. That's acceleration! And that's how O.J. propelled himself to the ground-gaining title.

Still, there was no way the Juice was happy. "In a losing year, you can't have a good feeling about something like this. The only redeeming factor is that we, the offense, can look back and say, 'Hey, we did it.'

"Our guys on defense need a lot of help. Management has dealt us some bad hands, and we've had to play with what we got. It's embarrassing. We have a positive thing, the rushing title, but it really doesn't make up for the season."

O.J. was asked at what point he knew the title was his. "One of our guys told me at the half that Payton had 45 yards [O.J. had 70], and later he told me he was out of the game with 49," he said. "I knew then I had the title wrapped up."

The Juice said center Mike Montler promised him the ground title in the third quarter. "Montler told me I was going to get it and that they were going to see to it," O.J. declared.

There was some discussion about O.J. returning to become the first back ever to gain 200 yards in three consecutive games. But when he knew the title was secure and the Colts had their second team playing, he stayed on the bench the last five minutes. "I don't want to go for a record against a second team," O.J. said.

Reggie McKenzie was clearly proud of the rushing title in the face of a 58-20 rout. "Once we saw the season was going to be one long struggle, we turned our goals to O.J.," his "main man" said. "We feel we salvaged something."

McKenzie showed that his feelings about O.J. run exceptionally deep.

"Until O.J., no backs got their linemen due credit for accomplishments," the muscular guard said. "He was the first. Now, everybody does it. This was harder still, doing what we did without Braxton. He's a super blocker and can run you into the ground. But O.J. got the title. That says it all."

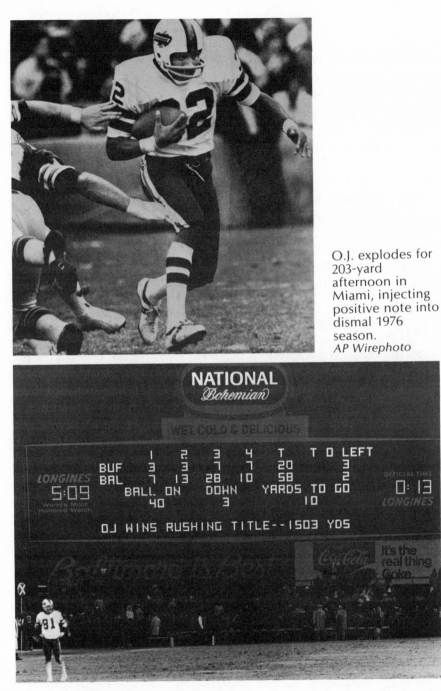

O.J. explodes for 203-yard afternoon in Miami, injecting positive note into dismal 1976 season.
AP Wirephoto

The scoreboard tells it all as 1976 season ends in Baltimore. The lonely Bill is wide receiver Bob Chandler.
Photo by Robert L. Smith,
Elma, N.Y.

Indeed it did. Even with a winless coach (Ringo was 0-9), a 10-game loss streak and 2-12 record, a "run-for-the-bus" defense, the Juice had injected a title ingredient into one of the most downbeat of seasons. He made the most of a horrible situation.

After eight years, the Juice had 9,626 yards, was pro football's second-leading ground-gainer of all time and trailed Jim Brown by 2,686 yards. With more rebuilding ahead, surpassing Brown was where O.J.'s sights were set.

"I felt I had to have 1,500 yards both this season and next in order to break Brown's record because I may slack off by 1978 and need the leeway," O.J. said.

O.J. also realized he needed a full training camp to be prepared for the season. That was his lesson of 1976—that he no longer possessed the youth to compensate for a lack of training. He once boasted he could get ready for a season in two weeks. That wasn't true anymore.

The Juice finished 1976 with 70 touchdowns (57 rushing, 12 receiving, one on a kickoff return). He had snared 159 passes for 1,786 yards and 12 touchdowns. And, recovering splendidly from those "three lost years" after being drafted No. 1 in 1969, he had carried 1,997 times for 9,626 yards and 57 touchdowns.

In all of pro football history, a back has exceeded 1,500 yards rushing in one season only seven times. Brown did it on three occasions and Simpson now has matched him, but O.J. is the first to realize back-to-back seasons (1975-76) of 1,500 or better.

Walter Payton (1977) is the only other runner to eclipse 1,500 yards within a 14-game season.

When the 1976 season ended, O.J.'s total of 100-yard games had reached 39, second only to Brown's 58. His half-dozen 200-yard afternoons were among 10 NFL records (seven still standing) he established. He owned no less than 22 single-game, season and career Bills' standards.

Clearly, O.J. was on course to fulfill the boyhood boast he made to Jim Brown that afternoon in a San Francisco ice cream shop. Though his team was light years from being a contender again, O.J. Simpson was just around the corner from becoming the all-time king of running backs—as promised!

CHAPTER TWENTY-SIX

The 10,000-Yard Man

Well before the first player walked into training camp at Niagara University, there were strong indications that 1977 would never be a year of recovery for the Bills.

O.J. sensed it by the moves which were not made during the off-season. The restructured front office never pulled off one major trade to import a player of quality.

About the biggest noise the Bills made in the bartering scene was to acquire defensive tackle Bill Dunstan from Philadelphia for a draft choice. Dunstan had warmed the bench for the defensively poor Eagles, yet would start with Buffalo.

Despite his 0-9 record, Ringo was retained and he assembled a staff of assistants who created a rah-rah atmosphere during summer training. Enthusiasm ran high, most players called this camp their best and the horrendous '76 season seemed all but forgotten—as if it hadn't happened.

But O.J. remembered. He did not join in the artificially festive spirit. He knew his team had not negotiated the necessary moves for a turnabout and said so in a surprisingly frank press interview. Some insiders reacted against O.J., indicating he should be a company man and convey optimism. But he was honest and on target: There was little reason for optimism.

Worse than the absence of bolstering moves was the continuing decay of assets. Now the offensive line which had opened all those holes for O.J. was springing leaks. Center Mike Montler and tackle Donnie Green became disenchanted and were traded to Denver and Philadelphia, respectively—for draft choices!

Two of the "Electric Company's" bulwark starters thus were unloaded within four weeks and not even a warm body was obtained for either. O.J.'s impression was correct: Management was continuing to deal the Bills' players a bad hand.

The draft was a perfect example. Ralph Wilson insisted his team would build through the draft, but of 52 collegians chosen since 1975 only five were starting. By contrast, Oakland won the Super Bowl with seven first-round and nine second-round selections.

The exhibition schedule began with another negative, a defeat at Pittsburgh, but far more ominous was O.J.'s absence. He was out with blurred vision in his left eye. O.J., obviously worried, was sent to the Wilmer Institute at Johns Hopkins Hospital in Baltimore for tests.

Suddenly, the Juice's career lay in doubt. Officials throughout the Bills' organization were worried and issued only guarded statements. It was a mysterious incident—no one knowing what caused the condition, but speculation centered on a jarring tackle during the second '76 loss to the Jets.

"I'd go back to sleep for a bit after the 6:30 wakeup call and when I'd wake up again, I couldn't focus on the clock in the room," O.J. complained.

But doctors gave O.J. a thorough examination and said the condition would heal itself within a month. He could play football without any restrictions. They called the problem "a benign self-limiting condition beneath the center of vision of the left eye."

In other words, the Juice had a small hole at the back of the eye behind the retina from which fluid dripped, causing the clouded vision. "I feel better. I don't see any better, but I feel better," O.J. reacted upon hearing the welcome news.

"The thought of knowing something was wrong and not knowing what it was weighed on me," O.J. went on. "I didn't know what was going to happen. I thought I could play. I only had one thing on my mind: Was this going to get worse?"

"The same disorder appears in a lot of healthy young people," explained Dr. Walter Stark, associate professor at the Wilmer Institute. He added that O.J.'s vision actually was only one line from perfect.

The Juice celebrated by scoring both Buffalo touchdowns in the next exhibition, darting one and 15 yards as the Bills ambushed Detroit, 17-10, for their first victory under Ringo. After 10 losses, even a pre-season win was major cause for jubilation and, to a man, the Bills celebrated while Maynard Ferguson's rendition of the "Rocky" theme blared over the dressing room's stereo system.

The negatives had only been interrupted briefly, however.

Hapless Tampa Bay was the only other team conquered in the 2-4 pre-season. And the Rich Stadium crowds, which from 1973-75 were the talk of the NFL, dwindled below 30,000. The victory over Detroit had been witnessed by a record-low 27,565 and smaller gatherings were to come. The fans were turned off and not just by the thought of paying regular-season prices for exhibitions.

Yet, when opening day arrived, hope was reborn and 76,097 showed in a downpour to watch the Bills self-destruct, 13-0, before Miami. These were the "new Bills." The result was the same—defeat—but the pattern had changed. Now, the defense was impressive and the offense pointless.

Phil Ranallo, columnist for the Buffalo *Courier-Express*, described the soggy scene splendidly with one sentence: "Fortunately," he wrote, "none of the Bills drowned."

O.J. found that minus Montler and Green, this was hardly the same "Electric Company" blocking for him. The front no longer turned loose the Juice. Willie Parker, previously Montler's understudy, and young Joe Devlin were the new starters, and proficiency suffered.

O.J. was unable to break a long-gainer, his biggest play a 12-yard reception of a Ferguson pass. He was the game's leading receiver (7 catches, 68 yards) and rusher (21 carries, 71 yards), but gained less than 3½ yards per carry.

Simpson reached the 2,000 mark in career carries during the first quarter. But, prophetic of the season in general, he sprained his right ankle on the next attempt.

O.J. also fumbled, but that was only one of seven Bills' bobbles. In all, the Bills crossed midfield seven times and never scored, repeatedly killing their own threats with miscues. They rolled up 16 first downs, 324 yards and had possession nearly 37 of the 60 minutes, but never advanced beyond the Dolphin 18-yard line.

With half the fourth quarter still to play, most of the huge crowd had "gonged" the show by leaving. The Bills would not see anywhere near that large a turnout at home again all season. So many had seen enough—a 15th straight loss to Miami over eight years and familiar futility.

"They didn't let us have anything to the outside," said the Juice, doubly disappointed since his friend, actor Elliot Gould, had journeyed to watch him from Toronto, where he was filming a movie, *The Silent Partner.*

"They were ready. In the first half, we wanted to run to our left, but they stopped that and when I started to cut back, their backside linebacker was always there to get me. We just made the bad plays at the worst time. But when you're a young team, you're going to make mistakes—especially on offense."

The post-game sound of misery became a weekly happening—as in 1976. The offense couldn't score the following Sunday in Denver and the Super Bowl-bound Broncos, with Montler at center, breezed 26-6. Even the PAT try failed after linebacker Bo Cornell scooped a fumble and scored the only Buffalo touchdown in two weeks.

O.J., bothered by that ankle sprain, was taken out after three periods with only 43 yards off 15 carries. Once again, a four-linebacker defense stymied the offense, concentrating on O.J. It was a real Rocky Mountain low except for one thing: Earlier in the day, Marquerite gave birth to their third child, a daughter, in California.

The Bills came closer a week later in Baltimore, but it was still no cigar with a 17-14 loss. O.J. was held to 52 yards on 16 thrusts and his team realized a milestone. The Bills had gone a full year without a regular season victory.

Bad ankle and all, O.J. rolled up 122 yards in 23 bursts against the New York Jets on the season's fourth Sunday. But the result was another defeat (24-19), only this time to a lightly regarded foe. The Bills seemed helpless. This time, they scored 10 late points to tie, 17-17, only to lose after Ferguson fumbled a snap at his own 17. That set up Clark Gaines' winning 14-yard touchdown two plays later.

So now the Bills were 0-4, O.J. was scoreless, the home crowd had dwindled to 32,046, the team was still winless under Ringo (in regular season play) with 13 straight defeats and 14 counting Saban's 1976 finale in New York. Ringo's job seemed in obvious jeopardy, but the stubborn Wilson stood by him—insisting he would remain the coach all season.

It was into this unfortunate backdrop that, ever so unexpectedly, another of O.J.'s most memorable games took place.

The Atlanta Falcons, a defensive powerhouse with a surprising 3-1 record, invaded Rich Stadium and only 27,348—another record low—turned out in bitter cold to watch.

The game figured to be dull—a real low-scoring affair. The Bills' offense was sputtering, and Atlanta, with former Bills' third-stringer Scott Hunter at quarterback, had just made one touchdown stand up for victory (7-0) over San Francisco.

O.J. remembered the last Atlanta meeting in 1973 ended a seven-game Falcon victory streak, dashed their playoff hopes and ignited a season-ending four-game Buffalo success streak in his 2,003-yard campaign.

But now things were so different. After the latest defeat to the Jets, O.J. sounded like he couldn't wait to retire. "I got 26 more games to play [over two seasons]," he said. "I just want to be healthy at the end of next year—get my 10 years in and get out."

He wasn't happy about several things. The run of 14 straight losses was the greatest thorn. But now he noted the Bills were de-emphasizing their most successful plays—his running—and Ferguson was filling the air with passes. "We haven't run the ball all that much," he declared.

Now the Bills were trying to dent Atlanta's armor and the early pattern was familiar. They reached the Falcon 15, but consecutive penalties killed the threat. Then they drove to the 10, but rookie Neil O'Donoghue hooked a 27-yard field goal wide.

Back came the Bills a third time, and O.J., running smoothly this day, fumbled a pitchout at the 17 and Atlanta's Ron McCarthy recovered.

Late in the second period, rookie John Kimbrough returned a punt 18 yards to the Falcon 36 and the Bills were "knocking" again. Six plays later, despite a sweeping crosswind, O'Donoghue clicked with a 30-yard field goal.

The Bills held a 3-0 lead . . . and they clung to it desperately. In the third quarter, the small crowd received a strong indication this game would be special when O.J. burst 11 yards up the middle. The game was stopped and O.J. was handed the ball by his teammates. He had just become the second player in pro football history, following Jim Brown, to pass the 10,000-yard rushing plateau.

O.J. trotted to the sideline, handed the ball to trainer Eddie Abramoski and grasped Ringo's right hand. "I had to shake his hand and thank him," he said later. "Ringo's been instrumental in just about all the yardage I've gained. I didn't have many yards until Ringo and Lou Saban came to this team."

The Juice continued to pile up the yardage, realizing his 41st 100-yard game in the NFL. But neither he nor the Bills could score a touchdown and the outcome remained in doubt. In fact, the pessimists were looking for the Bills to fold or self-destruct as they had so often while losing 14 straight.

Then with 5½ minutes to play, it happened!

Tackle Robert Pennywell crashed through untouched by human hands to block a Marv Bateman punt and Atlanta had possession at the Bills' 13. Ringo, who had seen similar disaster so many times, looked mortally wounded. He turned his back and paced the sideline. The crowd hooted, thinking another game was about to go down the tube.

But this was an afternoon of incredible happenings.

In three plays, the Falcons slashed nine yards to the Bills' four. That left them with a fourth-and-one. Unbelievably, Coach Leeman Bennett went contrary to his own conservative philosophy and disdained the almost certain field goal which would have tied the game and probably forced overtime.

Instead, he went for a first down.

Hunter took the snap and rolled out right behind two pulling guards. Hunter sliced in and was cut down by cornerback Keith Moody. Hunter thought he had the first down, and the Bills, waving wildly, were sure they had stopped him short. The crowd hushed as the officials beckoned for a measurement.

This time, finally, the Bills got the decision. They had held! After Tony Greene sealed a desperate Atlanta attempt with an interception at the Buffalo 29, the Bills celebrated victory for the first time in more than a year . . . the first time ever with Ringo as their head coach.

Ringo's 13-game nightmare was over. He was no longer a winless coach.

O.J. had eclipsed 10,000 yards—ripping off 138 in 23 carries, his best day of 1977.

And the day of elation for this offense-minded pair came off a game of tremendous defense with a most unusual score, 3-0.

In one dressing room, Ringo was filled with emotion. "I walked up that ramp or one like it with my head down 13 times," he said. "And each time I died. I died 13 times!"

There was no way a 3-0 game was dull for Jim Ringo . . . or the swarm of Bills who hugged him as he walked up that ramp a winner for the first time.

In the other dressing room, Bennett was second-guessing himself.

"We had a chance to tie the game up and keep from losing," he said. "I didn't follow my basic philosophy. It was my fault we got beat. It all boils down to a poor decision on my part."

Yet no one could deny the two most responsible for making Ringo a winner were Moody and Doug Jones, the strong safety. Jones eluded the blocks of both pulling guards and managed to slow down Hunter at the seven. Then Moody came up to nail the stumbling quarterback short of the first down inside the five.

"We were pinching in the middle, which means I usually go man-to-man and cover the tight end," Jones said. "But I saw the tight end block down and I had a feeling something was going to come outside. I looked up and there it was."

Now it was Moody's turn.

"They pulled both guards, one for each of us," he said. "But Doug made a helluva play. He took out both guards and still managed to get a hand on Hunter and slow him down. He turned the play back inside. All I had to do was make the tackle."

Both agreed a good deal of anticipation enabled them to deny Hunter the short-yard needed for a first down. "If we had played it normal, Hunter probably would have bootlegged it on in," Jones said.

"We didn't guess, we anticipated," Moody followed. "I was supposed to lay back more on that play, but I didn't think they were going to pass and I came up."

Just in time to nail Hunter on the rebound from Jones.

The decisive play and the final score were just two of a good number of unusual events surrounding the game. Before kickoff, Wilson and Ringo gave impassioned pep talks to the players. "We were so down after losing last week to the Jets, there's no telling what might have happened had we lost today," linebacker Dan Jilek explained.

He was saying the Bills appeared potentially "ripe" to quit on Ringo as they had in 1976. And, indeed, Wilson met with Ringo during the week to reassure him. "He was bleeding pretty badly," Wilson said. "I let him know that everybody was behind him."

Ironically, the game in which the Bills ended a 14-game tailspin also ended Bob Chandler's 31-game streak with at least one reception. The shutout was the Bills' first in nearly three years—since that 6-0 triumph over Baltimore in 1974 which clinched a playoff berth.

And then there was the ultimate irony for Neil O'Donoghue. It was his 30-yard field goal which wound up the game's only score. Yet, before the Bills would play again, he would be on waivers. Even though his field goal won the game, Ringo was disenchanted with his general ineffectiveness over five weeks and that 27-yard miss sealed his fate.

But except for O'Donoghue this was a day for rejoicing. As the game ended, Ringo embraced O.J., Ferguson, Parker and a group of others in their first really happy scene in over a year. "I can't tell you men how good this feels," Ringo told his players.

With the usual cluster of reporters all about him at his dressing room stall, O.J. searched for promising signs. With a 3-0 score, this was hardly a day for offense, but the Bills shook their pass-crazy tendency and reverted to what had worked so often in the past—strong rushing. O.J. responded with 138 yards, six per carry, and 218 of Buffalo's 314 yards came by land.

The tender ankle hadn't seemed to bother O.J. at all.

"I didn't tell Ringo anything special after the game, but I was happy for him," the Juice said. "This win was a long time coming and maybe it will get us going. But beating Atlanta was not special. If we had scored, say 27 points, that would have been special because they came in with the league's No. 1 defense.

"With all due respect to Atlanta, anytime you hold a team to three points, you should win. But our defense was something else. I still can't believe the play Doug Jones made."

And so the brightest spot O.J. could find was the defense. Easy to penetrate in 1976, now it was responsible for victory as the offense struggled for points—on O.J.'s best day of the season. And on a rare day when a 3-0 score wasn't boring but downright exciting because of that almost forgotten winning feeling.

One week later, however, it was back down to earth and reality for the Juice and his teammates. He ran effectively again, gaining 99 yards on 19 carries, but Cleveland used four possessions to dominate 23 of the second half's 30 minutes and breezed, 27-16.

The Bills were on offense only one minute and four seconds of the last quarter. That's being dominated! O.J. just stood there alongside Reggie McKenzie on the sidelines—helpless—as the Browns spun the clock by cranking out one first down after another. But afterward, something else bothered him.

Someone pointed out that Ferguson had tried more passes than any other AFC quarterback. Someone else suggested the Bills abandoned their running game when they fell 10 points behind early in the third quarter. Indeed, O.J. had only 28 yards off seven runs in the second half.

"There used to be a time when running the ball was the thing we did best, but it's obvious we don't feel that way now," O.J. said, clearly annoyed. "Most teams go to what they do best in tough situations, but we don't go to one thing. We go to everything.

"We started the year wanting to have a balanced attack and that's what is happening now. We've had some changes in the offense the last couple of years, but they haven't been that drastic. I'm a runner and naturally I would like to run more. I figure the tougher the situation, the more I want to run with the ball. But if you get way behind, you have to pass."

Ringo was being subjected to a new wave of criticism by the press and fans. A 10-point deficit early in the second half is not being "way behind." Yet, the rushing game was all but ignored thereafter.

"If the score were different, we could have run on these cats all day," O.J. declared. He obviously was pulling his verbal punches. He liked Ringo and did not want to criticize him publicly. But, just as obviously, he was very upset. He was also scoreless after six games—an incredible situation.

The fans watching didn't realize it, but that Browns' affair was O.J.'s final Buffalo appearance in a Bills' uniform. The next game, seventh of the season, would be against the problem-plagued Seahawks in Seattle. It seemed a fat chance to take out frustrations on a poor expansion outfit, but suddenly O.J. was a question mark.

He had amassed rushing yardage of 122, 138 and 99 in his last three games and seemingly was running smoothly. But his nagging leg injury was growing worse. The situation had deteriorated over a three-week period. After the Jets game, the club reported O.J. was bothered by leg cramps. After Atlanta, the report was he had "a slight calf muscle pull." Now, after 10 days of heat treatments, an arthrogram revealed "a derangement of the knee."

O.J. was regarded questionable for the Seattle game, but the fans there sold out the Kingdome to see him play. There was no sellout for the champion Oakland Raiders in Seattle, but there was for Buffalo because of O.J. So he played, but not for long.

It was a game none of the Bills could ever forget. Unquestionably, it was the low point of their franchise. The previously ragtag Seahawks, a 1½-year-old team, assembled an astounding 42-3 lead by halftime, tried to hold down the score thereafter and romped, 56–17.

O.J. was taken out late in the first half with nine carries for 32 yards. "There was no sense in humiliating a great athlete," Ringo explained. O.J. looked on in disgust as unheralded Jim Zorn fired four touchtown passes and scored himself—before coming out in the *third* quarter with 296 aerial yards.

The Bills were totally humiliated as supposedly inept Seattle scored almost at will—piling up 559 yards, the most ever allowed by a Buffalo team. The Seahawks had 30 first downs! They cracked 10 team and four individual records!

Afterward, the rumors flew furiously. Ringo had been reported wanting to quit at halftime and now it looked like Wilson would have to relieve him. O.J. didn't accompany the team back to Buffalo and some friends said his Bills' career might be over.

O.J. flew down the coast to Los Angeles, visited his family and Dr. Robert Kerlan, a prominent specialist who confirmed the Buffalo diagnosis of knee cartilage damage. It was soon decided that O.J. would undergo his first surgery in Buffalo. His ninth pro season was over at its midpoint.

It was likely that O.J. would have attempted to finish the season, if the Bills had something going. He probably could have played with limited effectiveness and without practice, but didn't want to risk further injury by playing out the string of a horrendous season.

"The cartilage is torn, but that's better than having ligament problems," O.J. told a press gathering upon his return to Buffalo. "I never wanted surgery in the past and I don't want it now. But if I must have it, this is the kind to have. I may be on crutches for three or four weeks, but I shouldn't need a cast."

The surgery followed and it went so well that O.J. was dancing at Studio 54, an exclusive New York disco club, before the season ended. Ringo lasted the full schedule and the Bills won two more games, shocking New England the week after the Seattle debacle and edging the Jets.

But 1977, without question, was a "downer" of a season for the Bills and O.J. The team finished with a 3–11 record and, in January, Ringo was replaced by Chuck Knox, who resigned as coach of the Los Angeles Rams.

O.J. finished his half-season with 126 carries, 557 yards and, most displeasing of all, not one touchdown! He saw his single-game rushing record, set in the 1976 Thanksgiving game in Detroit (273 yards), eclipsed by Chicago's Walter Payton, who rolled up a fantastic 275 yards against Minnesota. For the year, Payton had 339 carries, seven more than O.J.'s 1973 record.

The Juice nearly lost four records to Payton in '77. His 2,003-yard show of 1973 was in serious jeopardy, but the New York Giants' defense and an icy field held Payton to 47 in the season finale and he finished with 1,852—third best in NFL history. Walter also was one shy of O.J.'s record 11 100-yard games (1973).

O.J.'s single-season records now are exceptionally safe—if secured only by an asterisk in the official book. Because the NFL now employs 16-game schedules, the book has been closed on the 14-game format—of which O.J. was undisputed "King of the Seventies."

Now, his timetable seemingly delayed a year by the misfortunes of 1977, O.J. nevertheless can fulfill that dream and that boyhood ice cream shop boast to Brown by racing 2,130 yards before calling it a career. The honor of emerging as the sport's all-time No. 1 ground gainer remains within reach.

O.J. will pursue the rushing pinnacle in a different uniform, however. In a March 24 trade which shook the football world, his nine-year career with the Buffalo Bills came to a close. O.J. was sent home—to the San Francisco 49ers—for five draft choices.

The announcement of O.J.'s exit after nine years was hardly a surprise in Buffalo, where Knox would be rebuilding from the ground floor. Further, it had been well known for a couple of years that O.J. would prefer to finish his football career on the West Coast.

What was a surprise was the Bills' inability to obtain even one veteran player or a 1978 first-round draft choice for the sport's finest running back. Dealing with astutue 49ers' General Manager Joe Thomas, they received a second- and third-round choice in '78, a first- and fourth-round pick in '79 and the 49ers' second-round selection in 1980.

Of course, another large factor was that the 49ers would pick up O.J.'s $730,000 salary for 1978, the third and final season of the record contract he received from Ralph Wilson.

O.J. was wildly happy over the trade, walking into a jammed San Francisco press conference clapping his hands and exclaiming: "Home at last, thank God almighty I'm home at last! Obviously, I'm ecstatic. I was a 49er fan when I was a kid, and I'll never stop being a 49er fan."

But O.J. also had his "down" moments, surprising even himself. "After all these years, I thought I'd feel great coming to the West Coast," he said, "but my first reaction was a little sadness in leaving all the guys in Buffalo."

Without question, the most regretful figure in the transaction was Ralph Wilson. "Most of all, O.J. Simpson was a friend," the Bills' owner said. "We laughed together in moments of triumph and cried together in moments of pain.

"He made a contribution to professional football and to Buffalo that may never be matched. He wanted to play on the West Coast, where he has many personal ties and, at this stage of his career, he deserves that opportunity. He leaves Buffalo with tears in my eyes."

Meanwhile, Knox explained Buffalo's thinking behind the deal. "The decision to trade a player like O.J. was a difficult one," he declared. "We had to weigh his undeniable short-range value against the long-range prospect of building a challenging football team in Buffalo. We elected to go in the direction that, in our mind, best benefits the Bills."

Naturally, Thomas was ebullient at landing football's most popular player and one who figured to dramatically boost 49ers' home attendance. "The thing that appealed to me was we didn't have to give up any of our players or our No. 1 draft choice this year," the 49ers' GM said.

Edward DiBartolo Jr., the 49ers' owner, wore the broadest of smiles. "I'm ecstatic," he said. "This is great for the team and great for the Bay City. I'm very, very happy."

And then there was O.J., still reflecting on leaving his friends in Buffalo and the good times he enjoyed there. "In the 1973, '74 and '75 seasons, we were as close a team as you can have and the Electric Company was as good a line as any," he said. "It's too bad front office politics had to enter the picture.

"I've been a Buffalo Bill all of my pro football life," he continued. "I've always been proud to be a Bill and that will never change. I know that my most precious football memories, after I retire, will be those of the days when I was a Bill. Just as Babe Ruth will always be known as a New York Yankee and Willie Mays a San Francisco Giant, I will always be known as a Buffalo Bill."

That said, the Juice affirmed that he would continue playing at least through the 1979 season.

"I'll play two more years and see how I do," he said. "I know I'm good for two more years, maybe three."

And so entering the 1978 season at age 31, the opportunity for O.J. to surpass Jimmy Brown's career rushing milestone and become football's all-time top running back was clearly at hand. Two years could be plenty.

Brown's career standard of 12,312 yards could even fall with one super-productive 16-game season (2,130 yards) or via a pair averaging 1,065 each.

Further, as he donned a 49er uniform for the first time, he was only 236 attempts shy of Brown's record as the NFL player who carried more times than any other. The Cleveland ace rushed 2,359 times from 1957-65. With 2,123 attempts, O.J. needed only 15 per game to eclipse that peak in 1978.

Clearly, O.J. had gone home to become No. 1. The 49ers seemed only slightly stronger a team than the Bills, but O.J. would have no difficulty with incentive.

Whatever the length of playing time required, Jim Brown's record was there for the taking. One famed No. 32 had his sights set on the crowning achievement of a legend who wore the same number in another era.

Whatever the outcome, what great and memorable games Orenthal James Simpson has given the world of professional football! From this view, he truly is the king of running backs.

O. J.'s Record Summary

NATIONAL FOOTBALL LEAGUE RECORDS

Most Yards Gained, Season—2,003 (1973)
Most Games, 100 Yds. or more, Rushing, Season—11 (1973)
Most Games, 200 Yds. or more, Rushing, Season—3 (1973)
Most Consecutive Games, 100 Yds., or more, Rushing—7 (1973)
Most Consecutive Games, 200 Yds., or more, Rushing—2 (1973), (1976)
Most Touchdowns, Season—23 (1975)
Most Games, 200 Yds. or more, Rushing, Center—6

BUFFALO BILLS CLUB RECORDS

Most Rushing Attempts, Career—2,123 (1969-1977)
Most Rushing Attempts, Season—332 (1973)
Most Rushing Attempts, Single Game—39 vs. Kansas City, October 29, 1973
Most Yards Gained, Career—10,183 (1969-1977)
Most Yards Gained, Season—2,003 (1973)
Most Yards Gained, Single Game—273 vs. Detroit, Nov. 25, 1976
Best Rushing Average, Career—4.79 (1969-1977)
Best Rushing Average, Season—6.0 (1973)
Most Games, 100 Yds. or More, Rushing, Season—11 (1973)
Most Games, 200 Yards or More, Rushing, Season—3 (1973)
Most Consecutive Games, 100 Yds. or More, Rushing, Season—5 (1973)
Longest Run from Scrimmage—94 vs. Pittsburgh, Oct. 29, 1972
Most Touchdowns Rushing, Career—57 (1969-1977)
Most Games, 100 or More Rushing, Lifetime—41
Most Games, 200 or More Rushing, Lifetime—6
Total Points, Career—420 (1969-1977)
Most Points, Season—138 (1975)
Most Touchdowns, Career—70 (1969-1977)
Most Touchdowns, Season—23 (1975)
Most Consecutive Games, Touchdowns Scored—14 (1975 season)
Most Touchdowns Rushing, Season—16 (1975)
Most Consecutive Games Touchdown Rushing—7 (1975)

100-Yard Games

Date	Opponent	Carries	Yds.	Avg.	TD
9/28/69	Denver	24	110	4.6	0
11/1/70	@Boston	17	123	7.2	1
10/23/71	@San Diego	18	106	5.9	0
9/24/71	San Francisco	29	138	4.8	0
10/15/72	@Oakland	28	144	5.1	0
10/29/72	Pittsburgh	22	189	8.6	1
11/19/72	@New England	22	103	4.7	1
12/10/72	Detroit	27	116	4.3	0
12/17/72	@Washington	26	101	3.9	1
9/23/73	@San Diego	22	103	4.7	1
9/30/73	New York Jets	24	123	5.1	0
10/7/73	Philadelphia	27	171	6.3	1
10/14/73	Baltimore	22	166	7.5	2
10/29/73	Kansas City	39	157	4.0	2
11/18/73	Miami	20	120	6.0	0
11/25/73	@Baltimore	15	124	8.3	1
12/2/73	@Atlanta	24	137	5.7	0
9/29/74	New York Jets	31	117	3.8	0
10/13/74	@Baltimore	23	127	5.5	0
10/20/74	New England	32	122	3.8	0
11/24/74	@Cleveland	22	115	5.2	1
9/21/75	New York Jets	32	173	5.4	2
10/5/75	Denver	26	138	5.3	1
10/12/75	@Baltimore	32	159	5.0	1
10/20/75	New York Giants	34	126	3.7	1
11/9/75	Baltimore	19	123	6.5	1
11/17/75	@Cincinnati	17	197	11.6	2
12/14/75	@New England	21	185	8.9	1
10/3/76	Kansas City	24	130	5.4	2
10/24/76	New England	25	110	4.4	2
10/31/76	New York Jets	29	166	5.7	0
11/21/76	San Diego	25	118	4.7	0
12/12/76	@Baltimore	28	171	6.1	1
10/9/77	New York Jets	23	122	5.3	0
10/16/77	Atlanta	23	138	6.0	0

200-Yard Games

Date	Opponent	Carries	Yds.	Avg.	TD
9/16/73	@New England	29	250	8.6	2
12/19/73	New England	22	219	10.0	1
12/16/73	@New York Jets	34	200	5.7	1
9/28/75	@Pittsburgh	28	227	8.1	1
11/25/76	@Detroit	29	273	9.4	2
12/5/76	@Miami	24	203	8.5	1

O.J. vs. the NFL

	Games	Carries	Yds.	Avg.	TD
Atlanta	2	47	275	5.8	0
Baltimore	13	250	1197	4.7	7
Chicago	1	17	62	3.6	0
Cincinnati	4	60	371	6.2	4
Cleveland	3	68	307	4.5	2
Dallas	2	38	103	2.7	1
Denver	4	83	343	4.1	2
Detroit	2	56	389	6.9	2
Green Bay	1	16	62	3.9	0
Houston	5	77	209	2.7	1
Kansas City	5	104	458	4.4	5
Los Angeles	2	27	97	3.7	0
Miami	16	240	1177	4.9	4
Minnesota	2	24	102	4.3	1
N.Y. Giants	1	34	126	3.7	1
N.Y. Jets	17	350	1602	4.5	6
New England	14	280	1514	5.4	14
New Orleans	1	20	79	3.9	0
Oakland	3	46	272	5.9	0
Philadelphia	1	27	171	6.3	1
Pittsburgh	3	64	476	7.3	3
San Diego	4	72	354	4.9	1
San Francisco	1	29	138	4.8	0
Seattle	1	9	32	3.5	0
St. Louis	2	39	127	3.3	1
Tampa	1	20	39	2.0	0
Washington	1	26	101	3.9	1
Totals	112	2,123	10,183	4.8	57

1969 Season

Date	Opponent	Carries	Yds.	Avg.	TD
9/14	New York Jets	10	35	3.5	1
9/21	Houston Oilers	19	58	3.1	0
9/28	Denver Broncos	24	110	4.6	0
10/5	@Houston Oilers	13	27	2.1	0
10/11	Boston Patriots	Did not play			
10/19	@Oakland Raiders	6	50	8.3	0
10/26	@Miami Dolphins	10	12	1.2	0
11/2	Kansas City Chiefs	16	41	2.6	0
11/9	@New York Jets	14	70	5.0	0
11/16	Miami Dolphins	21	72	3.4	0
11/23	@Boston Patriots	17	98	5.8	0
11/30	Cinn. Bengals	13	35	2.7	0
12/7	@Kansas City Chiefs	11	62	5.6	1
12/14	@San Diego Chargers	7	27	3.9	0
Totals		181	697	3.9	2

1970 Season

Date	Opponent	Carries	Yds.	Avg.	TD
9/20	Denver Broncos	18	52	2.9	1
9/27	Los Angeles Rams	14	24	1.7	0
10/4	New York Jets	21	99	4.7	1
10/11	@Pittsburgh Steelers	14	60	4.3	1
10/18	Miami Dolphins	11	35	3.2	0
10/25	@New York Jets	15	55	3.7	0
11/1	@Boston Patriots	17	123	7.2	1
11/8	Cincinnati Bengals	10	40	4.0	1
11/15	@Baltimore Colts	Did not play			
11/22	@Chicago Bears	Did not play			
11/29	Boston Patriots	Did not play			
12/6	@New York Giants	Did not play			
12/13	Baltimore Colts	Did not play			
12/20	@Miami Dolphins	Did not play			
Totals		120	488	4.1	5

1971 Season

Date	Opponent	Carries	Yds.	Avg.	TD
9/19	Dallas Cowboys	14	25	1.8	1
9/26	Miami Dolphins	9	82	9.1	1
10/13	@Minnesota Vikings	12	45	3.8	0
10/10	Baltimore Colts	7	−10	−1.4	0
10/17	@New York Jets	18	69	3.8	1
10/23	@San Diego Chargers	18	106	5.9	0
10/31	St. Louis Cardinals	16	42	2.6	0
11/7	@Miami Dolphins	10	90	9.0	0
11/14	@New England Patriots	16	61	3.8	0
11/21	New York Jets	14	48	3.4	0
11/28	New England Patriots	14	61	4.4	1
12/5	@Baltimore Colts	9	26	2.9	0
12/12	Houston Oilers	12	29	2.4	1
12/19	@Kansas City Chiefs	14	68	4.9	0
Totals		183	742	4.1	5

1972 Season

Date	Opponent	Carries	Yds.	Avg.	TD
9/17	New York Jets	14	41	2.9	0
9/24	San Francisco 49ers	29	138	4.8	0
10/1	Baltimore Colts	21	78	3.7	0
10/8	New England Patriots	13	31	2.4	1
10/15	@Oakland Raiders	28	144	5.1	0
10/22	@Miami Dolphins	16	57	3.6	0
10/29	Pittsburgh Steelers	22	189	8.6	1
11/5	Miami Dolphins	13	45	3.5	0
11/12	@New York Jets	20	89	4.5	0
11/19	@New England Patriots	22	103	4.7	1
11/26	@Cleveland Browns	27	93	3.4	1
12/3	@Baltimore Colts	14	26	1.9	1
12/10	Detroit Lions	27	116	4.3	0
12/17	@Washington Redskins	26	101	3.9	1
Totals		292	1251	4.3	6

1973 Season

Date	Opponent	Carries	Yds.	Avg.	TD
9/16	@New England Patriots	29	250	8.6	2
9/23	@San Diego Chargers	22	103	4.7	1
9/30	New York Jets	24	123	5.1	0
10/7	Philadelphia Eagles	27	171	6.3	1
10/14	Baltimore Colts	22	166	7.5	2
10/23	@Miami Dolphins	14	55	3.9	0
10/29	Kansas City Chiefs	39	157	4.0	2
11/4	@New Orleans Saints	20	79	3.9	0
11/10	Cincinnati Bengals	20	99	4.9	1
11/18	Miami Dolphins	20	120	6.0	0
11/25	@Baltimore Colts	15	124	8.3	1
12/2	@Atlanta Falcons	24	137	5.7	0
12/9	New England Patriots	22	219	10.0	1
12/16	@New York Jets	34	200	5.7	1
Totals		332	2003	6.0	12

1974 Season

Date	Opponent	Carries	Yds.	Avg.	TD
9/16	Oakland Raiders	12	78	6.5	0
9/22	Miami Dolphins	15	63	4.2	0
9/29	New York Jets	31	117	3.8	0
10/6	@Green Bay Packers	16	62	3.9	0
10/13	@Baltimore Colts	23	127	5.5	0
10/20	New England Patriots	32	122	3.8	1
10/27	Chicago Bears	17	62	3.6	0
11/3	@New England Patriots	19	74	3.9	1
11/10	Houston Oilers	17	57	3.4	0
11/17	@Miami Dolphins	14	60	4.3	0
11/24	@Cleveland Browns	22	115	5.2	1
12/1	Baltimore Colts	24	67	2.8	0
12/8	@New York Jets	15	48	3.2	0
12/15	@Los Angeles Rams	13	73	5.6	0
Totals		270	1125	4.1	3

NFL POST-SEASON PLAYOFFS
(Playoff statistics are *not* included in career totals)

12/22	@Pittsburgh Steelers	15	49	3.3	0

1975 Season

Date	Opponent	Carries	Yds.	Avg.	TD
9/21	New York Jets	32	173	5.4	2
9/28	@Pittsburgh Steelers	28	227	8.1	1
10/5	Denver Broncos	26	138	5.3	1
10/12	@Baltimore Colts	32	159	5.0	1
10/20	New York Giants	34	126	3.7	1
10/26	Miami Dolphins	19	88	4.6	1
11/2	@New York Jets	21	94	4.5	0
11/9	Baltimore Colts	19	123	6.5	1
11/17	@Cincinnati Bengals	17	197	11.6	2
11/23	New England Patriots	27	69	2.6	2
11/27	@St. Louis Cardinals	23	85	3.7	1
12/7	@Miami Dolphins	18	96	5.3	1
12/14	@New England Patriots	21	185	8.8	1
12/20	Minnesota Vikings	12	57	4.5	1
Totals		329	1817	5.5	16

1976 Season

Date	Opponent	Carries	Yds.	Avg.	TD
9/13	Miami Dolphins	5	28	5.6	0
9/19	Houston Oilers	16	38	2.4	0
9/26	@Tampa Bay Buccaneers	20	39	2.0	0
10/3	Kansas City Chiefs	24	130	5.4	2
10/10	@N.Y. Jets	15	53	3.5	0
10/17	Baltimore Colts	20	88	4.4	0
10/24	New England Patriots	25	110	4.4	2
10/31	N.Y. Jets	29	166	5.7	0
11/7	@New England Patriots	6	8	1.3	0
11/15	@Dallas Cowboys	24	78	3.3	0
11/21	San Diego Chargers	25	118	4.7	0
11/25	@Detroit Lions	29	273	9.4	2
12/5	@Miami Dolphins	24	203	8.5	1
12/12	@Baltimore Colts	28	171	6.1	1
Totals		290	1503	5.4	8

1977 Season

Date	Opponent	Carries	Yds.	Avg.	TD
9/18	Miami Dolphins	21	71	3.3	0
9/25	@Denver Broncos	15	43	2.8	0
10/2	@Baltimore Colts	16	52	3.2	0
10/9	New York Jets	23	122	5.3	0
10/16	Atlanta Falcons	23	138	6.0	0
10/23	Cleveland Browns	19	99	5.2	0
10/30	@Seattle Seahawks	9	32	3.5	0
11/6	@New England Patriots	Did Not Play			
11/13	Baltimore Colts	Did Not Play			
11/20	New England Patriots	Did Not Play			
11/28	@Oakland Raiders	Did Not Play			
12/4	Washington Redskins	Did Not Play			
12/11	@New York Jets	Did Not Play			
12/17	@Miami Dolphins	Did Not Play			
Totals		126	557	4.4	0

UPDATED CAREER TOTALS:
   Rushing—2,123 carries for 10,183 yards and 57 touchdowns.
   Receiving—175 catches for 1,924 yards and 12 touchdowns.
   Kickoff Returns (None since 1971)—33 for 991 yards and one
   touchdown.
   Passing—6 of 16 for 110 yards and one touchdown.
   Scoring—70 touchdowns (57 rushing, 12 receiving, one return)
   for 420 points.